Chris Larson

Failure

HATJE
CANTZ

Acknowledgements

Sarah Stauder

The Rochester Art Center is honored to present this exhibition and catalogue highlighting the work of Chris Larson. Larson, a Minnesota native, is known both in the United States and in Europe for his provocative and challenging work developed over the past decade and a half. In keeping with our vision to be a premier center for contemporary art, we welcome the opportunity to exhibit the work of this accomplished artist at a pivotal point in his career. We are grateful that Chris has chosen a location near his hometown of St. Paul, Minnesota, to show his recently created films, sculptures, and photographs; it has been a pleasure to work with him throughout this process.

This catalogue, the culmination of nearly a year of work, is the first major publication dedicated to documenting the work of Chris Larson. Without the generous support of the National Endowment for the Arts and Think Community Foundation, we would not have been able to present this exhibition. We also thank Wells Fargo for its support of Larson's work as part of the 2008 Wells Fargo Atrium Series.

We are deeply grateful to everyone at the gallery magnus müller in Berlin, Germany, and in particular Sönke Magnus Müller, who has been instrumental in the development and organization of this publication. Constanze Korb, Irini Toussemiti, and Thomas Köhler have provided invaluable advice and support, and Constanze has worked tirelessly to gather all the documents and photographs for this catalogue.

Our gratitude also goes out to Wayne Roosa, Tamatha Sopinski Perlman, and Marc Glöde for their thoughtful contributions to this publication.

We would like to take this opportunity to recognize the efforts of Chief Curator Kris Douglas, whose ongoing quest for excellence has made it possible for us to put on quality exhibitions of the work of regionally, nationally, and internationally recognized contemporary artists. Kris's ability to find a perfect balance between the needs of the institution and the desires of the artist is apparent in the content of every exhibition he produces.

Our thanks also go to everyone at Hatje Cantz Verlag, especially Cristina Steingräber and Julika Zimmermann of the Hatje Cantz Berlin office, for their gracious support and their belief in this project. Their design and printing of this catalogue are of the highest quality.

We would like to thank the corporate and individual members of the Rochester Art Center. Their generous and constant support enables us to carry out our mission to foster an appreciation and understanding of contemporary art and to effectively engage our regional audience.

Finally, we would like to express our warmest thanks to Chris Larson himself for his extraordinary vision and dedication to this project. Without his tireless efforts, neither the exhibition nor this publication would have been possible.

Foreword

Sönke Magnus Müller

When I showed Chris Larson's piece *County Line* in a group exhibition at my gallery in 2004, I was astounded by the complexity of his artistic approach. Both the obsessiveness in his work and its aesthetic realization impressed me deeply. Larson belongs to that group of artists who do not limit themselves to a single media. Besides performance, film, drawings, and photography, Larson mainly produces sculptures; his choice of media makes it clear that the exploration of pictorial and corporeal space is an essential aspect of his work. It is impossible to categorize his work within a single traditional concept. He consciously leaves the exhibition space behind and intervenes in the public space, installing for example disturbing, anarchic elements such as the 2006 sculpture of a piano in a tree situated in front

current events can be drawn upon to trigger the execution of his pieces. Larson is noncommittal about their interpretations. But time and again it seems very obvious that it is the collision, the violent encounter between different worlds, that stimulates Larson. It is the collision of human beings, ideals, thoughts, races, convictions, as well as the clashes of religions and political outlooks that Larson stages as a test arrangement to find out what happens during these often violent confrontations.

His piece *Crush Collision* conclusively shifts attention away from the project results and toward the processuality and enigmatic procedures within the thirteen-minute video and, in the end, toward the subjectivity of the project's author.

The present publication has been produced to accompany the presentation of Larson's new film *Deep North* at the Rochester Art Center and gallery magnus müller in fall 2008. The book also introduces the reader to Larson's mechanistic narrations and attempts to provide a long-overdue assessment of the artist's work.

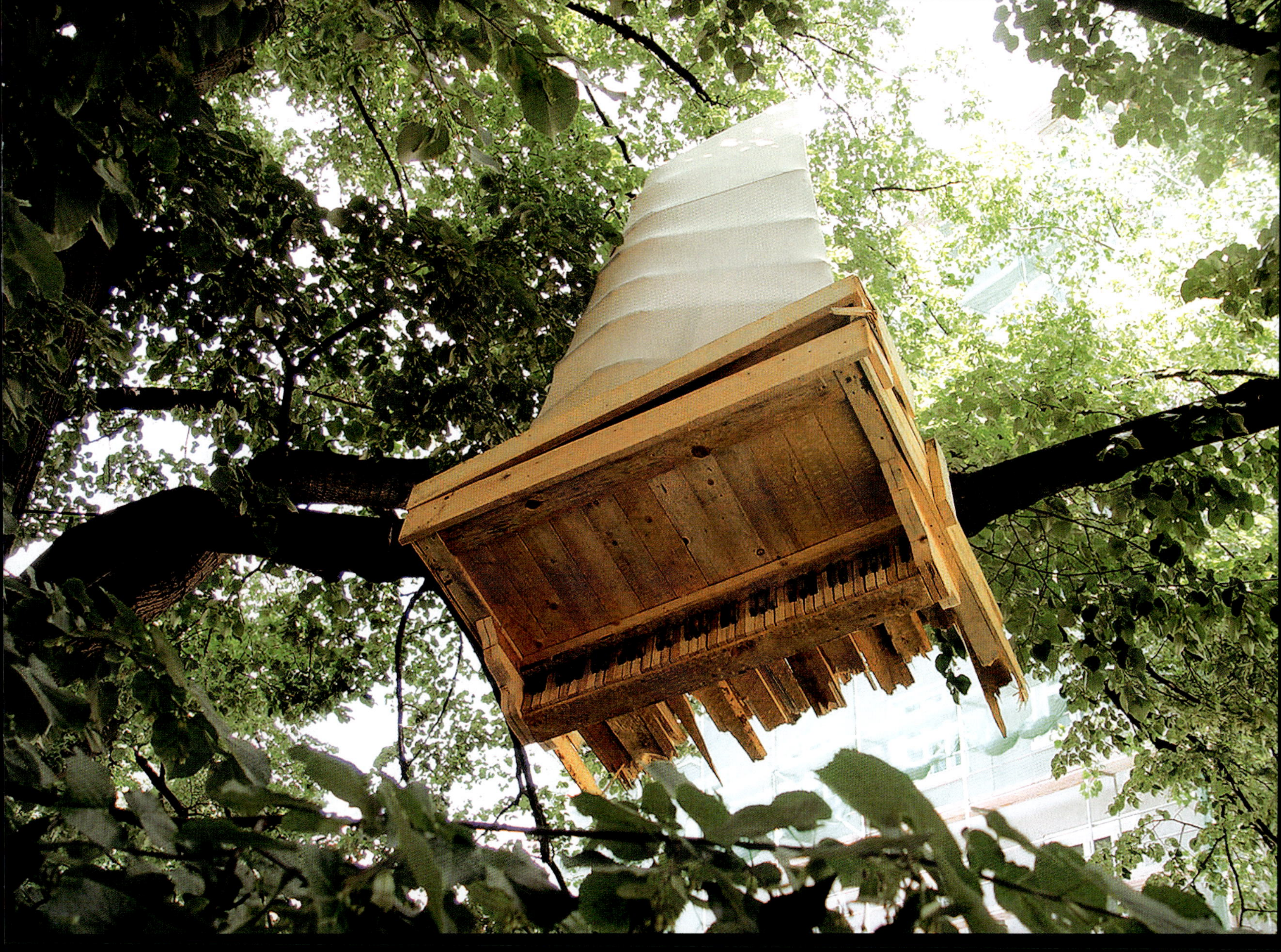

Flügel
2006 * Wood, mixed media * 150 x 180 x 300 cm
Site-specific installation at magnus müller, 2006

Introduction

Kris Douglas

The interdependent relationship of man versus machine is a profoundly complex subject frequently explored by artists, writers, and theorists. The interplay between technological advances and their implications for the individual invites consideration of ethics and humanity. Bertrand Russell, the English logician and philosopher, stated, "Machines are worshipped because they are beautiful, and valued because they confer power; they are hated because they are hideous, and loathed because they impose slavery." Chris Larson's work often includes a constructed machine that requires strenuous human labor for some ominous purpose that is emphatically unclear. Consequently, these issues of power, technology, and mechanization can be considered in his work, and provide metaphors for progress within the individual and society or lack thereof.

Larson is perhaps best known for his elaborately constructed, large-scale sculptures built with wood (rather than the metal more characteristic of modern machines) and given a raw natural finish or painted a monochrome, flat black. Shown as either stand-alone sculptures or as integral characters within his films, the machines yield no clues as to their purpose and consequence. Many of Larson's machines are seemingly designed to operate in perpetuity via human power. With individuals literally becoming part of the machine to operate it—many being strapped in and using their arms, legs, hands, and mouths to make the machine function—one wonders why and how the protagonists in the unfolding story entered into this bizarre environment. It becomes the responsibility of the viewer to ascertain the function of the apparatus and to determine the consequences of its operation. One questions the functioning of the machine and whether it will ever have a definitive outcome or if it is meant to operate ceaselessly without an end or purpose. The viewer likely questions to what extent do machines serve us, or we them, and to what end?

Beyond man versus machine, the formal and conceptual content of Larson's work invites consideration of numerous other contrasting themes, such as the beautiful and the grotesque, darkness and light, the observable and the unseen, stability and instability, vulnerability and strength, and cohesion and isolation. All media included within his work contributes to a grim suspense and a heightening of these challenging dichotomies. Exemplifying this within his film *Crush Collision* is the melodious music with bleak lyrics, the seemingly safe and comfortable images of the well-dressed family in prayer at mealtime by the light of day while their house precariously floats on water, and the technically sophisticated yet crude appearance of the machine. Because of the ambiguity of the situations Larson represents, and because individuals are present or their presence is implied, the viewer is led to attempt construction of some narrative. Objects and locations take on a disorienting, surreal character, blurring the boundaries between the real and the imagined. Although often unsettling, challenging, and uncertain, the works compel further consideration after viewing.

Chris Larson thoughtfully examines these themes and others in his exhibition at the Rochester Art Center. These considerations are both a continuation of his characteristic modes of production and theoretical points of departure, but also a progression into new territory, both methodologically and conceptually. While machines are an important formal and metaphorical component of the works included in the exhibition, his consideration of human behavior and history along with a careful exploration of aesthetics and spatial development provide the overall structure to the exhibition. To put it into simpler terms, Larson is a builder. He builds not only intricate physical objects, but also the complex conceptual foundation for creation of meaning over time within his works. His sculptural, video, and photographic works are constructions of contrasting elements that layer upon and juxtapose each other to create a technically and conceptually multifaceted whole.

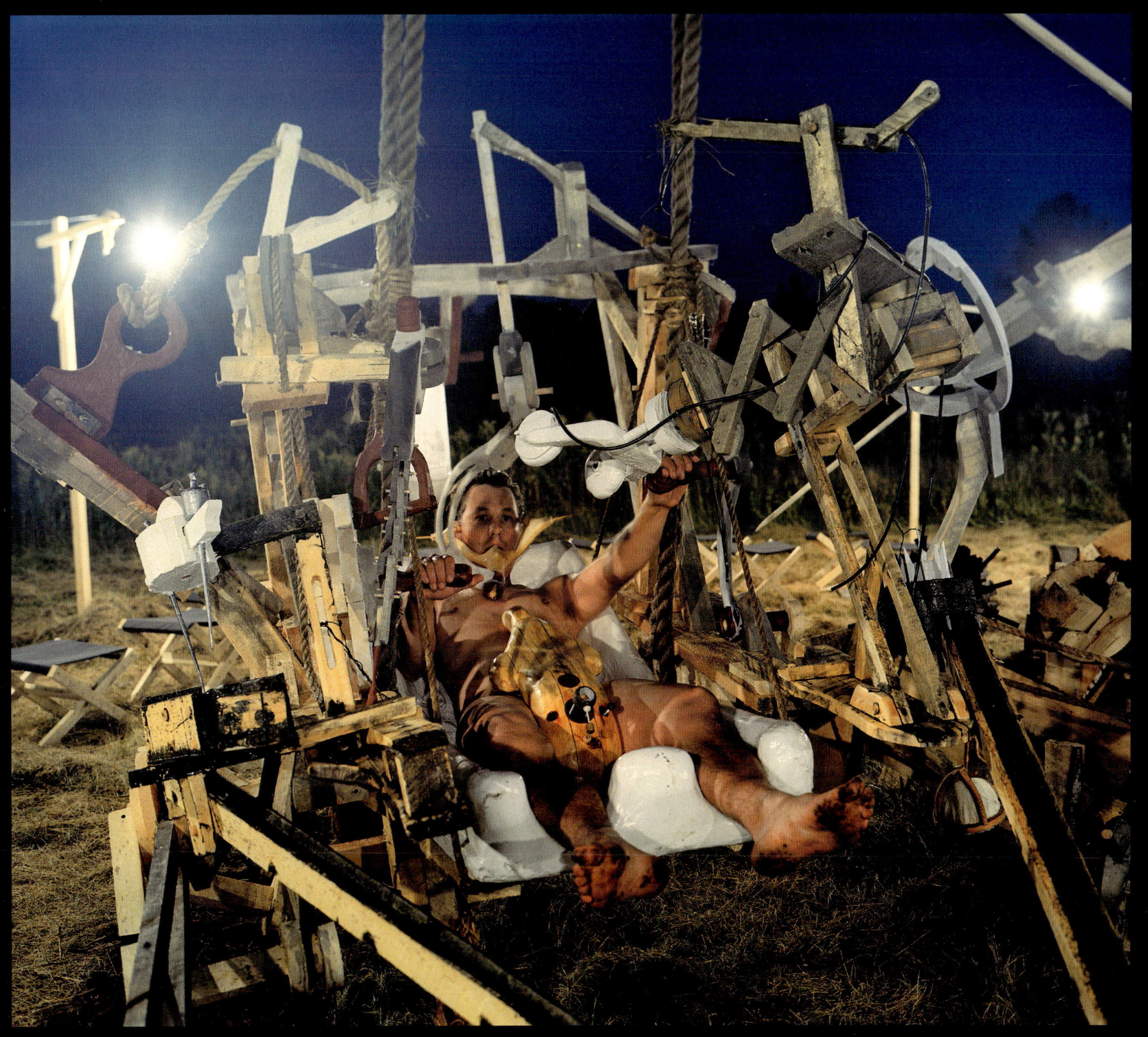

Bogus Brook Township (SatSun Midnight)
2002 • C-print • 102 x 152 cm

'Yet That Things Go Round and Again Go Round': In Praise of Failure

Wayne L. Roosa

In the life of an artist one makes a complete circle . . .
Motifs reoccur and objects become interwoven.
Marina Abramović[1]

Any viewer who considers "failure" deeply, that is, who thinks about these last fifteen or more years of Chris Larson's art as a whole, will quickly discover that his work "makes complete circles" and that there are core motifs and objects that "reoccur and become interwoven." In fact, one of the overall formal impressions that linger in the memory's eye after seeing Larson's work is a powerful and relentless sense of circular movement. This is not only true work by work, but also repeatedly over the long trajectory of nearly twenty years of work. Of course, coming full circle is not a simple matter of using a motif and then returning to it to create variations. It is, rather, a complex matter of visiting and revisiting core ideas and their forms over time, allowing us to enter more and more fully into their nature until their mysteries begin to yield.

But perhaps the image of "making a complete circle" is not quite right, for in looking at Larson's work, that image may be too flat and too static. Perhaps a better image is that of a spiral, where the artist comes back around but with each pass returns on a different or more complex plane of expression and understanding. A circle, after all, ends precisely where it began, with no change or complexity and, therefore, with no epiphany. A circle is complete in itself. In this, the circle—which in Western art has been the emblem of eternity, the dome of heaven—speaks of our need for peace and resolution. But a spiral fails to return precisely to its beginning. It is incomplete in itself. The spiral is emblematic of organic processes, of restless evolution, of dialogue and argument. It is less the emblem of eternal heaven and more the emblem of this world's temporal struggles. While it does come round again and again, it also labors forward through time and matter. If the circle's beauty is a spiritual and mathematical perfection, all centric and stable, then a spiral's beauty is an organic and evolutionary dynamism, all eccentric and troubled. If the circle speaks of our desire for heaven, then the spiral confesses our hunger for desire. And if we think of them both as together and in tension, then we have the right image of what Larson's art embodies. What lingers, then, as the overall formal impression in memory's eye is this sense of highly fraught circular motions.

Hence the Wallace Stevens line in the title, "Yet that things go round and again go round," borrowed from a poem, "The Pleasures of Merely Circulating," in his collection *Ideas of Order*. Nothing could be more appropriate in thinking through Larson's work than to set the stage with a strong sense of circular unrest set against questions about the order of things.

All of this began quietly enough in Larson's earliest works, where these matters were still latent or implied. For example in *Untitled*, from 1990 (ill. p. 11), a central shaft rises as a vertical axis while a cagelike structure of extended arms radiates out, tilting and spiraling around it. Larson speaks of these early works as "scanners," and indeed, they do imply some sort of strange medical equipment that is half machine and half organic figure. Their arms define a void that invites entry and is sized to hold the human body. Hindsight makes clear how this early work prefigures later sculptures and video sets, in which real human bodies will indeed be strapped into rotating machines where they will labor inside mechanisms that produce highly organic processes. Already implied in the "scanners" are several of the central tensions that will emerge and drive Larson's art: the human body played against the machine, the mechanistic pitted against the organic, the intense labor—even futility—required to produce visceral life fluids, and a dark sense of determinism interwoven with a yearning toward freedom.

Larson has said that one of the great sculptures from the past that had an impact on him is Giacometti's *Hands Holding the Void (Invisible Object)*, of 1934. In that work we sense a kindred spirit, both formally and metaphorically, even though Larson's work looks very different and emerges from an entirely different social context. What is shared is the fundamental psychological metaphor of some kind of architectural structure that houses the human body and its efforts—both as a home and an entrapment. Further shared s the formal energy of that figure working at the center of he structure, using its arms and feet in an attempt to discern omething greater than itself, some purpose, but unsure whether that mystery exists transcendently, as a wholly "other" realm (a heaven/void), or immanently, within the elation of the human body and the world's mechanistic order. Even more, Larson's work shares with Giacometti's figure a sense of a terrible suspension between opposite possibili-ies, namely whether all our efforts as humans striving at the center of our "machines" will prove to be redemptive or, on he contrary, futile.

These ideas were initiated on a very intuitive level by Larson's early works. He has said that it was not really clear to him exactly what he was working on, but that it made sense o build more and more elaborate "machines" with implied human presence. With each subsequent work, he found himself circling back around into the same handful of essential elements, but always at richer levels of complexity. One of hose core elements, of course, is the tension between circular and spiraling movements. A second is the formal tension between a strong, upward-rising verticality versus a down-ward-pulling, earthbound horizontality. Another is the con-versation—or perhaps argument—between machine forms which we expect to be precise and metallic) and the wood and leather used by Larson to build his machines, materials hat we associate more with bodies and flesh. And a fourth s an ambiguity in meaning. That is, the "scanners," like the later "machines," are riven with a sense of having a purpose as opposed to being useless. Nascent within this last tension s a larger, though still undeveloped, idea that will haunt all of Larson's work: namely, a feeling that motion, which is to say energy or life, is held taut between a sense of freedom versus entrapment, between a kind of hope and redemption versus futility and determinism.

From 1992 through 1998, Larson completed several more monumentally scaled machines constructed of wood (ills. pp. 41–43, 46–49). These works have a heroic quality to them, due partly to their scale and the complexity of their structures, and partly to the feeling that they are old and have been worked hard. The sense that they could still function, but are now inert and exhausted, gives a certain pathos or tragedy to hem. During this period he experimented with ash and soap as remnants left in the machines' hoppers, gears, and "paddle wheels" (ills. pp. 17, 41). The ash and soap not only added a patina of age and work; they also implied something about what these machines produced. That product, however, re-mains enigmatic, though there is a sense of something about death and cleansing, something transformational, hinting at a kind of alchemical transformation.

Interestingly, Larson says that in these works he was test-ing ideas about alchemy, which have been widely used in the "shamanistic" leanings of some modern art, particularly in the work of Joseph Beuys. But ultimately he found those ideas too occult for his own sensibility. This makes sense, given where his art has taken him since that time. In the end, his work and sense of meaning is not linked to magic or mysticism. It is more about the struggle between freedom and determinism within the existential rawness of organic life, sweat and labor in relation to the mechanistic. When something transformative or spiritually redemptive does occur within his work, it is prob-ably closer to traditions such as "the grotesque," as exempli-fied by the southern American writer Flannery O'Connor, than it is to the alchemical, as exemplified by an artist like Beuys.

This phase of "machines" peaked, in a way, with a large installation he built in 1998 at the Walker Art Center in Minneapolis, Minnesota, for their *Sculpture on Site* exhibi-tion (ills. pp. 44–45). For Larson, the building and exhibiting of these structures proved to be a turning point, where the ideas developed thus far not only came full circle, but also were clarified in a way that would take them to a new level. Several significant elements made this possible. One was that while each of the previous large-scale machines had essentially been a single mechanism, the Walker work ended up as two parallel machines. Standing side by side, they had obvious similarities. Yet because there were two of them, a new kind of tension or duality began to assert itself. Both seemed to have the same structural elements and the same purpose/non-purpose. That is, each machine had a verti-cal stack of equipment involving circular gear wheels, cams, rods, and levers, with arms that plunged in and out; and each seemed to produce something that flowed down long chutes standing on stilts and extending far into the gallery space. But because they were two distinct structures, inevitably their difference within their sameness began to create a dialogue or conversation, even an argument between them. These parallel machines were the beginning of what would later develop in Larson's work into single structures containing dual worlds that operate in contrast to each other.

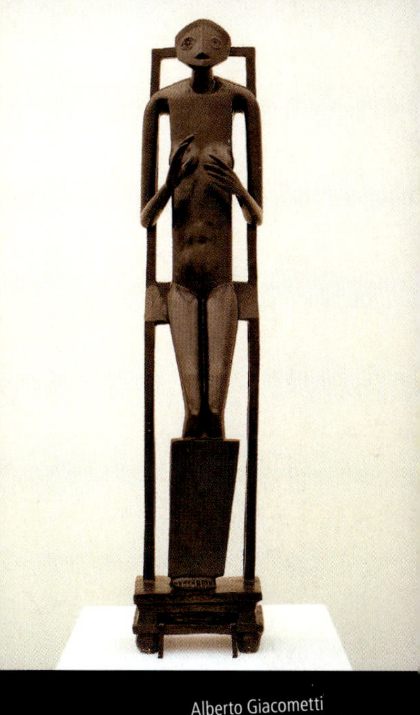

Alberto Giacometti
Hands Holding the Void (Invisible Object)
1934–35 • Bronze • 153 x 32 x 29 cm

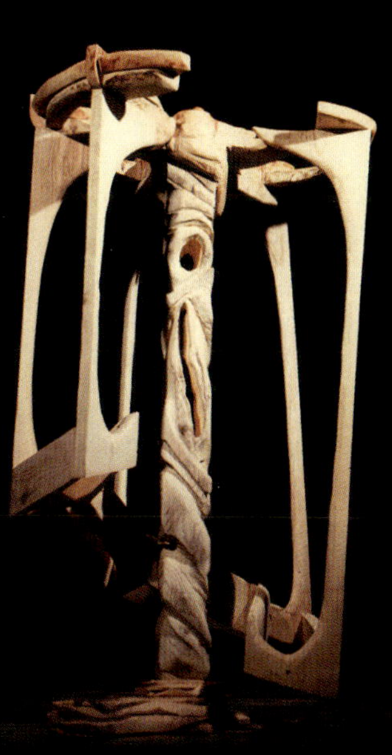

Untitled
1990 • Wood • 180 x 100 x 100 cm

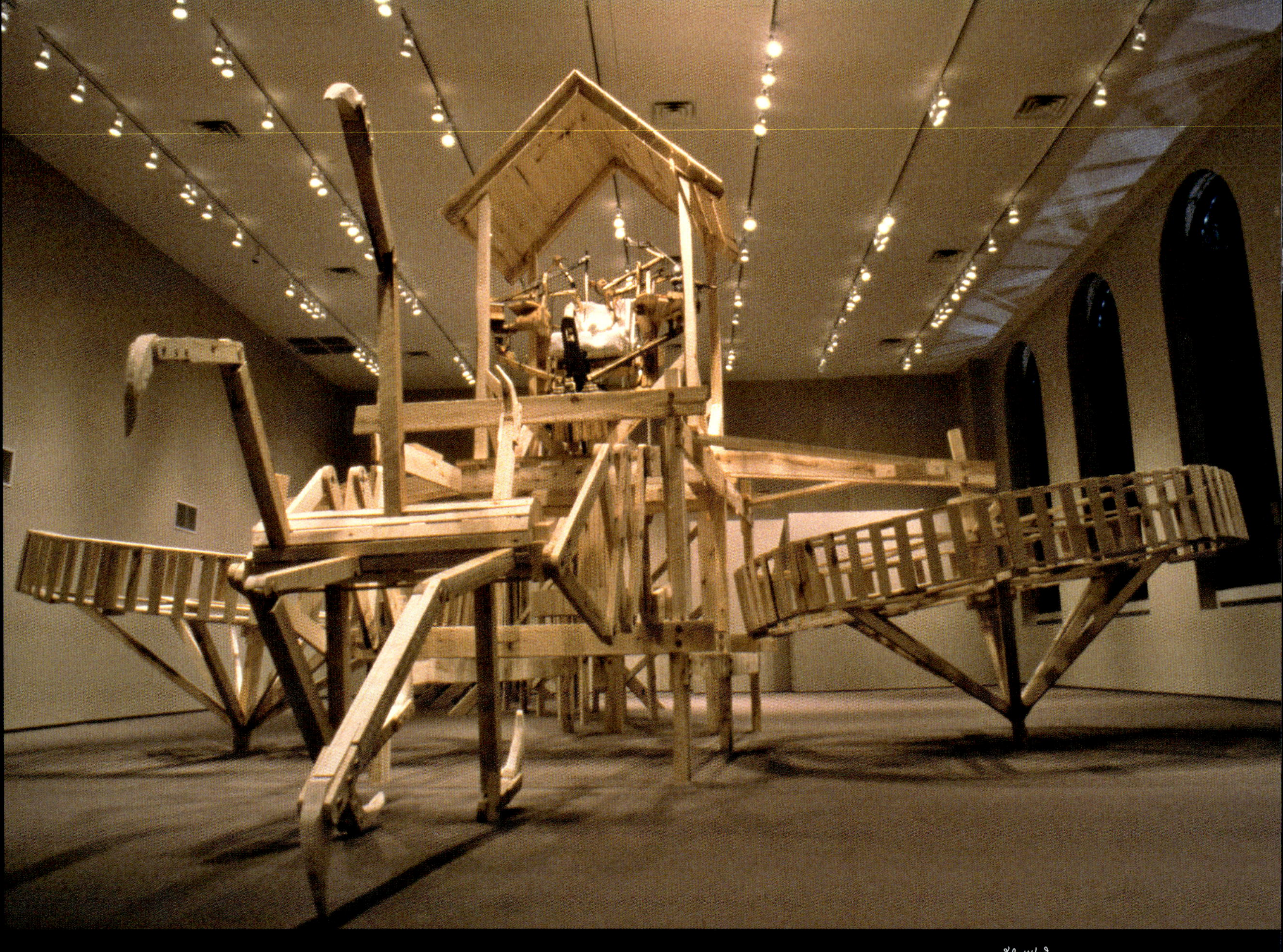

Untitled
2000 * Wood * 701 x 1371 x 2438 cm
Installation view, Washington Pavilion of Arts and Science,
Sioux Falls, SD

It is important to know that this duality emerged out of Larson's working processes. All the previous pieces (including, in fact, the Walker piece) were made without preparatory drawings or plans. Part of their meaning, which Larson felt he had not yet fully understood, had to do with the paradox of them seeming both useful and useless. In that light, it had always made sense simply to start building without a plan or purpose, until the machines felt complete, standing there in all their ambiguity. As a metaphor, this nicely expressed the sense that human culture involves monumental industriousness, all with apparent clarity about where the human race is going, but in fact plagued by an unnerving sense that civilization may be entirely ad hoc. This ambiguity is also why all the early machines had officially been titled, "Untitled."

But by now he had built enough of these that the problems of their structures had become easier to solve. And the overall nature seemed clearer. As a result, with the Walker pieces, the expressive energy was poured into the fact that with two parallel machines a new opportunity to wrestle with the tensions between things was possible. Each machine thus took on a different and more individual "character." This was the first installation where, so to speak, "two worlds" that interrelate and yet are in opposition to each other forcefully came into his work. One machine is smoother, one rougher. One has more perfect materials while the other has broken and crude materials. Although the human operators of these machines are still only implied, one can clearly see here the seed for the powerful polarities created in his later videos through the use of actual human operators versus the machines they operate.

A further element in the Walker installation that would also change Larson's later work is that while building these machines, Larson met Jason Spafford, who was working at the Walker. Larson mentioned to him that given the new clarity of these structures and their parts, he now wished they might actually move. To which Spafford replied that if Larson would build one that actually worked, he could make a film of it.

This possibility ratcheted Larson's work up several levels, as movement required actors to operate the machines, and actors plus movement required his work to enter into the medium of video. And, of course, the inherent nature of video as a medium turned the implied narratives and time element of the earlier work into real narrative and time as video. It also played the circular forms and spiral energies of the early work into a richer tension perfectly suited to the time-based and "circular" feel of how video "rolls forward." That is, in the videos, within each individual scene a human operator labors inside a machine that goes nowhere, giving a sense of futility. The camera shifts back and forth between one operator and another. Each machine thus seems isolated in its circular frenzy. And yet as a whole, the video itself struggles forward in a dialogue between the two operators, their conversation acting more as a spiraling forward, as if in hope that their labor will produce a meaningful resolution.

The subsequent works in the exhibitions that followed, from 2000 to the present, reveal the flourishing of all these possibilities. In 2000, for example, Larson began a more multimedia exploration of his interests, not only beginning his body of videos, but also treating the objects made for the sets of those videos as sculptures in their own right. His first solo show in New York at the RARE Gallery featured his first video, *The Gastral Colony*, alongside the actual "Gastral Machines" and houses used in the video (ills. pp. 30–35).

Another new element that came into being with *The Gastral Colony* was the introduction of an actual "text" of sorts. Unlike the Walker Art Center, which gave Larson free reign just to start building, New York's Art in General asked for a proposal. So Larson submitted a one-page "story" that was purportedly a single page torn from a four-chapter book about a place called the "Gastral Colony." The whole book is nonexistent, of course, but by combining a textual fragment as a source of clues about a place and its meanings, together with a video supplying a pseudo-narrative of that place alongside sculptures and installations based on it, Larson created a number of elements that all conspired together to make his work far more multidimensional and complex.

This combination of the machine, the house form, a supposed textual source, and a video established Larson's repertoire of archetypal images. More importantly, it established his use of these together in order to create an entire "world" or implied reality. In the *Gastral Colony* work, the house forms suggest all the basic functions of a community: house, school, city hall, and library. Corresponding to these are four different machines that give the bizarre impression that a person could either operate or be operated on while sitting in them. The ambivalence of the relation of the human to the machine to the community becomes a central motif. Implicit in this is the ambivalence between human freedom, in which we in our mastery are able to build machines, versus the sense that humans are merely part of a larger deterministic mechanism of nature.

Larson's video *The Gastral Colony* embodies all these elements. While there is not space here to describe all his videos in detail, it is helpful to the reader who has not seen them to describe one in enough detail to convey the texture and density of these rich works. The opening scenes of *The Gastral Colony* are set in nature, in the farmlands of the American Midwest. A tractor pulls farming equipment across a stubbly farm field, which we view through a car window traveling across this agrarian landscape. The scene then shifts to a barn, where the viewer is taken inside and the camera pans over the equipment and tools used by a farmer to work the land. The metaphor of what happens outside in nature versus what happens inside in human artifice—this being both literal and psychological—is a central idea for Larson. Once inside the barn, we encounter one of the gastral machines standing there like a strange harvesting machine. But instead of a farmer in the driver's seat, we find a man half sitting, half lying in its seat, silently waiting. Mostly naked, his skin and the machine parts juxtaposed, he sits as if he is both operator and victim.

A sound track, steadily increasing in volume, shifts between what sounds like a human heart beating and a tractor motor coughing into action and revving up its rpms. The man begins to operate the machine's levers with his hands. Its rods, bound in fabric so that they resemble the ligaments of the human body, plunge in and out of wet orifices while rounded wooden hammers pound on moist pouches or sacs filled with something soft.

There is a long pause in the motion, while the heartbeat sound continues. The man takes what look like crudely carved wood auger bits, lubricates their tips with a black greaselike substance, and drills them into black sacs, puncturing them until dark liquids flow freely from them. The camera views are always of details taken close up, which prevents the viewer from achieving a clear spatial orientation. As the video proceeds, the man works the machine, operating it on increasingly intimate terms. He dips his fingers into its lubricants and then slips them into metal collars attached to cables. These he pulls until he has pulled out some plugs in liquid-laden sacs, allowing more liquid to gush out. Black fluids ooze and then flow. The heartbeat and the tractor motor thump and rev.

At this point the man dons wooden headphones, the sound track falls silent, and the viewer feels that he or she has now been taken more internally into this man and machine. He inserts wooden parts into his nose and takes a mouthpiece between his lips. His feet are inserted into crude pedals. As he starts to pump the pedals, it seems that he is now operating the machine with his legs and arms while literally breathing life into it from nose and mouth. The boundary between man and mechanism softens. As he accelerates, the sound track returns with a driving noise, and we are shown a black tube protruding from his crotch, his pedaling action driving a phalluslike rod in and out of a tightly stretched membrane, until it bursts the membrane. As this happens, dark fluid—like both blood and crude oil at the same time—flows from his crotch, his mouth, and his nose, while his hands dip in and out of a clear fluid.

As these fluids flow, blood, sweat, urine, semen, but also oil, water, and sap, are all somehow implied, as if in his striving with the machine he is also striving with nature, desiring to produce some fecund, life-giving juice. Finally, this fluid flows into a main tube, where it is routed down through a hole in the barn floor into another realm or world. The camera then shifts to that other world, which is outside, in the dark night. There we see a small model of a white farmhouse, with the tube pouring fluids snaking into its chimney. The man continues to pump until the fluids fill the house, bulging out its walls and roof in bubbles and herniated distensions, until fluid literally pours out the doors and windows—out the orifices—of the house itself.

In this total video image, man is an extension of the machine as much as the machine is an extension of man. Interiors and exteriors are conflated as we shift between physical realities and psychological constructs. It is not clear whether this man who works the "farming" equipment in the barn is not also equally inside the house; whether this is his labor or his dream, his nightmare or his fantasy. His hard labor seems both futile, even Sisyphean, and productive, even heroic. It reaches some torturous ecstatic climax that is mostly painful and exhausting, but is also a needed release. The question that remains for the viewer is, "What was achieved?" The hard labor certainly filled the house to overflowing; and yet we are left with a sense of darkness, as if the cost to this man was too high, as if he will have to do this again every day merely to survive in a deterministic, endless circling of work.

Larson leaves open the question of whether this was somehow revelatory or redemptive. As will become increasingly apparent in his work, this is part of what Larson means by "failure." That is, if epiphany is reached, it does not come from the traditional plot structure of initial incident, struggle, and then bright victory. Rather, it comes more through the tradition of the "grotesque," through a less transparent, much darker paradox. Given his fascination with the grotesque, any moments of grace will have to be wrenched more darkly out of the fabric of failure, not triumph.

Looking back with hindsight, the layered complexity of Larson's metaphors here seems to have been already latent in the early "scanner" pieces. But looking forward, these metaphors are played out even more extensively in the later videos, drawings, and sculptures created between 2000 and 2006. In these years, Larson works in a kind of alternating rhythm between large sculptures, elaborate drawings of sculptures too big to build (recalling the fantastic scale of Piranesi's *Imaginary Prisons*), and videos.

What distinguishes the maturation of these more recent works is a fuller flowering of the provocative dualities initiated by the Walker installation and *Gastral Colony*. Larson ramps up his work by increasing the layers and intensity of worlds that collide and struggle. He does this by increasing the number of actors, making them more diverse (in race and gender), complicating the layers of enigmatic space and machines in which they operate, and extending his metaphoric references out into populist culture.

In the video *County Line* (2004), he creates a different conflict of two worlds. Here two machines exist in a hierarchy, one above, one below, built as a strange tower. The upper machine encases a white man as operator; the lower one encases a black man (ills. pp. 53–55). It remains ambiguous whether they are laboring in a collaborative effort or in outright opposition to each other. In two major sculptures, *Pause (The Dukes of Hazzard '69 Charger and Ted Kaczynski's Montana Refuge)* (2004) and *Spaceship and Shack* (2004) (ills. pp. 20–21, 22–23), irrationally opposite worlds collide. For example, in *Pause*, the car from the television show *The Dukes of Hazzard* falls out of the sky and crashes into the shack of the Unabomber, Ted Kaczynski. If the "Dukes" belong to the Deep South—two outlaw "good ol' boys," whose law-breaking is a "good" because the authorities are corrupt—then Ted Kaczynski belongs to what Flannery O'Connor scholar Ralph Woods calls the "Deep North." Kaczynski also was an outlaw who felt he was doing "good" in defiance of corrupt authorities. But as a real person killing innocent victims, he becomes a humorless and demented terrorist, played by Larson against the hilarious and fictive Duke boys. This room-sized sculpture plays on video and television in its name, *Pause*, which suggests our use of the remote control to pause the action so that we can savor the details of violent destruction-as-entertainment.

In the midst of these works, as Larson amplifies the complexity of his art and ideas, a new dimension begins to emerge. Inevitably, something more than mere collision between opposing elements had to happen. Somehow a new thing, a metamorphosis, had to be birthed out of the conflict of opposites. Some move out of the two-dimensional circle of violence and into a three-dimensional spiraling elsewhere needed to occur. The clearest place that such a metamorphosis first occurs is in *American Gothic (Saturday Night/Sunday Morning)* (ills. pp. 24–27).

This video begins with the clashing of opposite forces, the Man in Black versus the Farmer in Gold. The conflict of these characters is amplified by the back-to-back opposite social structures of "Saturday Night" as a time of moral abandonment versus "Sunday Morning" as a spiritual time of hymns and prayer. The secular and lurid versus the religious and pure of this metaphor is drawn from one of Larson's other interests, which is country gospel music. Specifically, this imagery comes from an album by country western and gospel singer Ralph Stanley, titled *Saturday Night and Sunday Morning*. On one side of that album, Stanley recorded his dissolute drinking songs, while on the other side he recorded his redemptive gospel songs. These spiritual opposites are bound together since they exist on the same circular vinyl disc. As such, they posit a distinction between good and evil, as well as a clear choice the listener must make in deciding which side to play. But at the same time, these opposites exist inseparably as one album. Every listener knows we will indulge both sides at one time or another.

Larson gives these collisions concreteness by rooting them directly in populist Midwest American culture and the "low art" of film noir, country western and gospel music, and vaudeville and fundamentalist Christian church services. The Man in Black is a stylized figure for darkness. He is the vaudevillian personification of evil. He is based on Charles

Laughton's gothic film noir, *The Night of the Hunter* (1955), a biblical tale of greed, innocence, seduction, sin, and corruption, where the preacher is also a mass murderer. The imagery in the Man in Black's machinery comes from the gambling hall, the saloon, and the magician's stage. In contrast, The Farmer is the typology of good as one who works the soil and nurtures life. The imagery in his machinery comes from the farm, the land, and the country church with its gothic windows and baptismal font full of healing water.

As they confront each other, each character operates his machinery, the Man in Black sweating heavily, the Farmer in Gold wet with the water of baptism. With tubes hooked up or failing to hook up, fluids flowing, they pump their machines vigorously, until the Man in Black—accompanied by honky-tonk music—reaches a frenzy, and the Farmer in Gold—accompanied by lyrical hymns—slips into a meditative trance. At the full crescendo of their pumping motion, a large white membrane inflates and bursts open, birthing an unexpected, hybrid man who rises up like a Frankenstein out of their contest. He is like the gangly, awkward offspring of farm animals, with spindly legs that seem too long. Dressed in a white suit and cowboy hat made of cheap, shiny vinyl embroidered with conflicting symbols—an apple, two dice with snake eyes, playing cards—this "too-tall Texan in White," as Larson refers to him, strangely blends religious iconography with the devices of gambling and sin that Midwest religion forbids. He is a bizarre hybrid of the Man in Black and the Farmer. He is, in short, a metamorphosis emerging from a weird cocoon.

As this ungainly, deformed man tries to get up from his birth bed, he falls backward. The camera pans up his six-foot-long legs, over his body, to his hideous face. His huge lips are rouged, his bloodshot blue eyes stare, and a hideous leering grin reveals enormous buckteeth crudely capped in gold. It is as if this monstrous man is a strange synthesis of good and evil. Or perhaps more, he is the deformed result of human efforts to resolve good and evil, even as we crave both—a kind of new and strange creature, morally and spiritually ambiguous. He is the repulsive personification of "failure."

And yet, as this strangely deranged Man in White towers over us, the camera holding on his face from a low viewing point so that we must look up into his visage, an unwelcome fascination rises up in the viewer. A strange expressive "beauty"—a grotesque beauty like the kind that writer Flannery O'Connor reveals—is felt. Such grotesque beauty is birthed by a collision of good and evil, a collision that is not a reconciliation, but rather a metamorphic twisting together into a new hybrid. And, as in O'Connor's stories, this kind of ugly beauty always seems a disaster, a moral failure. But that disaster also fascinates, almost as if it is somehow an unexpected occasion for an outrageous epiphany of grace. A perplexing, troubling grace: this is not the grace of the perfect eternal circle; it is the grace of ugliness, of the spiraling struggle. As the camera holds on his face, the Man in White seems to awaken to his existence, his red lipsticked mouth, his huge gold teeth, his stupid, leering grin, and his weirdly staring blue eyes that are both idiotic and ecstatic, all radiating weirdness and light while the film becomes so overexposed that he disappears in what is either apotheosis or destruction.

In Larson's subsequent work, this enrichment of conflicts by way of metamorphosis comes to fruition, especially in the video *Crush Collision* (2006). But to get at that, we must address what I see as one of the most fundamental layers of his thinking. A layer in which the narrative expressiveness of metamorphosis links profoundly with another kind of metamorphosis, which is his transformation of materials.

Thus far we have followed Larson's work via an organizing matrix of core ideas—the circle and spiral, the tensions between human freedom and determinism, purpose and uselessness, failure and epiphany. But to speak of these as abstract ideas too separately from the way that Larson handles materials risks missing the heart of his accomplishment. Of course, much has already been said about the impact of his visceral use of fluids, lubricants, gears, levers, and so on. But the danger is in letting that impact operate too much at the narrative and emotive levels. There is a more fundamental level of using materials that underwrites these things.

This more fundamental level is his "translation" of one material into another. Larson insists upon building his mechanisms in wood, fabric, and other organic materials. On the obvious level, these are expressive materials for him. At the same time, it should be pointed out that the things he builds are not, in their real world counterparts, built of wood. They are machines, which are typically made of metal because metal has greater precision, tighter tolerance in its moving parts, and greater durability. Larson goes against this by building everything more crudely in wood. The obvious result is a more raw and primitive quality, which increases

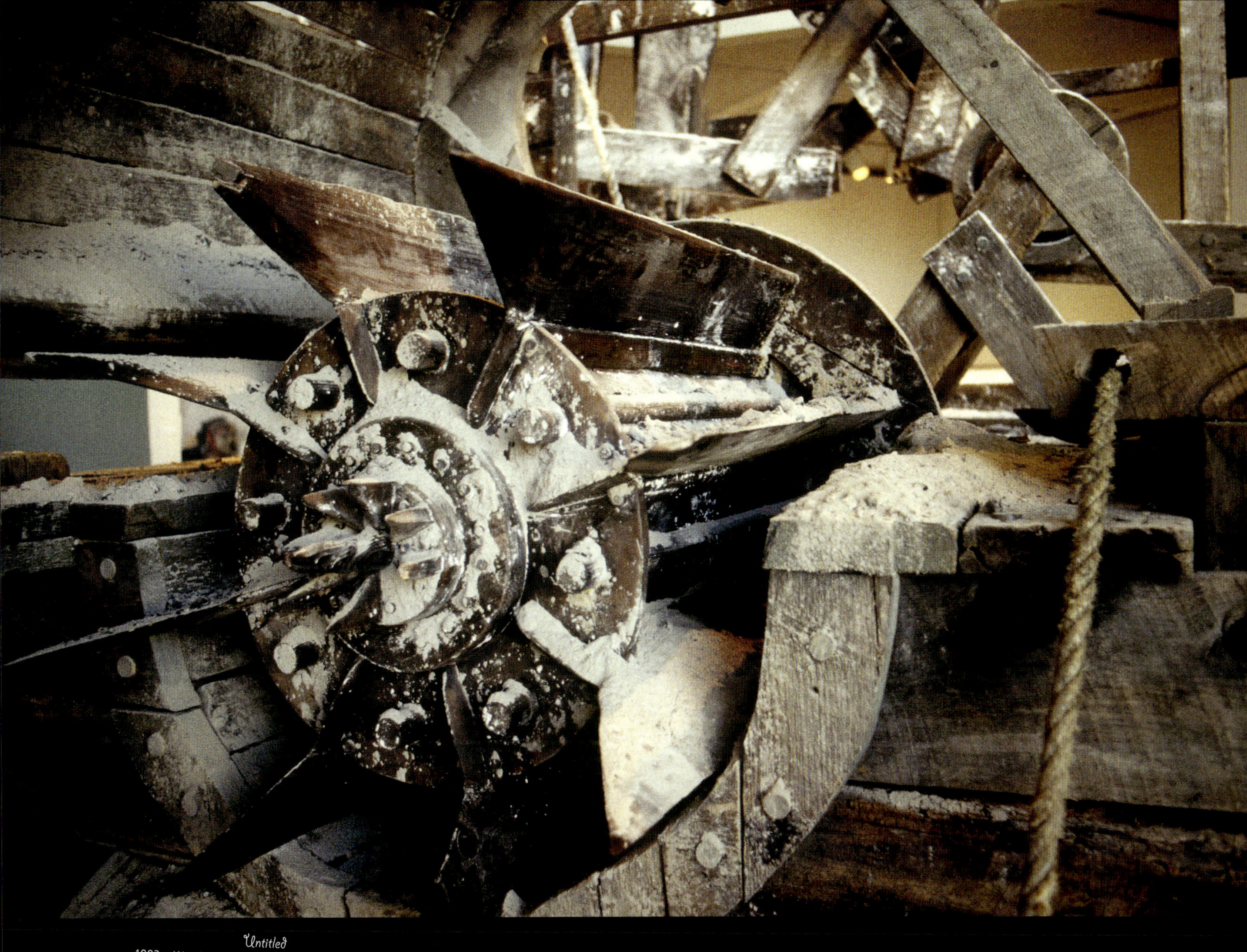

Untitled
1993 • Wood, salt, ash, soap • 580 x 366 x 275 cm
Detail, installation view (see p. 41)
Minneapolis College of Art and Design, Minneapolis, MN

our emotional engagement. But this use of wood is not simply about "getting a good effect."

Indeed, it is a cul-de-sac to say that Larson "builds his machines out of wood." The real energy of what he is doing is better revealed by saying that he "translates" machines into wood. He translates from the "hard language" of metal and precision into the "soft language" of body and vulnerability. In this he carries us from what is mechanistic and rational into what is organic and of the heart. And in doing so, he blurs the boundaries between structures, persons, and meanings.

The word "translate" must be insisted upon. In today's common parlance (which interestingly enough is the second meaning given by the *Oxford English Dictionary*), "to translate," means to change into another language while retaining the sense of the first. Of course, everyone knows that a translation also loses something inherent, something that is true to its meaning as embodied within the first language and yet difficult to capture in the second. Indeed, as Daniel Taylor pointed out to me, translators understand well the Italian pun between "*traduttore, traditore*" ("translator, traitor"). To translate is to betray as well as to convey. For the professional translator, this is a pragmatic problem with an unfortunate result.

But for the artist, it is a metaphor and an opportunity of great value. For as a metaphor, it is in the uncertain *place* between one language and another, where "translation" is simultaneously a success and a failure, that *a disruption* occurs. At the most primal level, "translation-as-disruption" is not only part of Larson's working method, it *is* his *content*. It is the formal equivalent of "failure-as-epiphany." That disruption itself becomes an important experience. In fact, that disruption comes to exist as a *new form*, which is what Larson's hybrid machines are. They indicate "a realm" or meaning that is neither the one language nor the other, that is neither goodness nor evil. This is what Martin Buber called "the realm of the between." And as Buber demonstrated, it is art that gives form to that realm. Such form signifies a "suspension" between the known and fixed meanings of the first language and the known and fixed meanings intended in the second language. Larson, it seems to me, seeks to suspend us between languages, between states of being, by way of "translation."

All of which brings us to the first meaning of "translate" given in the *Oxford English Dictionary*, which is, "to bear, convey or remove from one person, place or condition to another." This idea of being conveyed from one condition of being to another is central to Larson's "translations" from metal to wood, just as it is central to metamorphosis. Indeed, in that sense, being "translated" or "changed" might be the central content for Larson. His work is asking if life is a mere circling in futility, a laboring round and round on the material plane, or a spiraling transformation brought about by struggle, a laboring toward redemption.

It is this sense of "translate" that was used, for example, by the poet John Donne, in his *Meditation XVII*, where he speaks of our conveyance from this earthly body, which is a site of some futility, into a heavenly body as "being translated." That is, as a *being changed* from one meaning or form into another precisely by the effort of laboring through our travails. "Some," he wrote, "are translated by age, some by sickness, some by war, some by justice." While this usage of the word is no longer common in our era, it is still felt intuitively. And Larson's translation of materials bears that intuition. For what is balanced precisely at the fulcrum point of his translation between metal machine and organic body is the tension between deterministic structure and humanistic freedom, between us as laboring animals caught in an endless circle and us as spiritual animals passing upward in a spiral.

This teetering and turning between meanings, between struggle and suffering versus hope and redemption, is what Larson's video *Crush Collision* fully embodies. In the beginning of *Crush Collision*, we encounter another bi-level machine. This time it is operated by a male and a female. They work their machines in tandem, laboring in an endless circular motion. Yet their coupled efforts do seem to produce something: a giant ring of some breadlike substance. Even so, they work repetitively in an ambiguous, enclosed space, surrounded by their machines, without reprieve.

While this dual structure sufficed in the earlier videos, in *Crush Collision* it is only half of the levels involved. While the male-female couple work rhythmically, the camera shifts from the enclosed space of their machinery to an entirely new kind of space, with a new kind of bifurcated level. It takes us to a house floating on water in an open landscape (ills. pp. 79, 84–85).

For the first time in all of Larson's work, an expansive, sunlit, green and blue natural space is offered as a powerful release to the viewers' eyes. And for the first time, the house form is large enough to be inhabited as a home, in direct opposition to the machine-as-housing. This does not mean, though, that we are safe, for this house lacks foundations and stability. It floats on the water, quietly turning in a circling motion as it spirals downriver. We are taken inside where we see a black family, a mother and father and two girls, seated at a dinner table. Apparently they wait for food. As they wait, they pray and sing, while the floor of the room is strangely open to the water directly beneath their feet. A pianist plays the piano in the attic level of the house, and they sing a spiritual about pain and suffering, about not being able to bear pain any longer, about the desire for release to Heaven and Zion.

As these elements play back and forth between each other, the house is floating across the water, turning and spiraling. One feels that the movement of the video camera and the time-based quality of this medium become part of its content, as if we are being translated somewhere, from one state to another.

Crush Collision is not Larson's final statement. It remains to be seen where his working process will take him. Certainly his most recent video, *Deep North* (2008), throws us back into a far bleaker world, where everything is frozen and the human figures seem to work mechanically to no purpose whatsoever (ills. pp. 87–97). They take ice in at the front of the house and work it; then the ice exits at the rear of the house. Everything is covered in thick, unrelenting ice.

While one thinks of the most brutal of Minnesota winters up North and the struggle to survive such weather, one also thinks of Dante's *Inferno*. Interestingly, the spatial structure of Dante's Hell is a downward spiral through which he must labor, with Virgil as his guide. When they finally descend to the lowest rings of damnation, they find there not the cliché of Hell as fire, but Hell as the absence of all life: Hell as an utterly frozen realm of ice.

And yet, when Dante reaches that terrible place, we are not finished, though it seems to get worse. It is at this most bleak, frozen, and lifeless level of Hell that his companion, Virgil—who stands for reason as the human capacity to guide us through evil and suffering—is forced to leave poor Dante altogether. For reason can only lead us as far as the worst depths of human behavior. Beyond that, reason is a failure. Only faith and the beatific vision of his love, Beatrice, can guide Dante on to Purgatory, and to the hope of his translation into the ascending circle of Heaven's dome.

Deep North promises no Beatrice. Nor do we find Virgil there. It remains to be seen where Larson's next twenty years of art will translate us.

---

1 *Marina Abramović, Public Body: Installation and Objects*, 1965–2001, text by Germano Celant (Milan, 2001), pp. 26, 29.

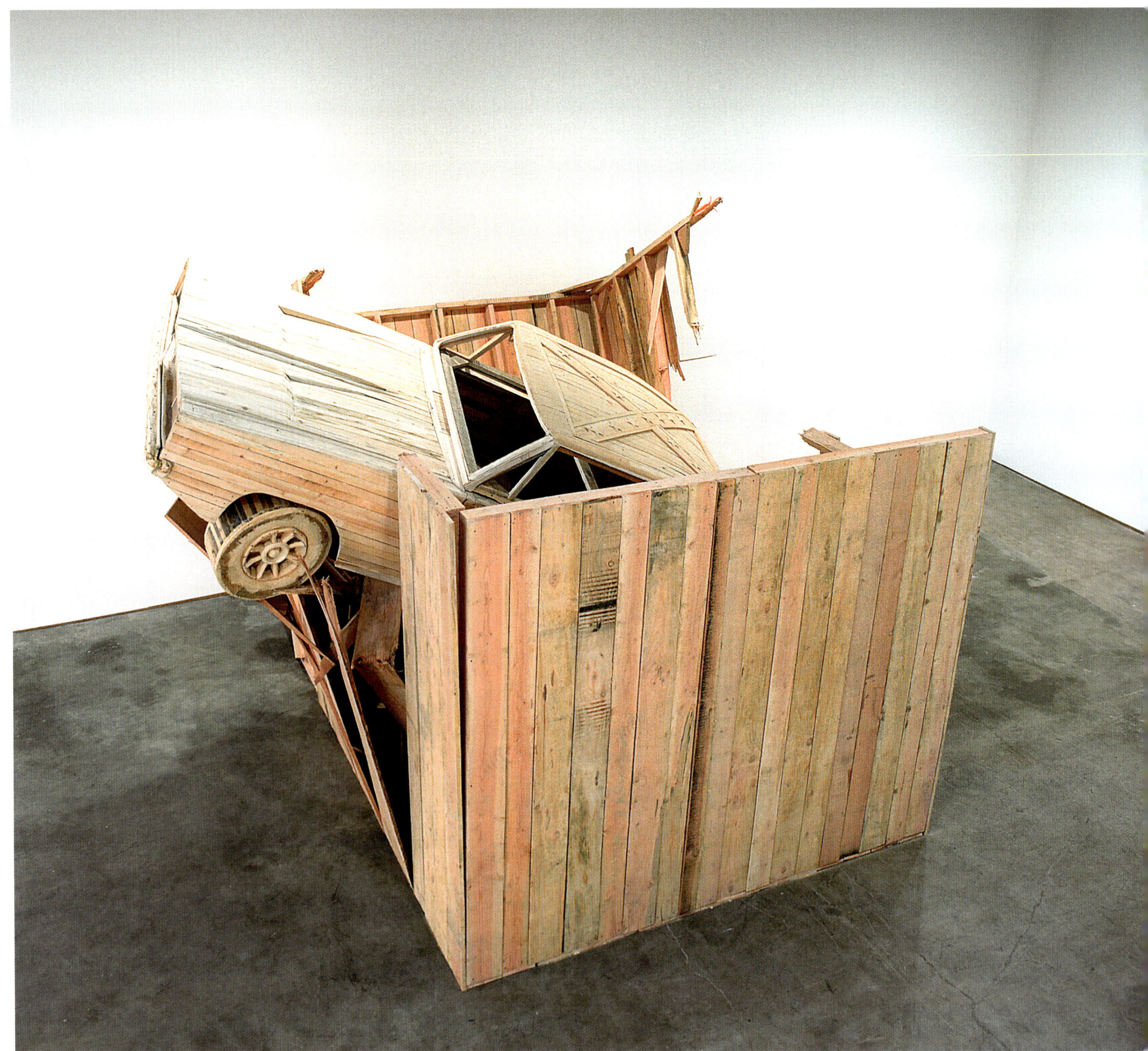

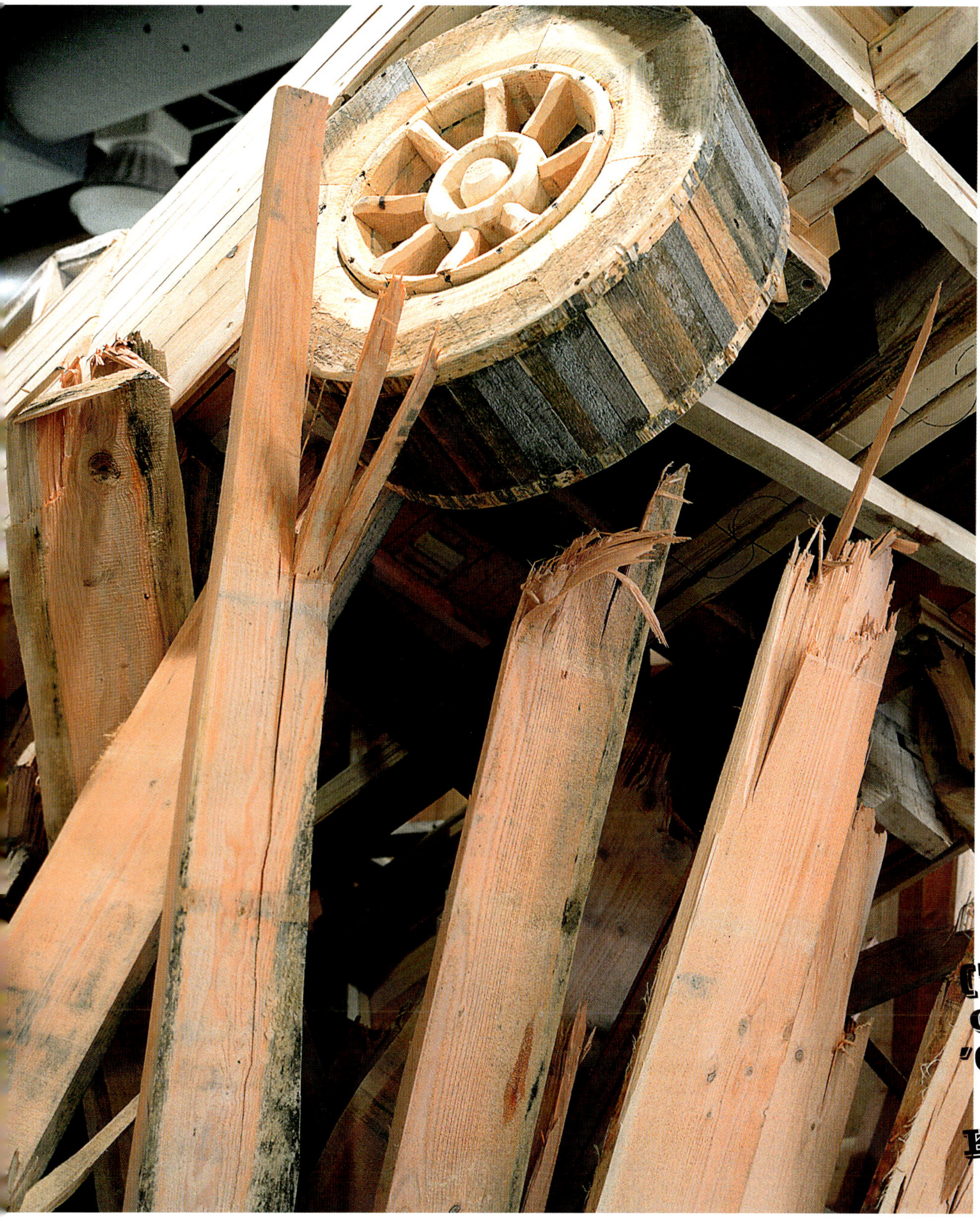

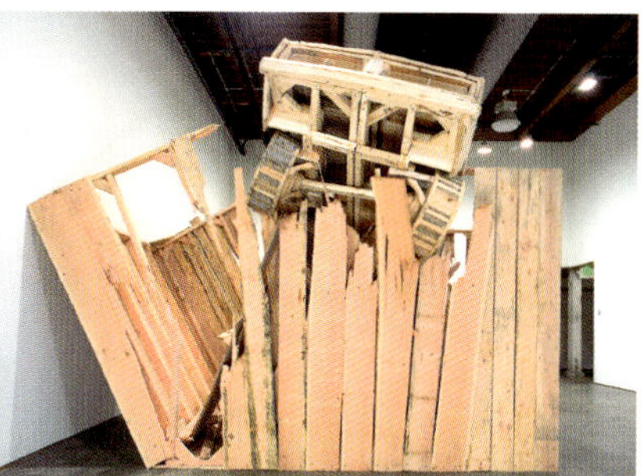

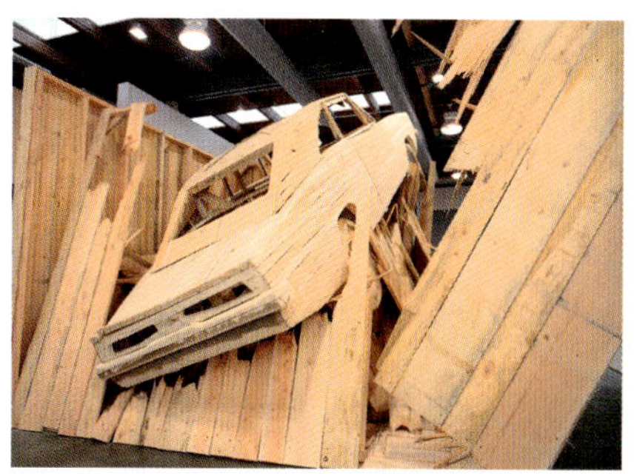

Pause (The Dukes of Hazzard '69 Charger and Ted Kaczynski's Montana Refuge)

2004 • Wood • 518 x 457 x 305 cm
Installation views, Western Bridge, Seattle, WA

Spaceship Shack

2004 • Wood • 701 x 640 x 488 cm
Installation views, Franklin Artworks, Minneapolis, MN

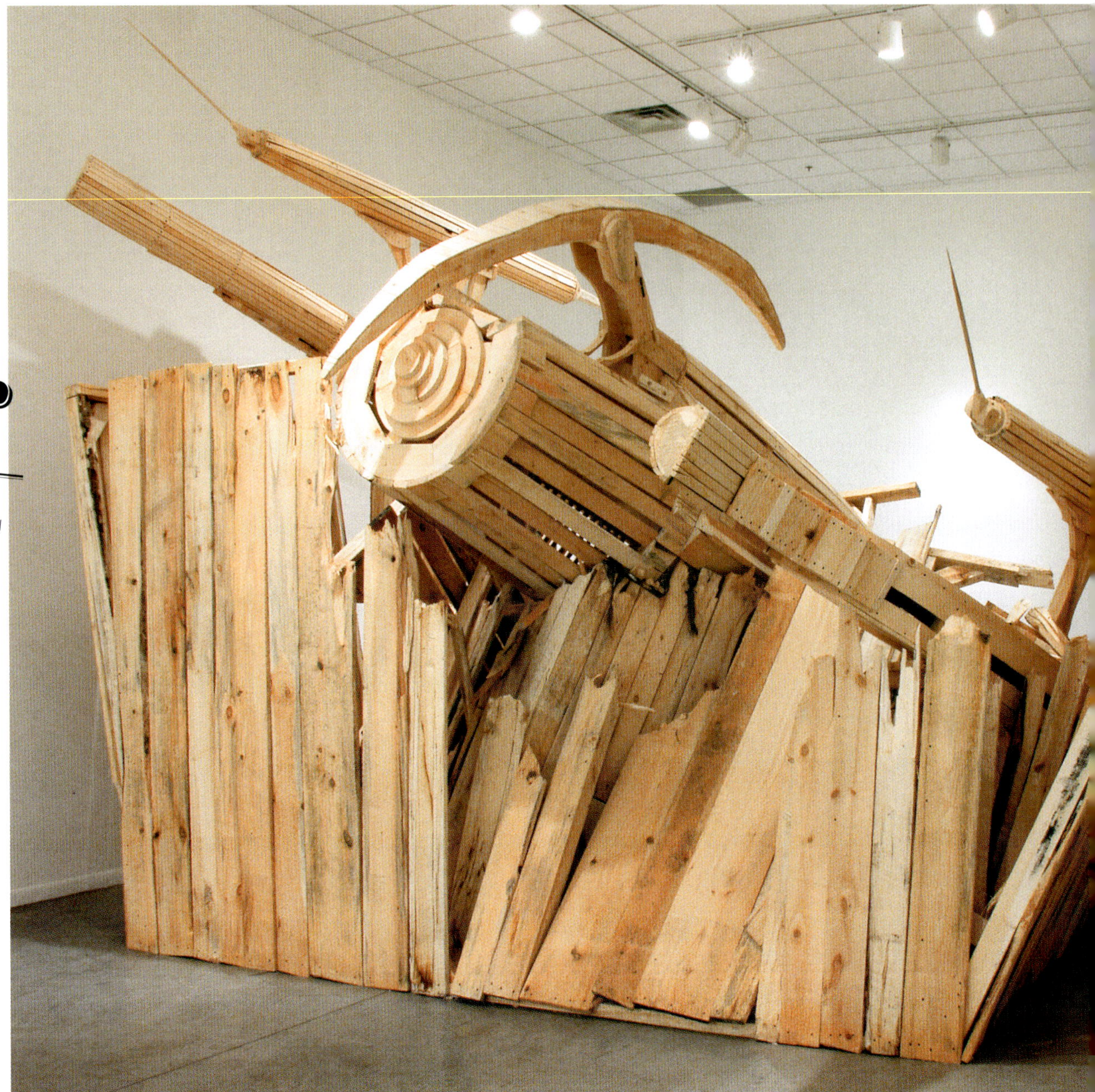

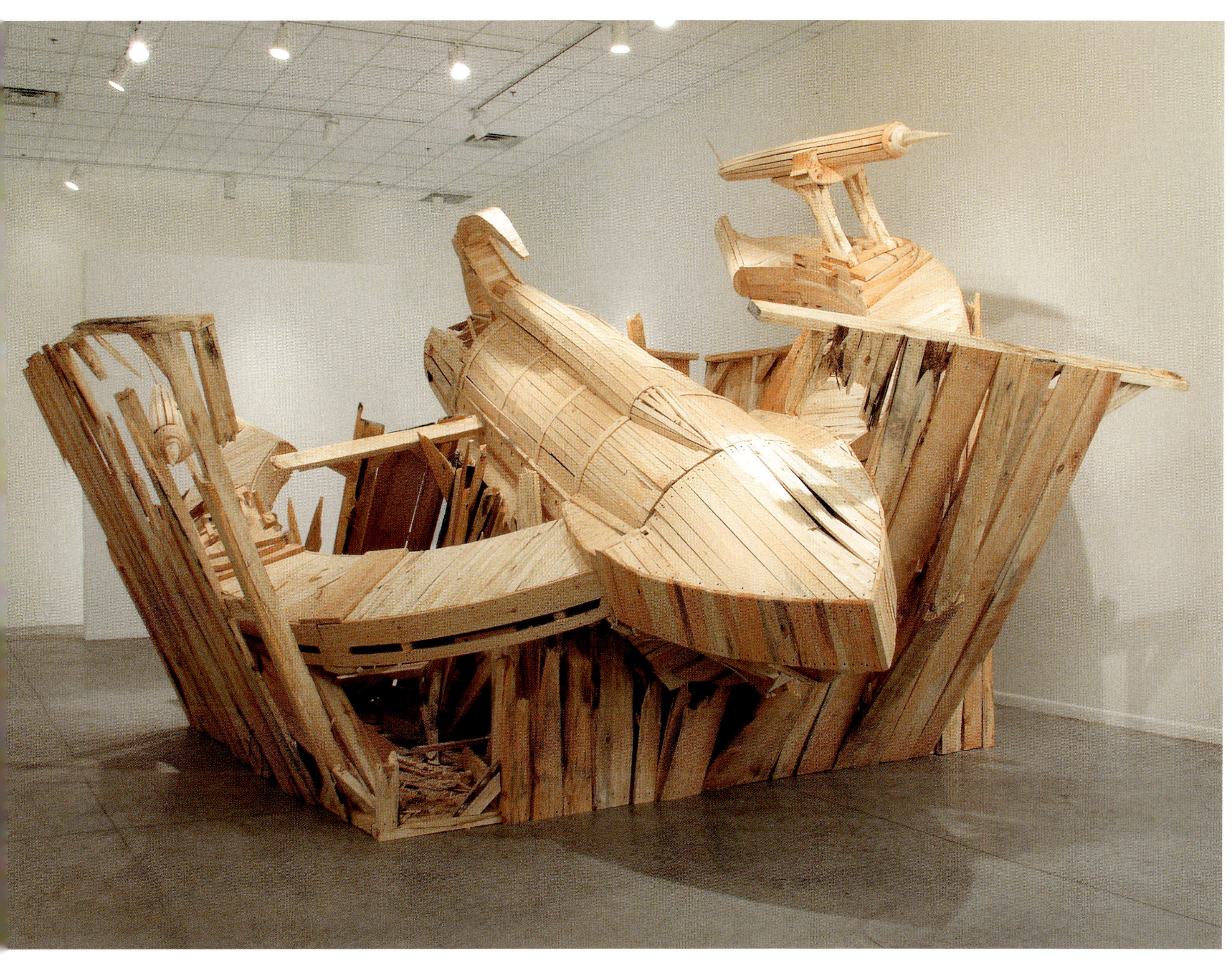

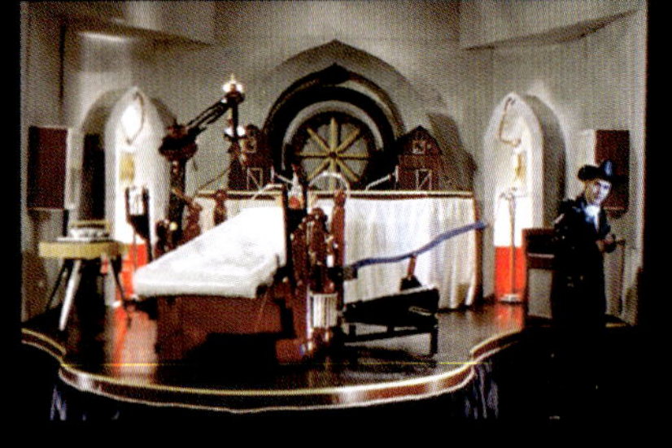
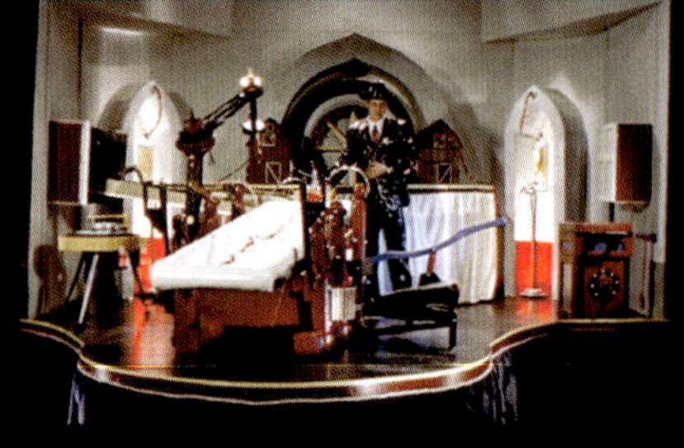
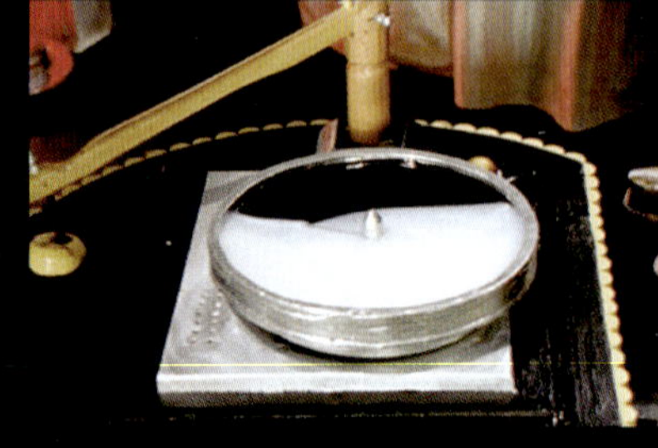

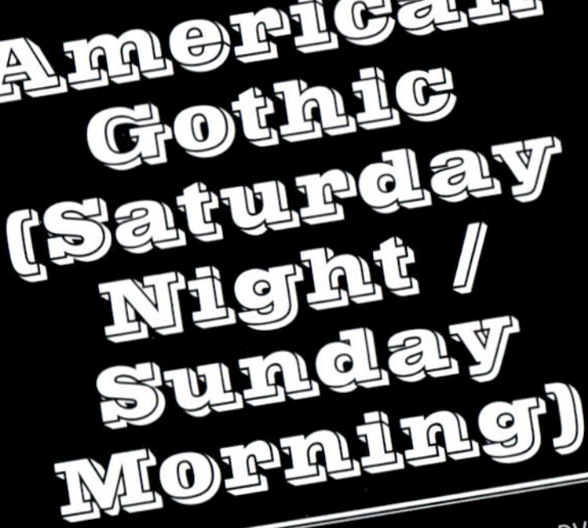

American Gothic (Saturday Night / Sunday Morning)

2001 • Super 16 mm color film transferred to DVD
Running time: 10:45 min.
Video stills

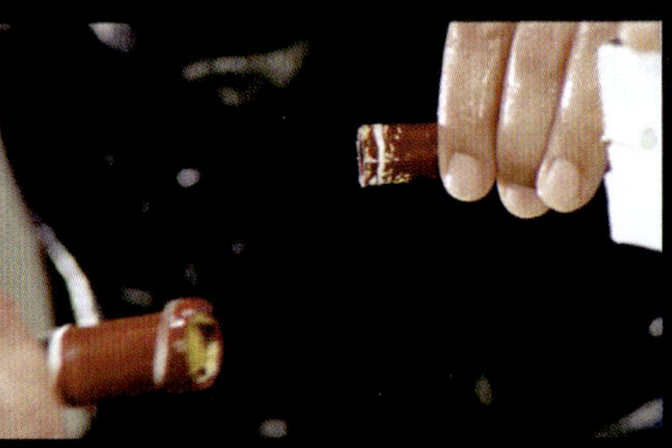
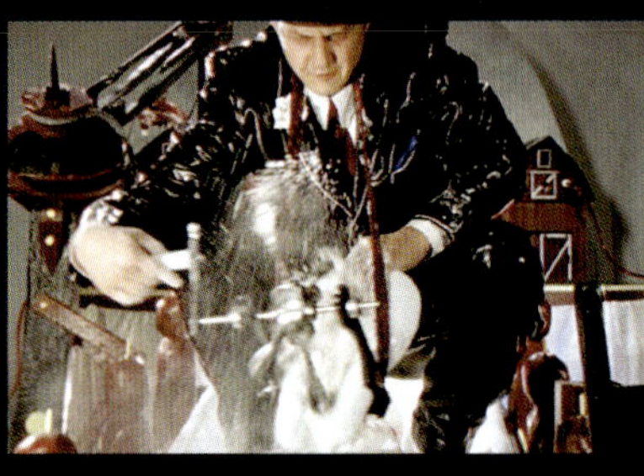

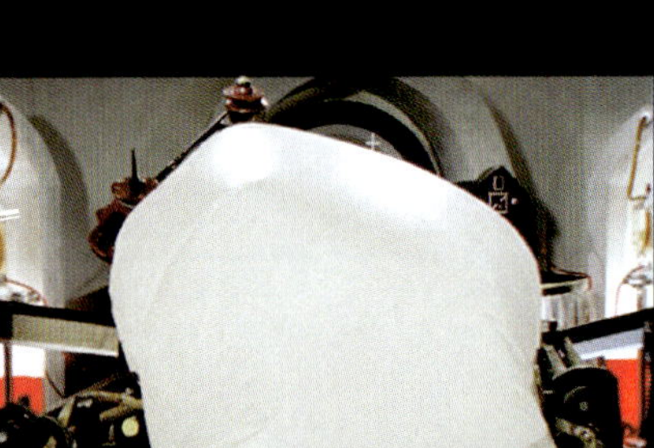
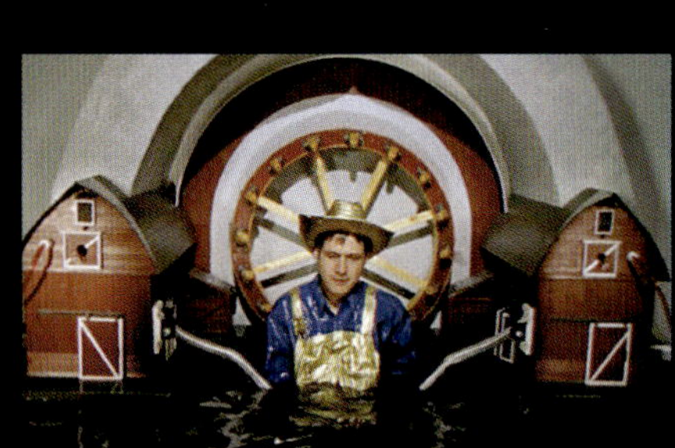
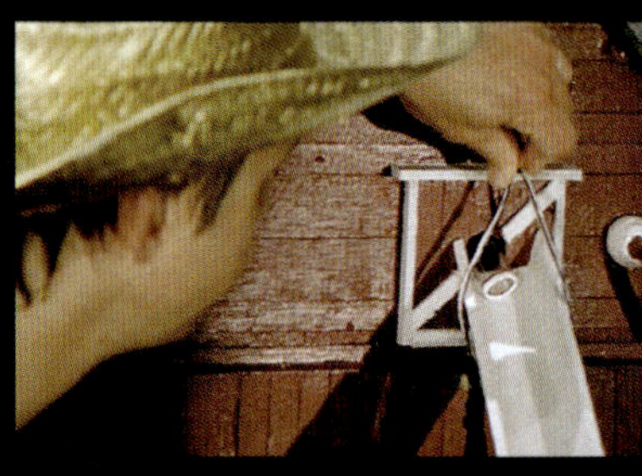

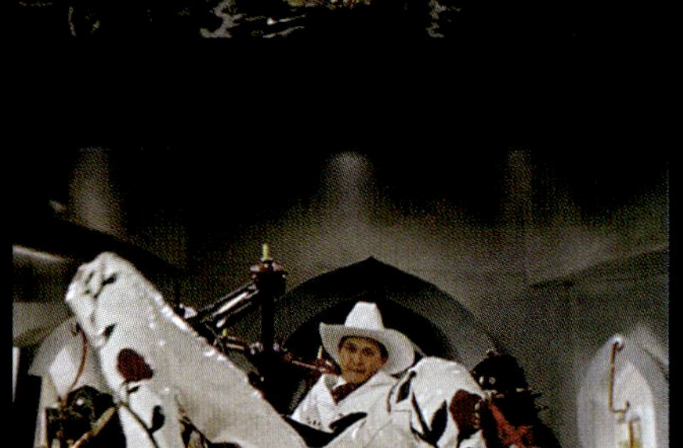
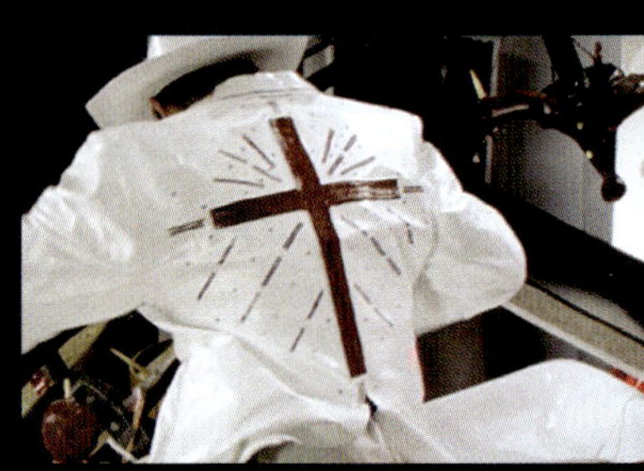

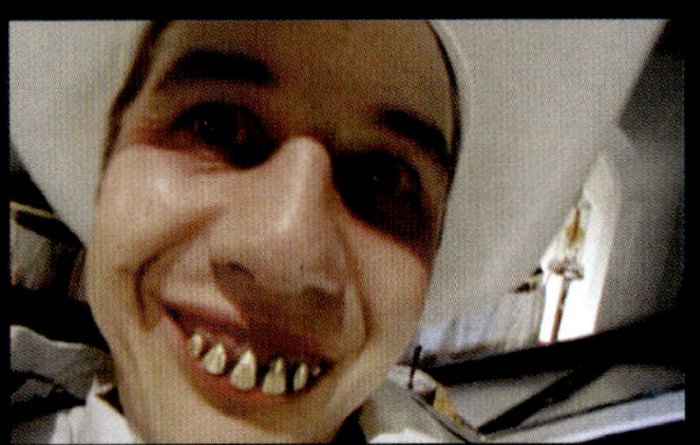

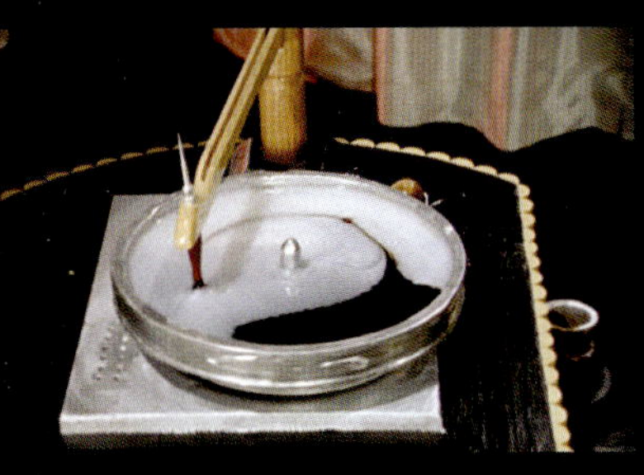
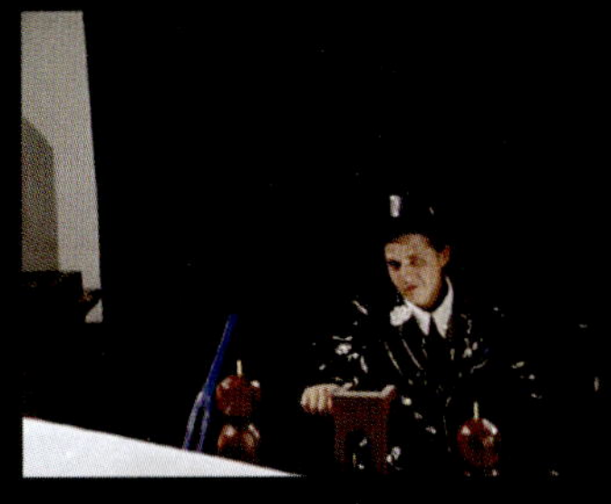
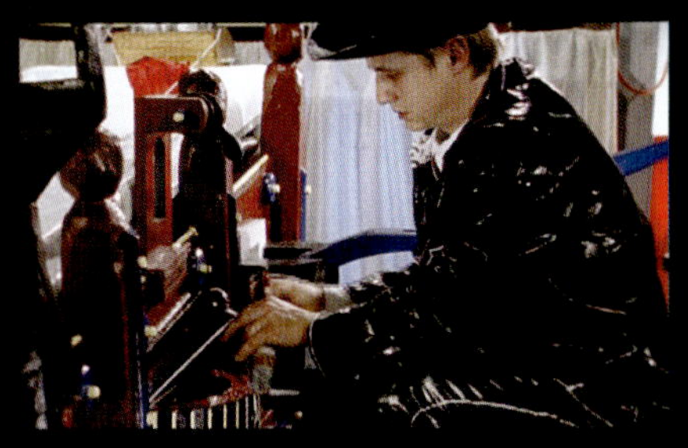
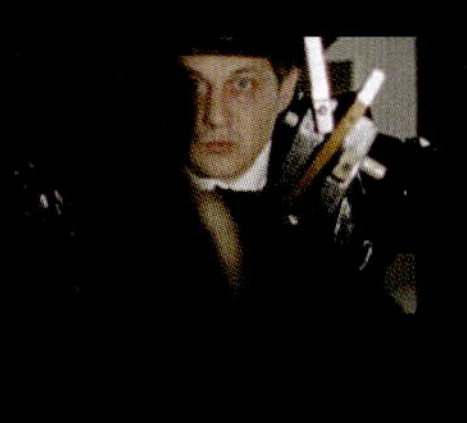
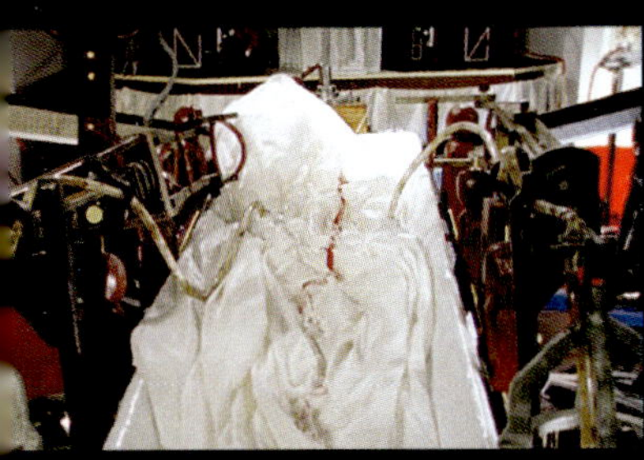
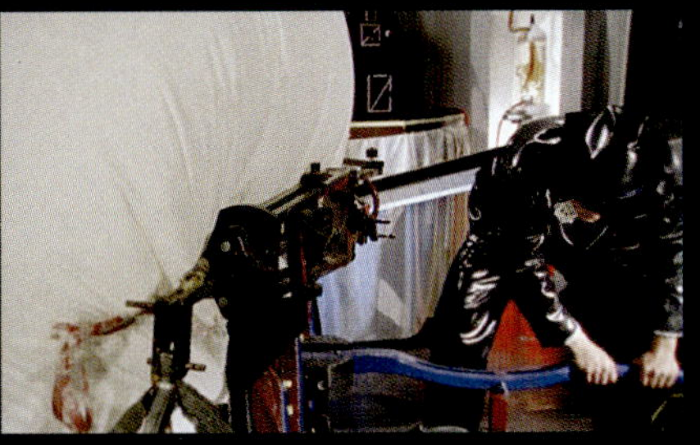
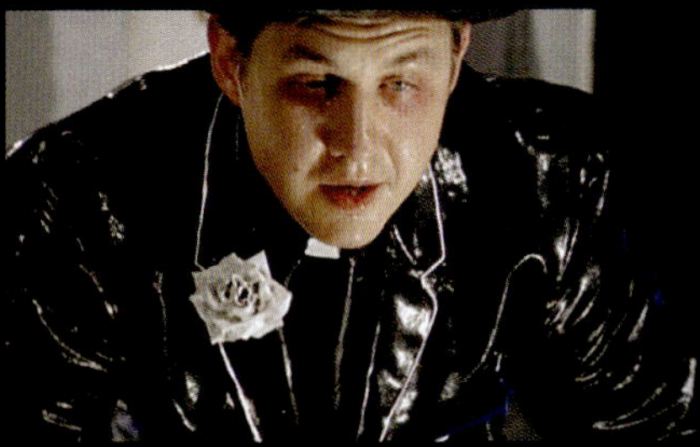
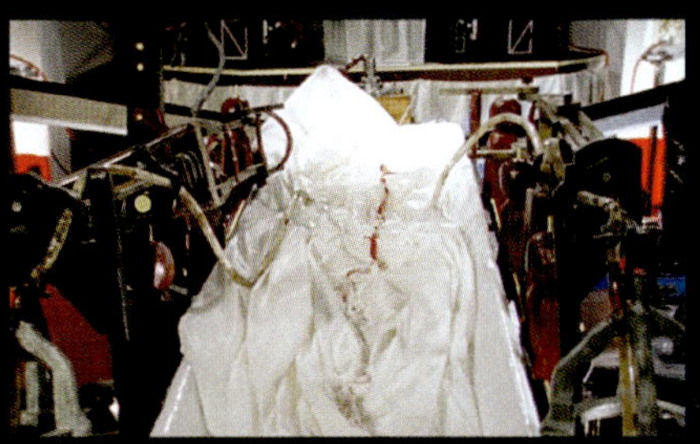
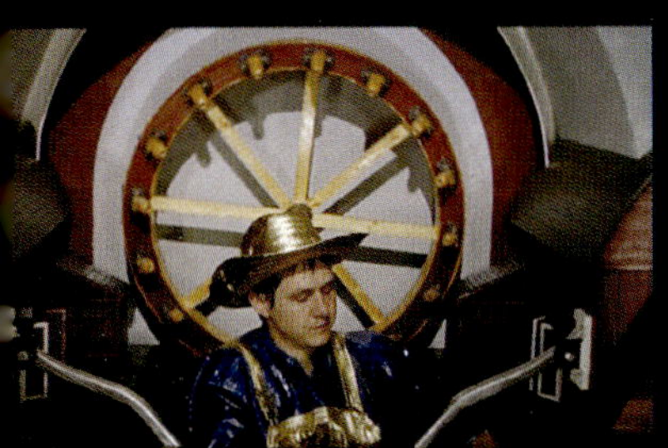
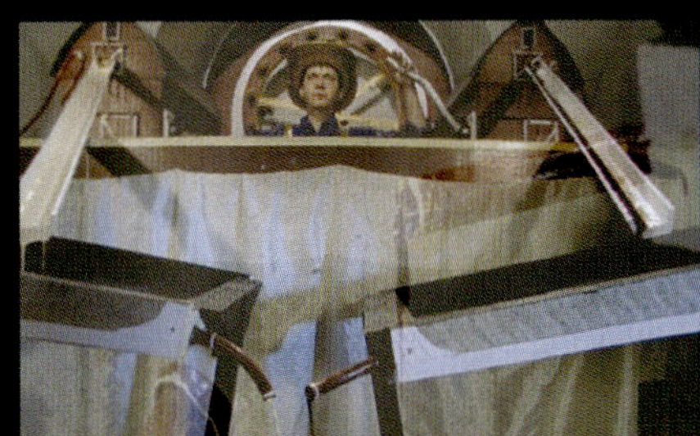
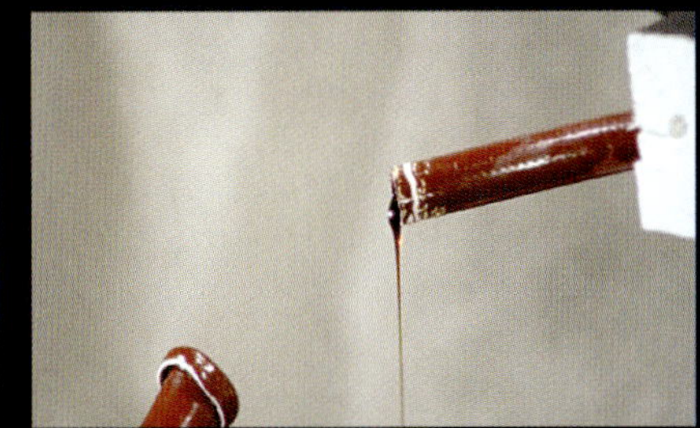
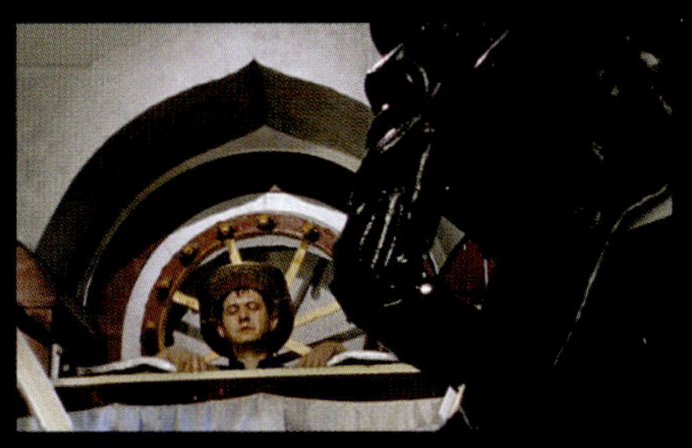
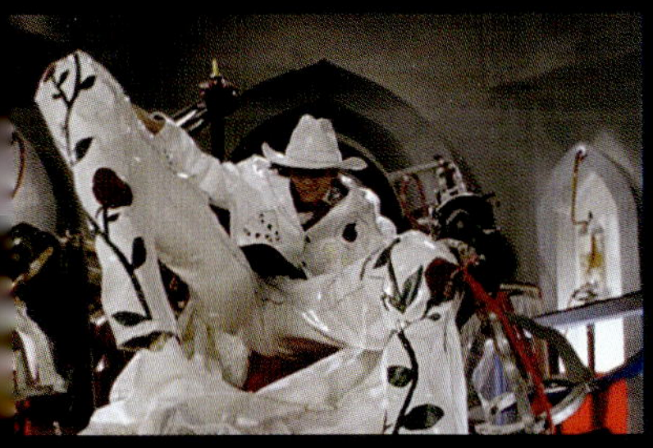
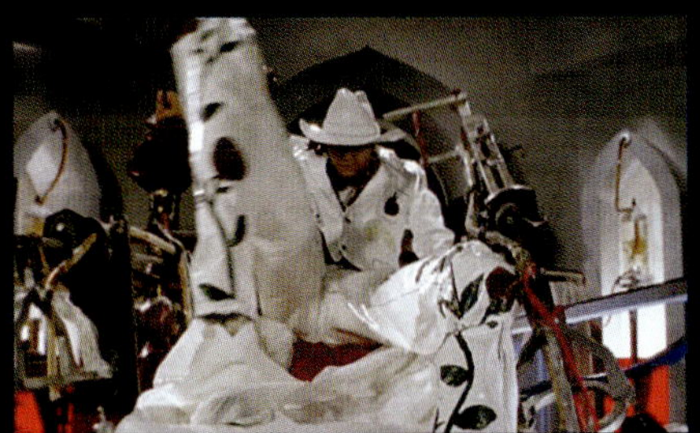
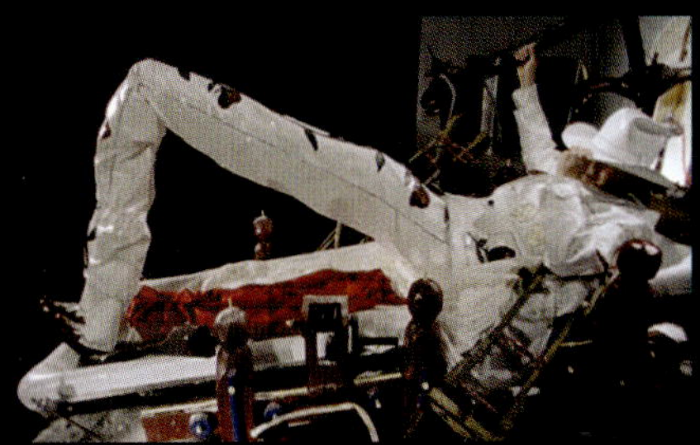
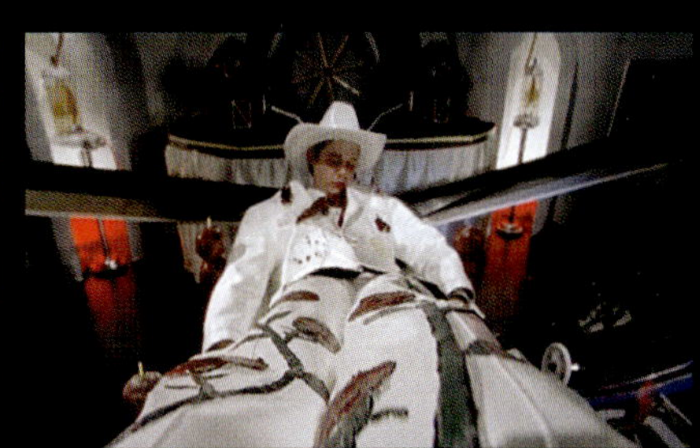

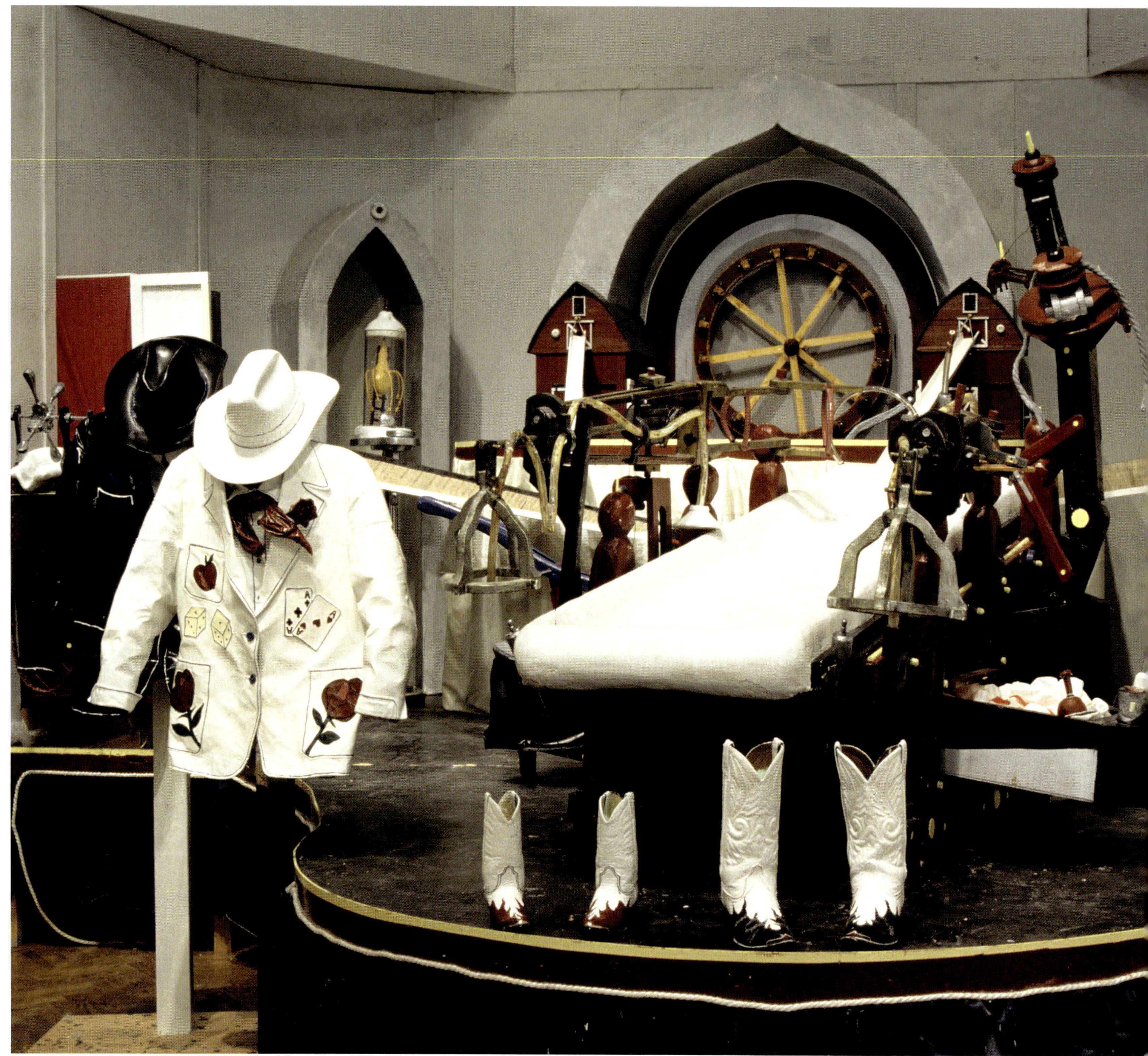

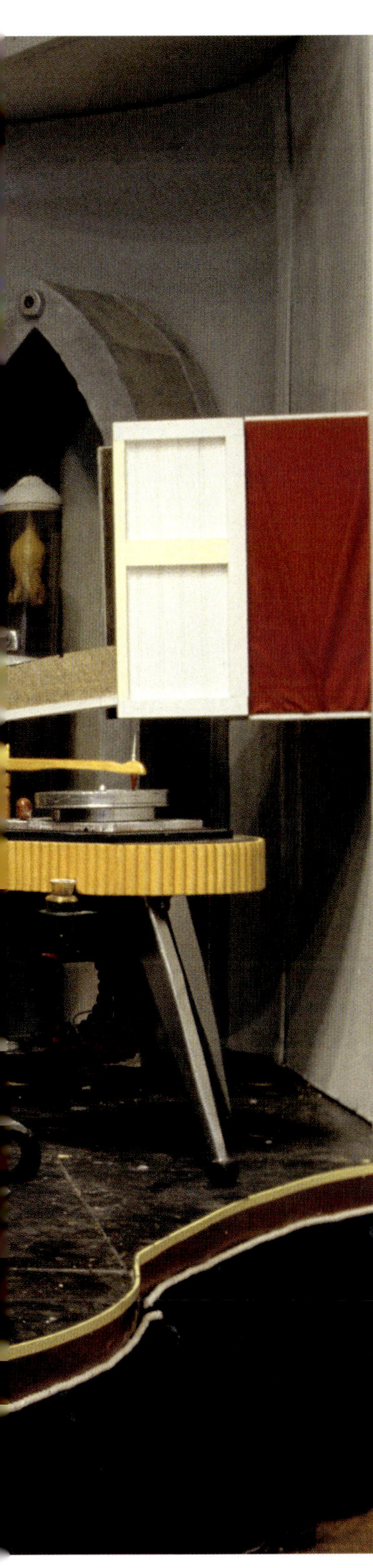

American Gothic (Saturday Night / Sunday Morning)

2001 * Set, installation view
Minneapolis Institute of Arts, Minneapolis, MN

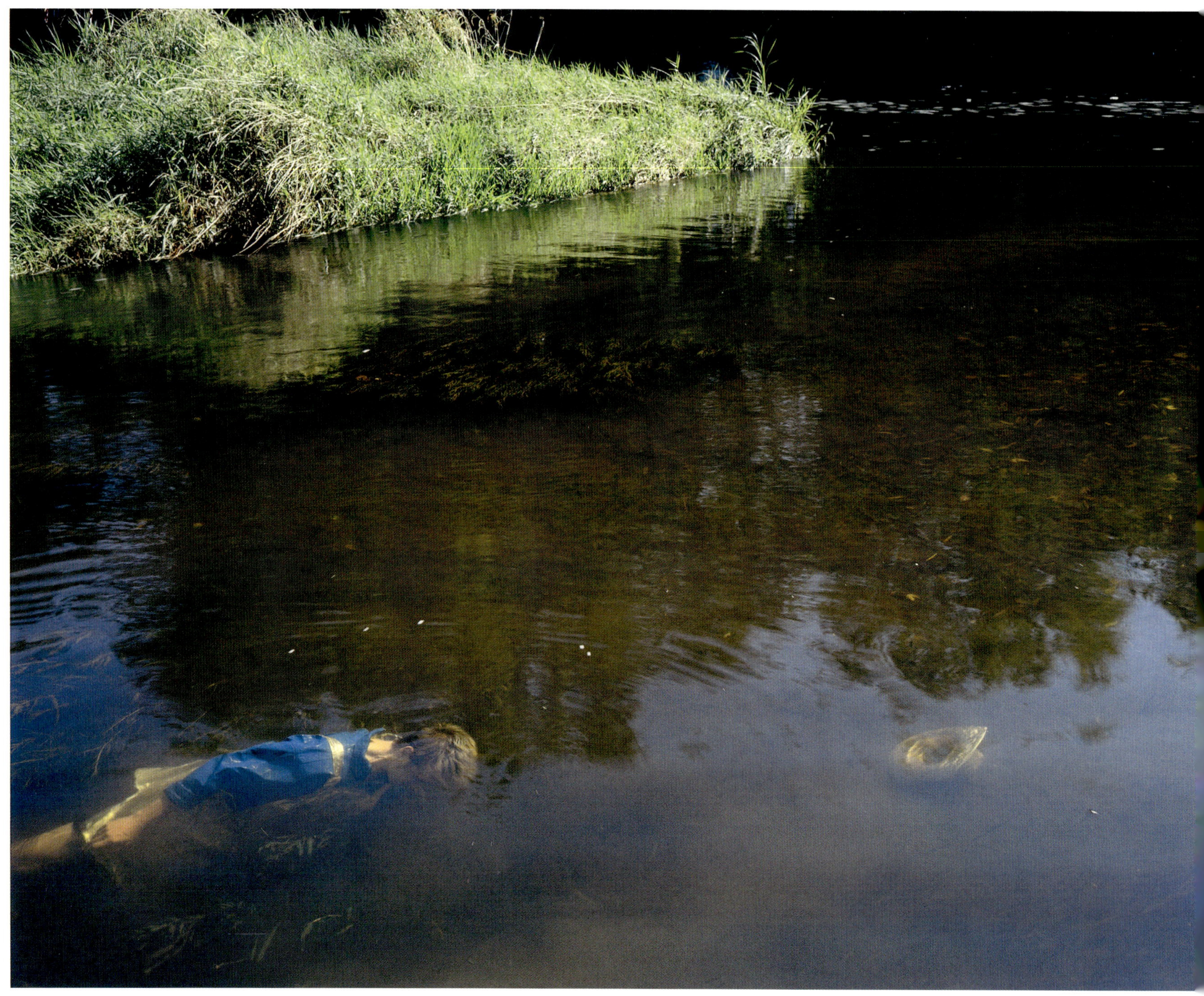

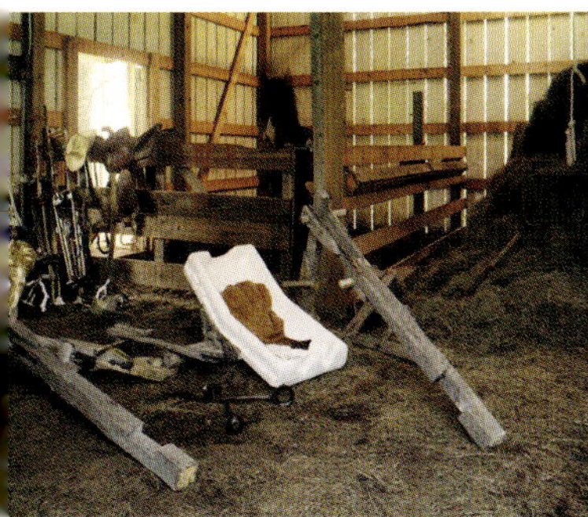

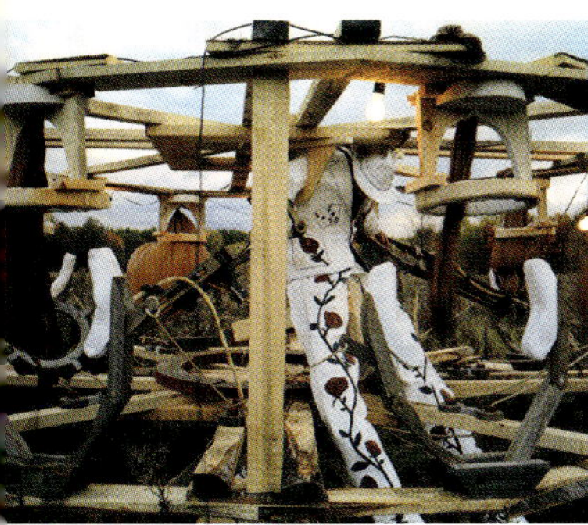

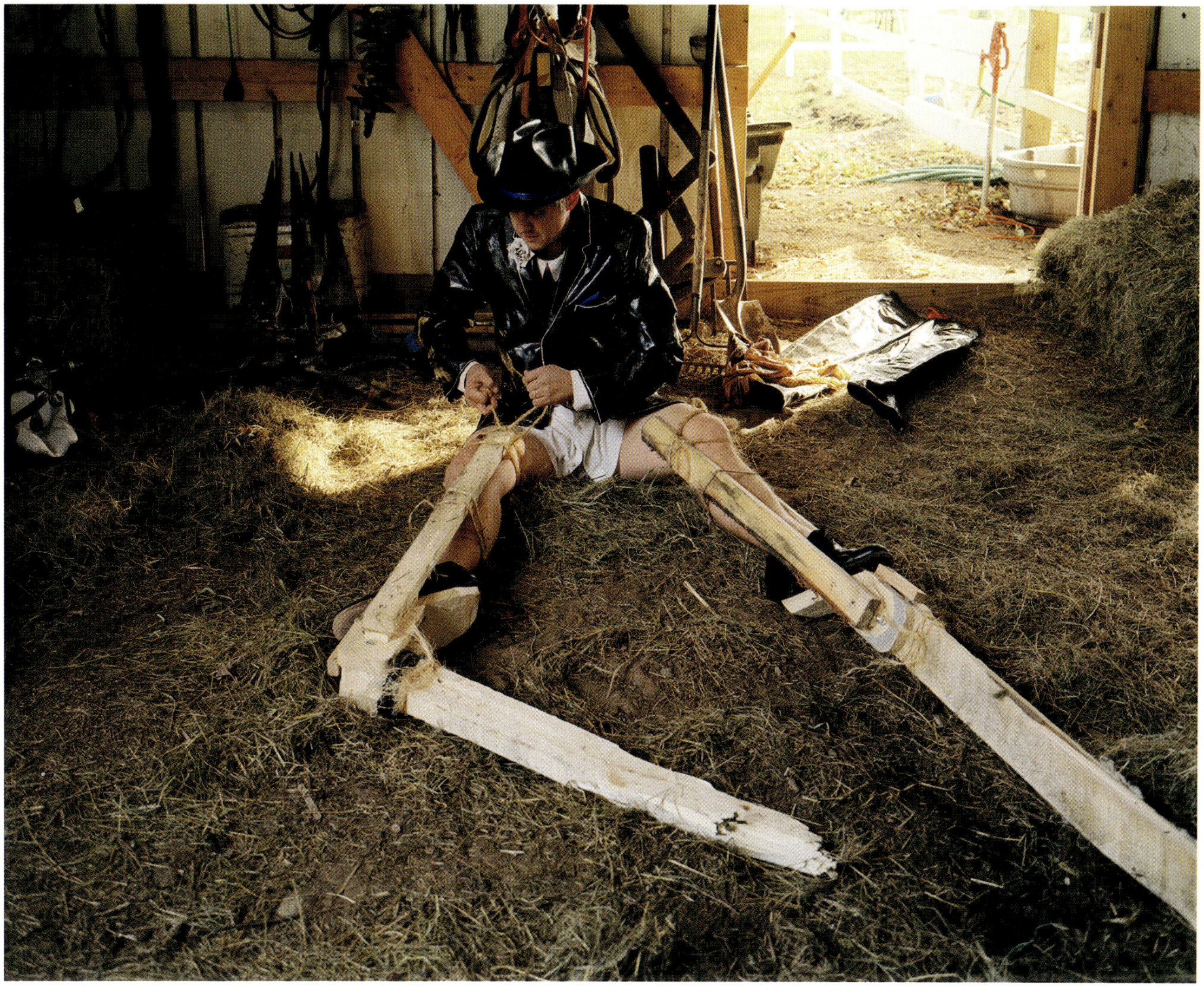

Bogus Brook Township

2002 * C-prints * Each 102 x 152 cm

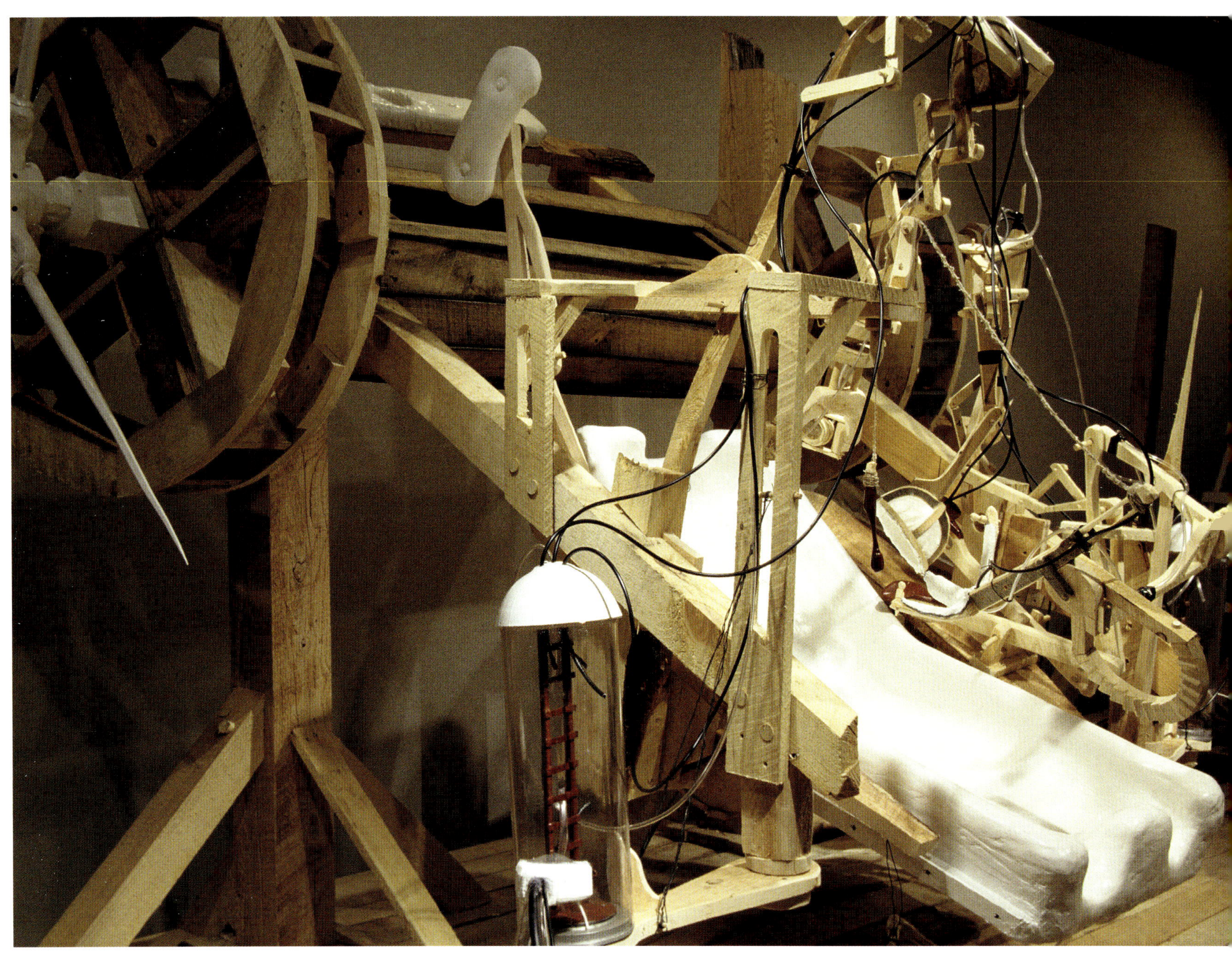

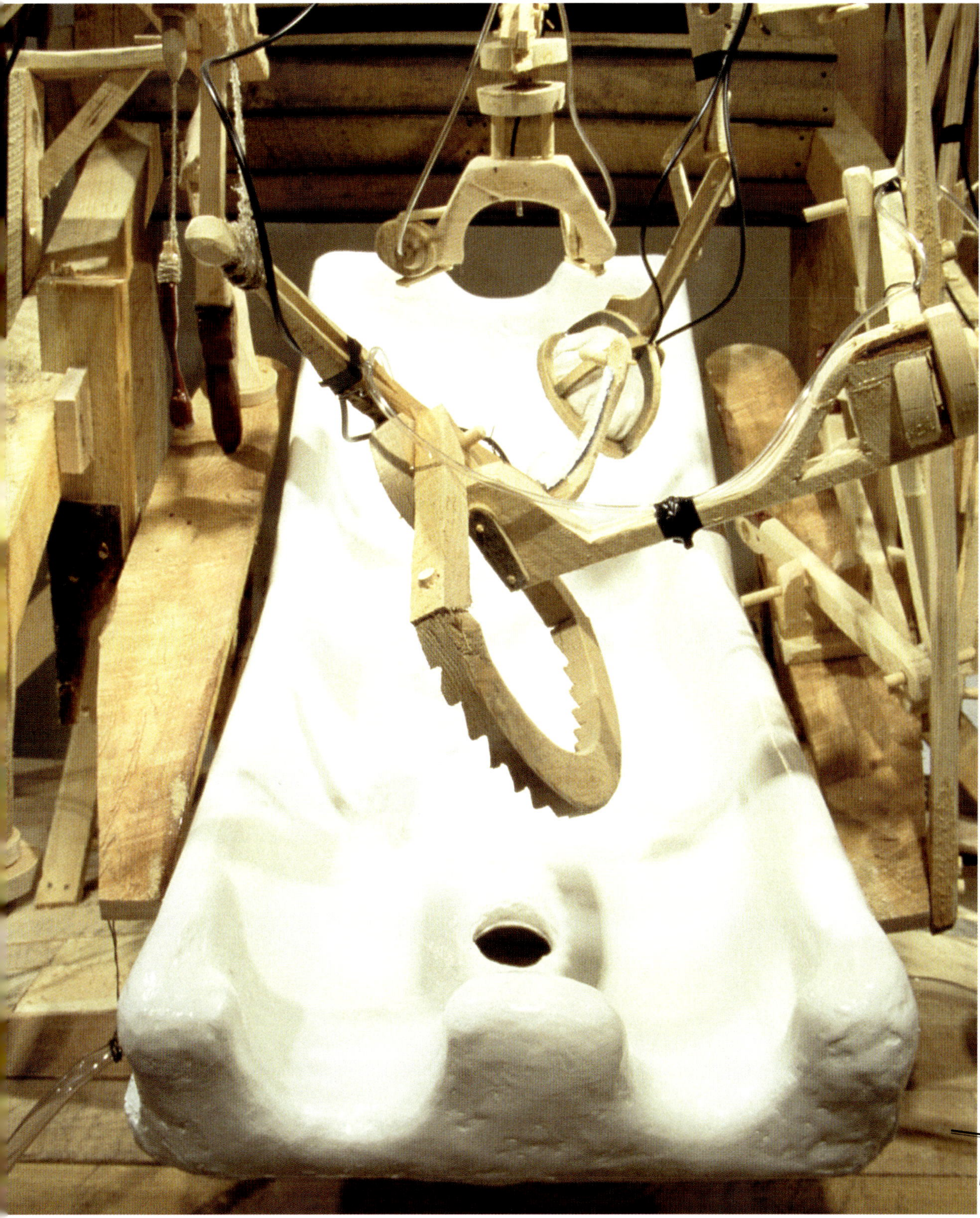

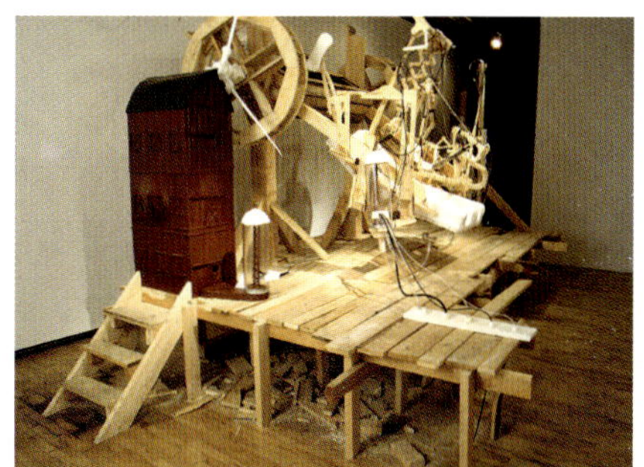

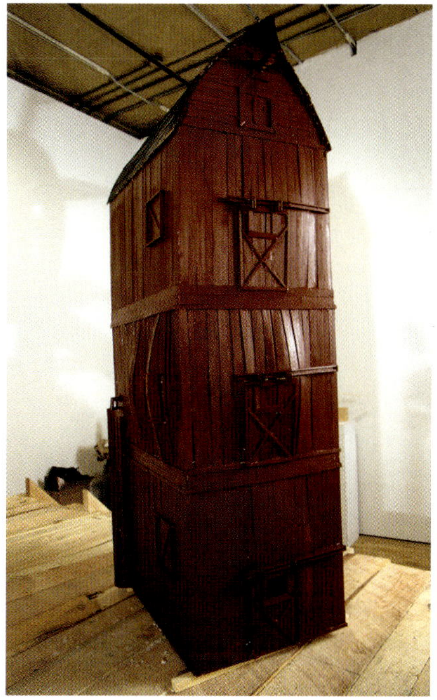

Gastral Machines (Bellmay Barn)

2000 • Wood, plaster
Installation views, Art in General, New York, NY

Gastral Machines

2001 * Wood, plaster * Each 183 x 121 x 244 cm

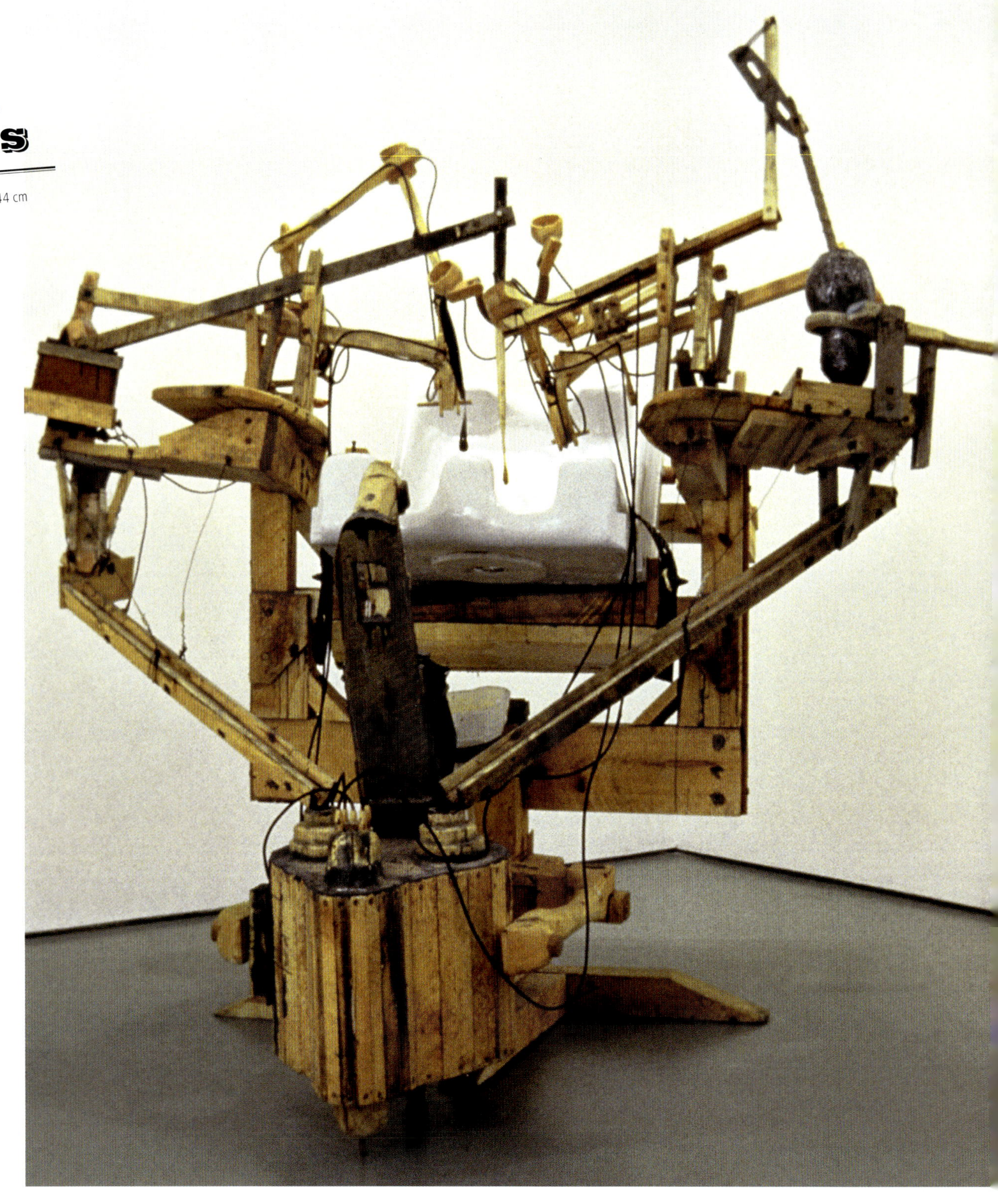

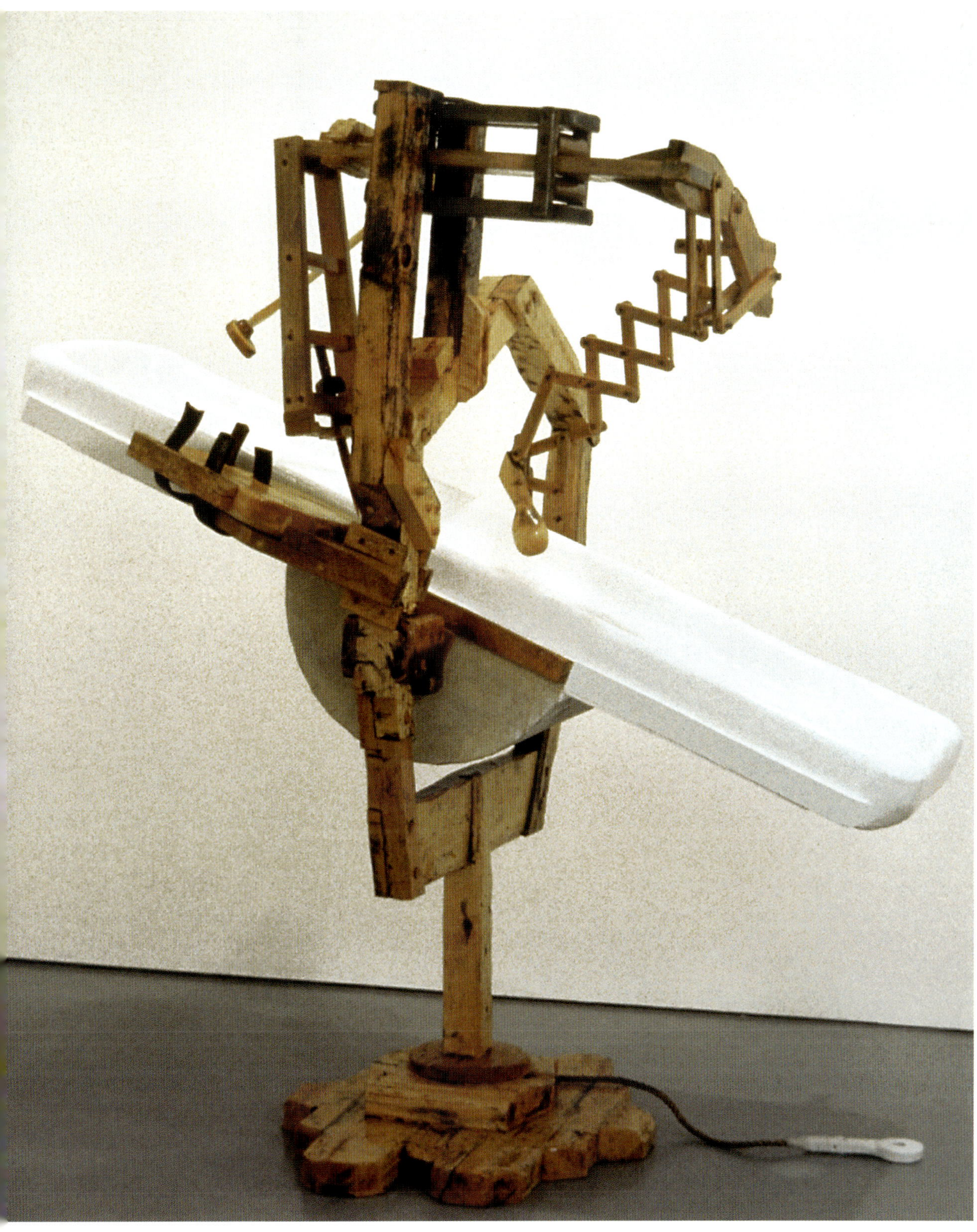

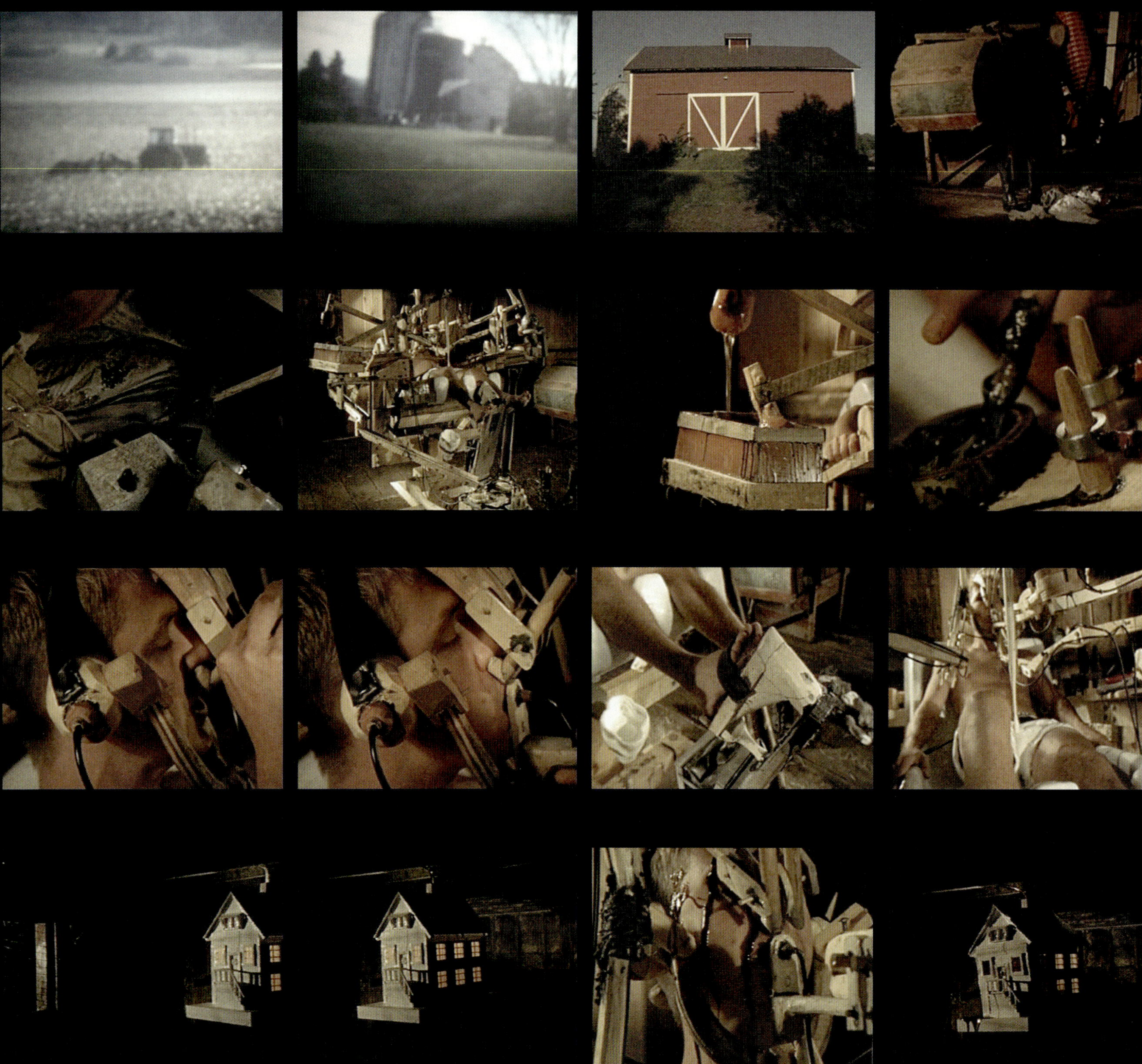

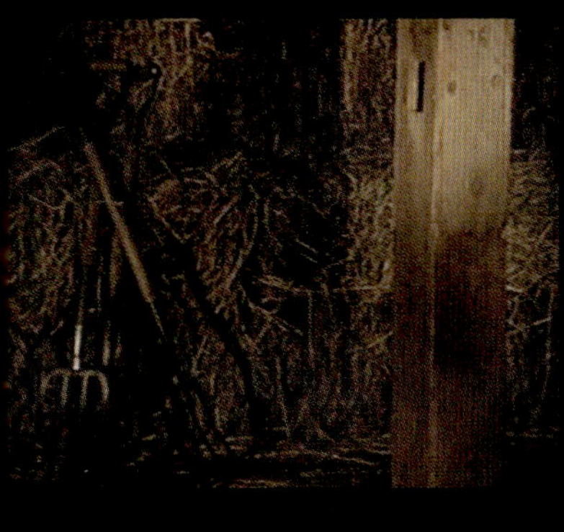
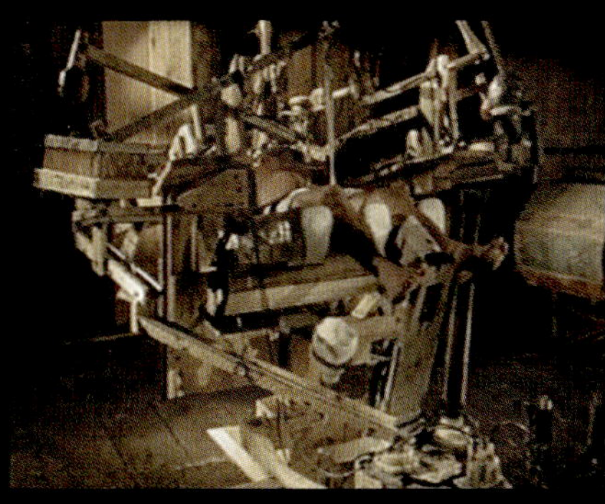
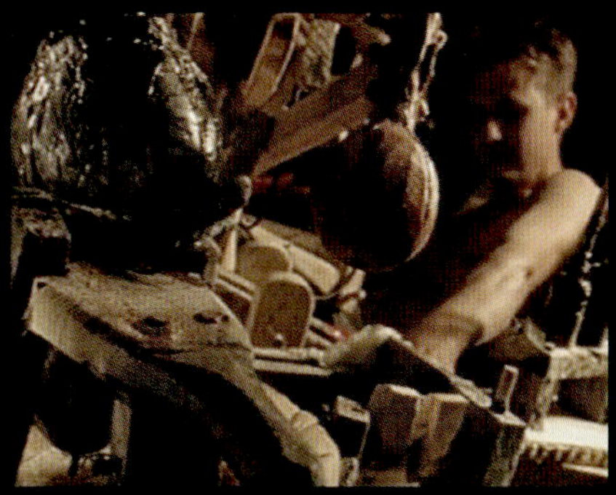
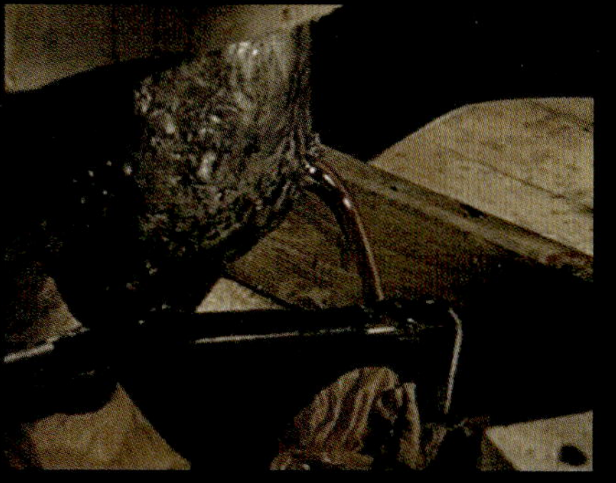
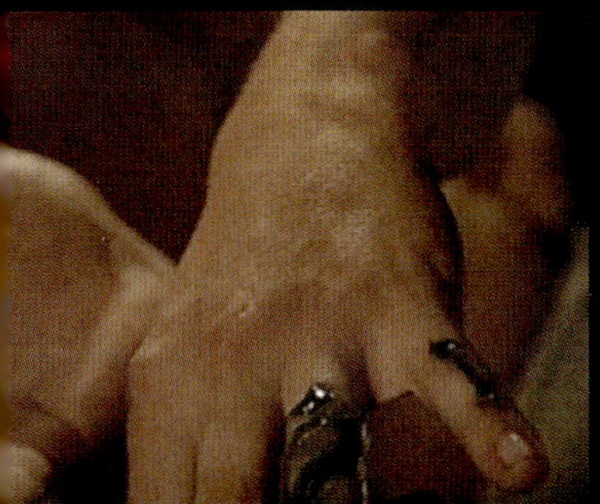
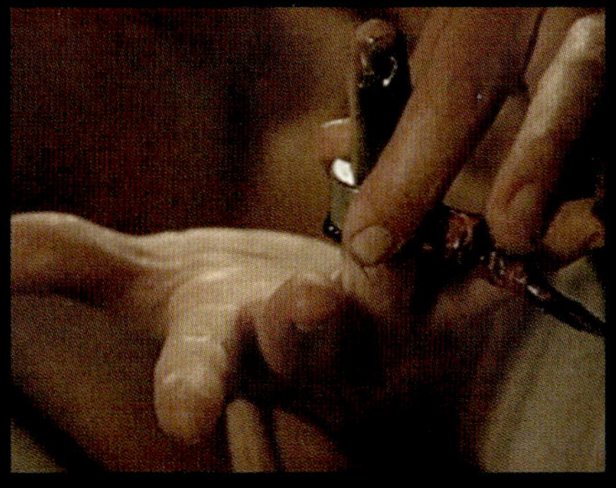
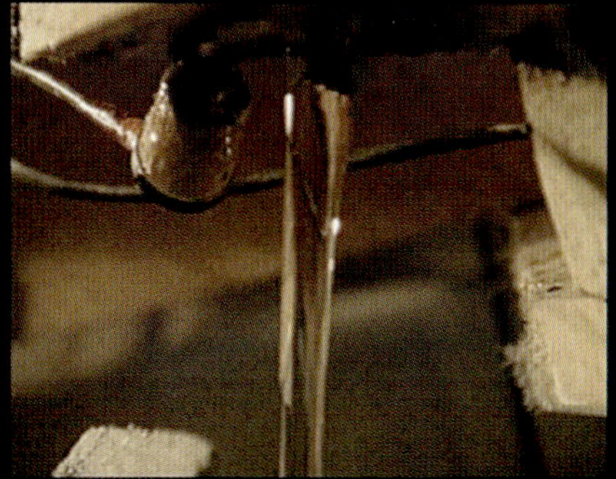
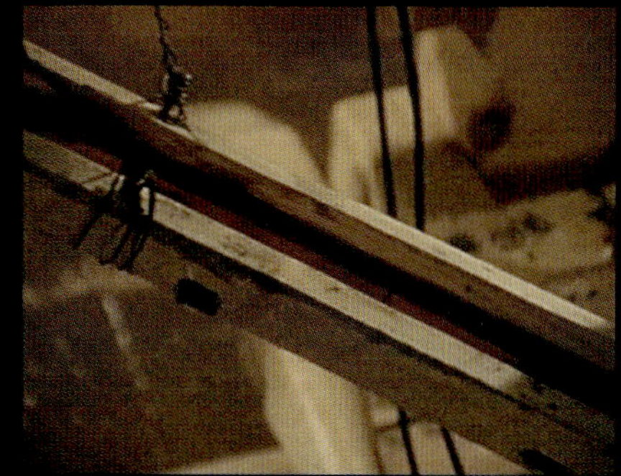
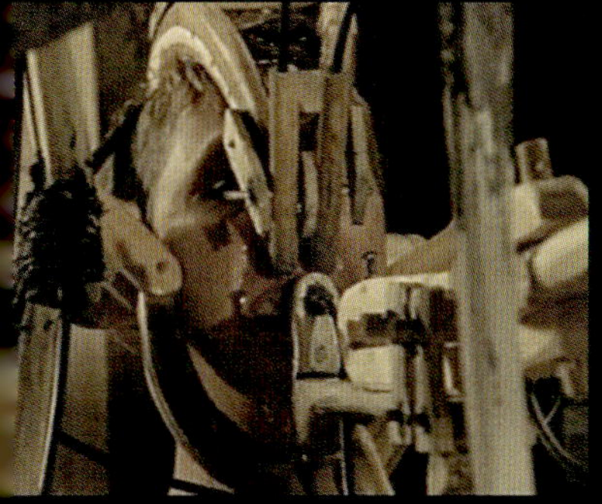
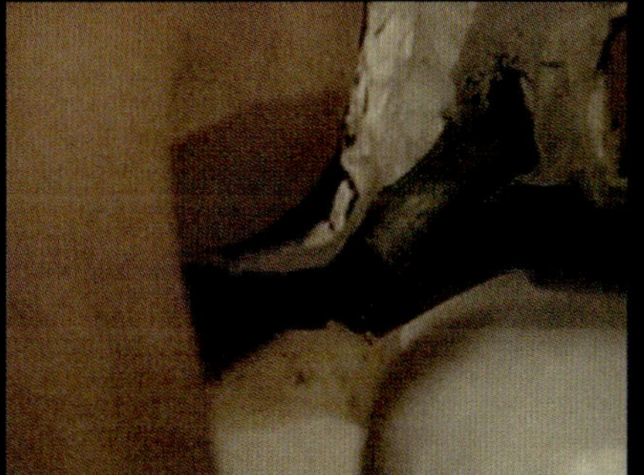
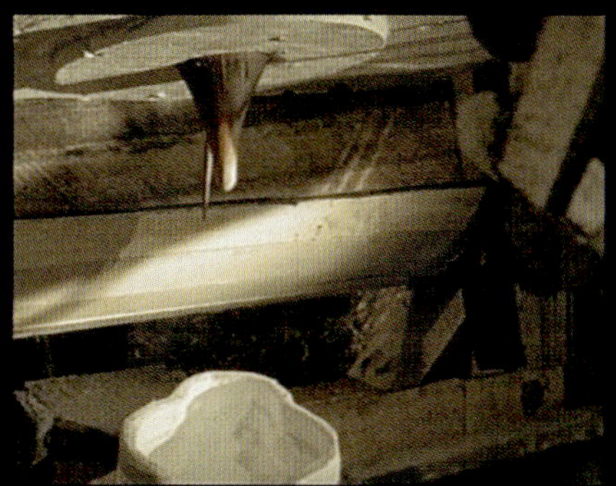
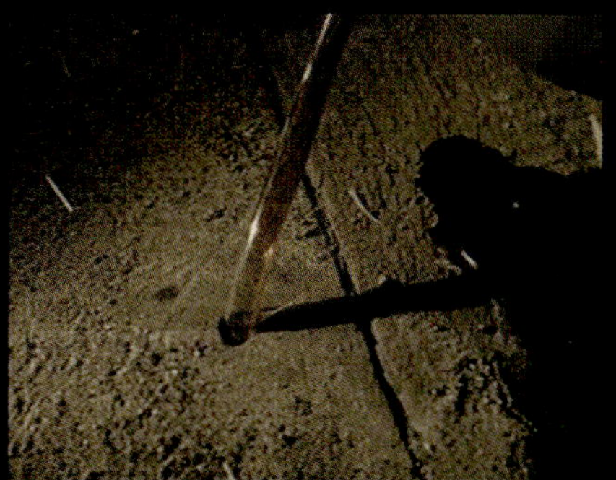
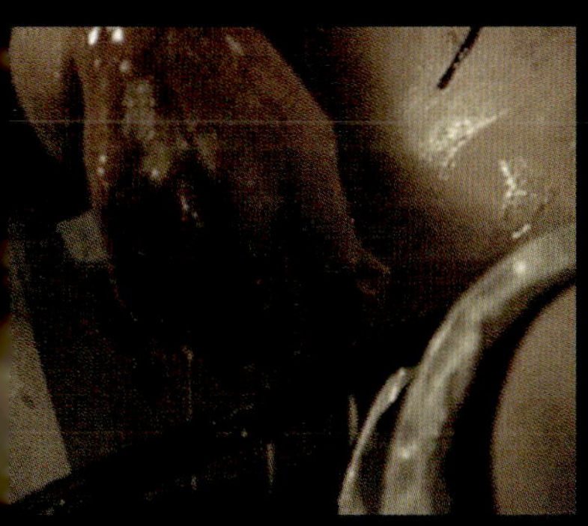
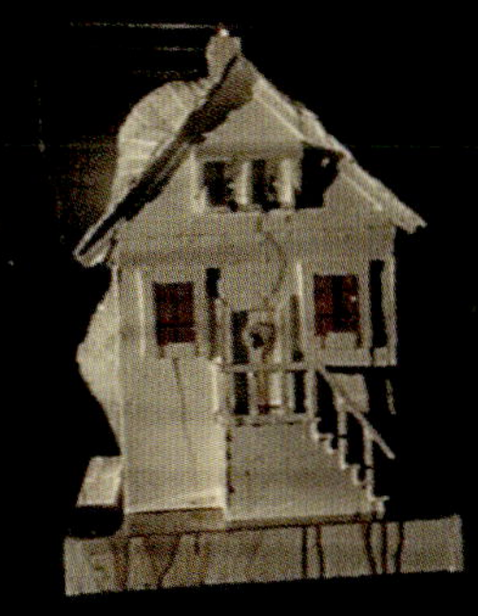

The Gastral Colony

2000 * 16 mm color film transferred to DVD
Running time: 13:41 min.
Video stills

Indeed, in order to get over this fascination with technology and the deathlike dimension it sometimes takes, we have to reapprehend and reconceptualize the machine differently, beginning by considering the "being" of the machine as something that is at a crossroads, one that is as much "being," in its inertia and in its character of nothingness, as "subject," subjective individuation or collective subjectivity.

Félix Guattari,
On Machines[1]

Chris Larson's Machine Park

Marc Glöde

When, in their 1930–31 film *Architectures d'aujourd'hui*, Le Corbusier and Pierre Chenal attempted to record the advantages of modern architecture or the fundamental ideas of modernism, one thing seemed to get to the heart of this new way of thinking better than any other: the concept of the machine. To Le Corbusier and Chenal, the car was primarily a machine for driving, an airplane was a machine for flying, and the house was a machine in which to live. In turn, the materials mainly associated with these machines (glass, steel, and concrete) became essential elements through which this new way of thinking was manifested, and the duo sought to capture the precision of these elements on film (that particular machine for seeing).[2]

The confrontation with machines and the way they influence our thinking is also of central importance to Chris Larson's artistic structures. Again and again, in works such as *Gastral Machine* (2000), *American Gothic (Saturday Night/Sunday Morning)* (2001), *Machine with Horse* (2003), *Crush Collision* (2006), and *Deep North* (2008) he produces complex technical installations, in which processes of energy transfer are incisively carried out. Although, like Le Corbusier and Chenal, Larson often employs the medium of film to capture visual images of his own mechanical worlds, the materials of his structures do not take the viewer into the modern era, but back into another age altogether. The materials in his works have nothing in common with the steel machines of the Industrial Age, let alone the delicate, clinically sanitized, high-tech machines of the twenty-first century. Instead, Larson's wooden wheelworks open up worlds that bring to mind earlier concepts of the mechanical—the siege machines used in war, medieval torture rigs, elaborate preindustrial devices, and other spectacular stage works, especially the ones found in the first extensive books on machines published in the sixteenth and seventeenth centuries.

Besides this purely material, aesthetic aspect, however, there is another noticeable parallel that also seems to play an equally significant role in Larson's work. If we look more closely at antique books of machinery, we can see that the old descriptions, especially the illustrations, were not solely concerned with a primarily technical analysis and understanding of the machine; they did not present a perspective that made it possible to construct and master the machine.[3] Instead, there is just as much focus on the mechanical spectacle—meaning, the effect of a machine, its ability to amaze, or the aesthetics of a machine itself[4] (ills. p. 37).

We are also confronted with this kind of situation when considering Larson's artistic approaches. Both his mechanical installations as well as his filmed mediations of these installations do not seem to pertain to a scientific understanding of such constructions, processes, or even their more precise functions, but rather they are continually independent of purpose and meaning. Instead, the operation of the machines and the use of the body in them are turned into spectacles with their own unique dynamics. However, referring to the question of the body in the machine, it becomes clear that there is a fundamental difference in the media Larson employs. Even though Larson himself is a protagonist in his films, interacting with the machines and demonstrating their applications, the status of the body in the museum installation always remains a blank. Nonetheless, because there is a correspondence between the film and the installation in the space, a situation is created in which the viewer of Larson's installations is always drawn into the mechanical setting. Just as in the old books of machines, where people increasingly became elements of the mechanical, Larson's world is capable of seducing viewers into a moment in which they abandon themselves to technology, letting the self be dissolved inside it. In this, the artist is in accordance, to a certain degree, with the philosophy of Julien Offray de La Mettrie, author of the book *L'homme machine* (1747), in which he sought to overcome the fundamental distinction between man and machine. In Larson's works, it becomes obvious that he is not only dealing with a metaphorical level of references—in the sense that he conceives of layering categorically separate areas—, but also that this relatedness can be understood in metonymical terms, too. Through artistic exaggeration, it becomes clear that people and machines are not simply in a relationship involving the transference of similarities (the human body and the mechanical body), but that they are also increasingly interdependent, emphatically inscribed in each other. This is an important reason why Jonathan Crary referred to the human being as caught in a "relation of contiguity" to the machine, as a "part to other parts."[5]

However, it would be limiting to reduce Larson's works merely to their ability to create dynamic relationships between the installation and the body. It would mean ignoring a very crucial aspect that is an element in almost all of his works: the fact that Larson always sets up an exploration of film or photography next to almost every one of his installations or performances. The film or photographs become more than just a documentary aspect of his work. On the contrary: the film and the photograph take a far more independent position, which not only comments on the confrontation between body and sculpture or between man and machine, but also expands into an exploration of one's own dependency on machines or a redefinition of the self as machine. For instance, the film machine in *Gastral Colony* (2000) permits a view into Larson's body and into the machine he is in, but after a while, it becomes equally obvious that viewers are just as involved, that Larson's work actively targets them. Inside the intriguing space containing sculpture, film image, and Larson's present/absent body, the viewer's own body and his own involvement in the machine park are increasingly drawn into the field of view. Larson turns the combination of installation, film, photograph, and viewer's body into a complex construct, which in turn makes it possible to think about machines in a different way. And so the house—which for Le Corbusier and Chenal was only a machine for living—turns into something much more complex in Larson's *Crush Collision* (2006): Larson's house shows that living is already a far more complicated process, a process whose many components have been so taken for granted that they can no longer be easily named. In his surreal configuration, he instead shows the potential inherent in the categories of house, film, and body and, in the process, discovers in a more vital way a radical machine for conceiving the physical body.

---

1 Félix Guattari, "À propos des machines," *Chimères* 19 (Spring 1993), pp. 85–96, here p. 86. Our translation. Guattari's article was published in English in *Complexity: Art, Architecture, Philosophy*, edited by Andrew Benjamin, translated by Vivian Constantinopoulos, special issue, *Journal of Philosophy and the Visual Arts* 6 (1995), pp. 8–12.

2 For more on the special approaches to architecture and film, see Andres Janser, "'Only Film Can Make the New Architecture Intelligible!' Hans Richter's *Die neue Wohnung and the Early Documentary Film on Modern Architecture*," in *Cinema & Architecture*, edited by François Penz and Maureen Thomas (London, 1997), pp. 34–46, esp. pp. 42–44.

3 For more on this, see Wolfgang Pircher, "Das Bild der Maschine," in *Wunschmaschine—Welterfindung. Eine Geschichte der Technikvisionen seit dem 18. Jahrhundert*, edited by Brigitte Felderer (Vienna, 1996), pp. 93–108.

4 For more on this, see Jan Lazardzig, "Paradoxe Maschinen—Bracelli, Tzara und der Ursprung des Fragens," in *Spuren der Avantgarde. Theatrum Machinarum*, edited by Helmar Schramm, Ludger Schwarte, and Jan Lazardzig (Berlin, 2008).

5 Jonathan Crary, *Techniques of the Observer: On Vision and Modernity in the Nineteenth Century* (Cambridge, Mass., 1999 [first ed., 1990]), p. 131: "In the factory, Marx contended, the machine makes use of man by subjecting him to a relation of contiguity, of part to other parts, and of exchangeability."

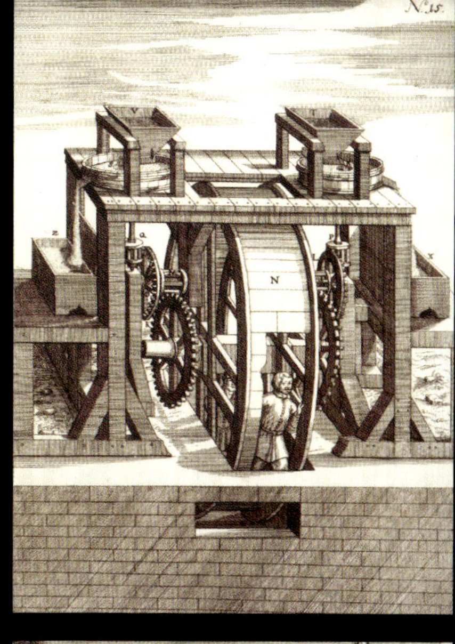

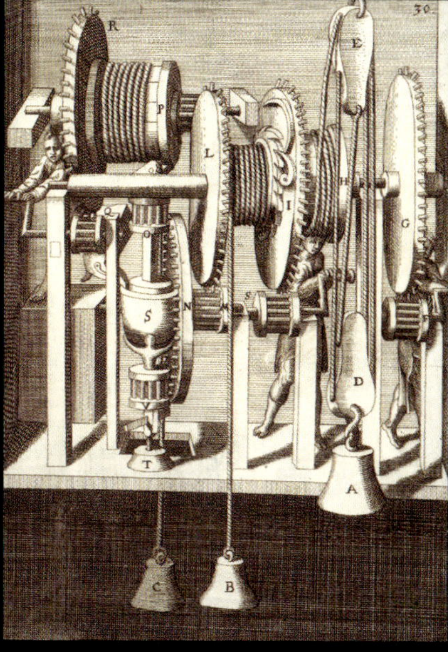

Georg Andreas Böckler
Theatrum Machinarum Novum
(Nuremberg, 1661)

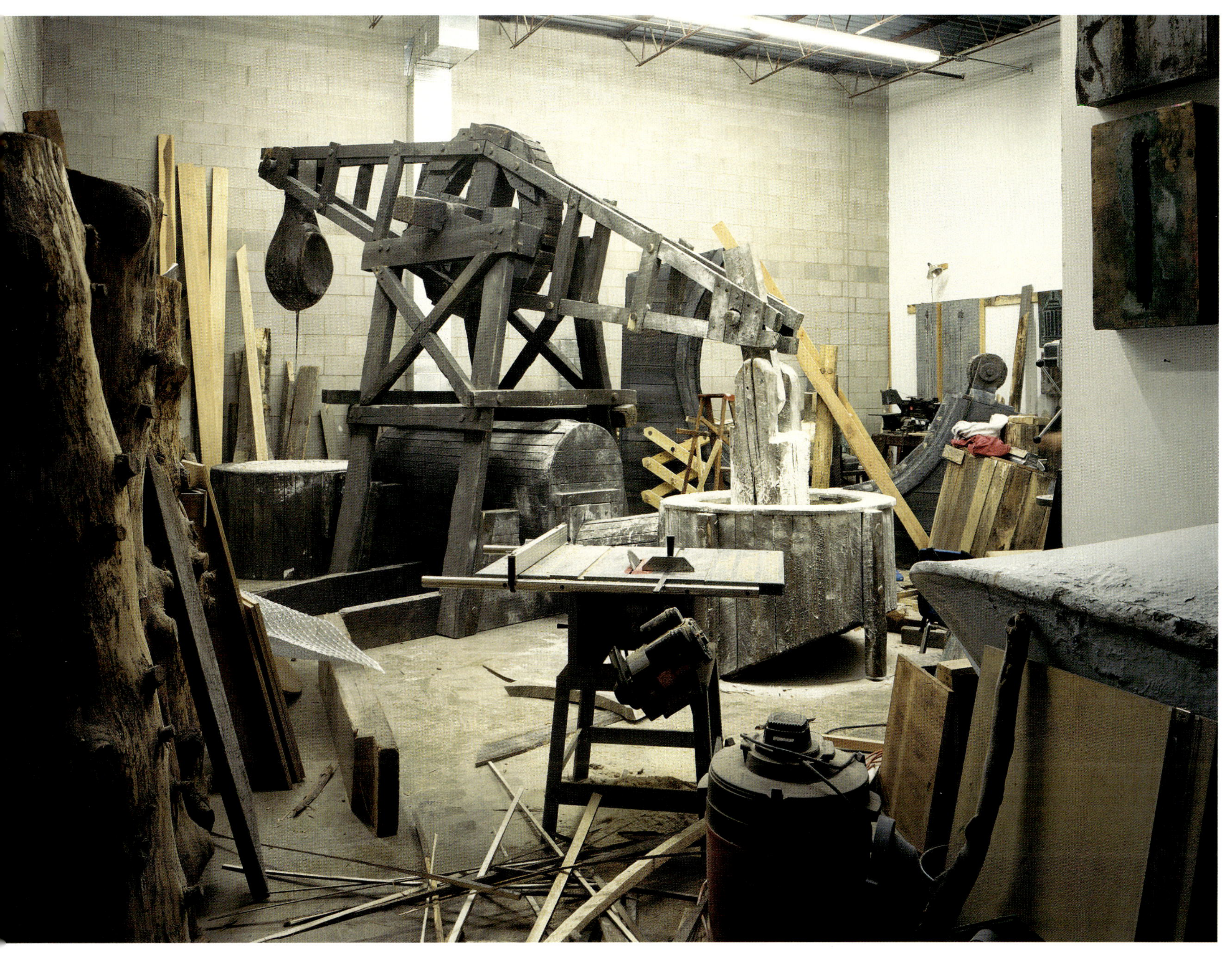

Untitled

1998 • Wood • 1067 x 304 x 640 cm
Installation view, artist's studio, St. Paul, MN

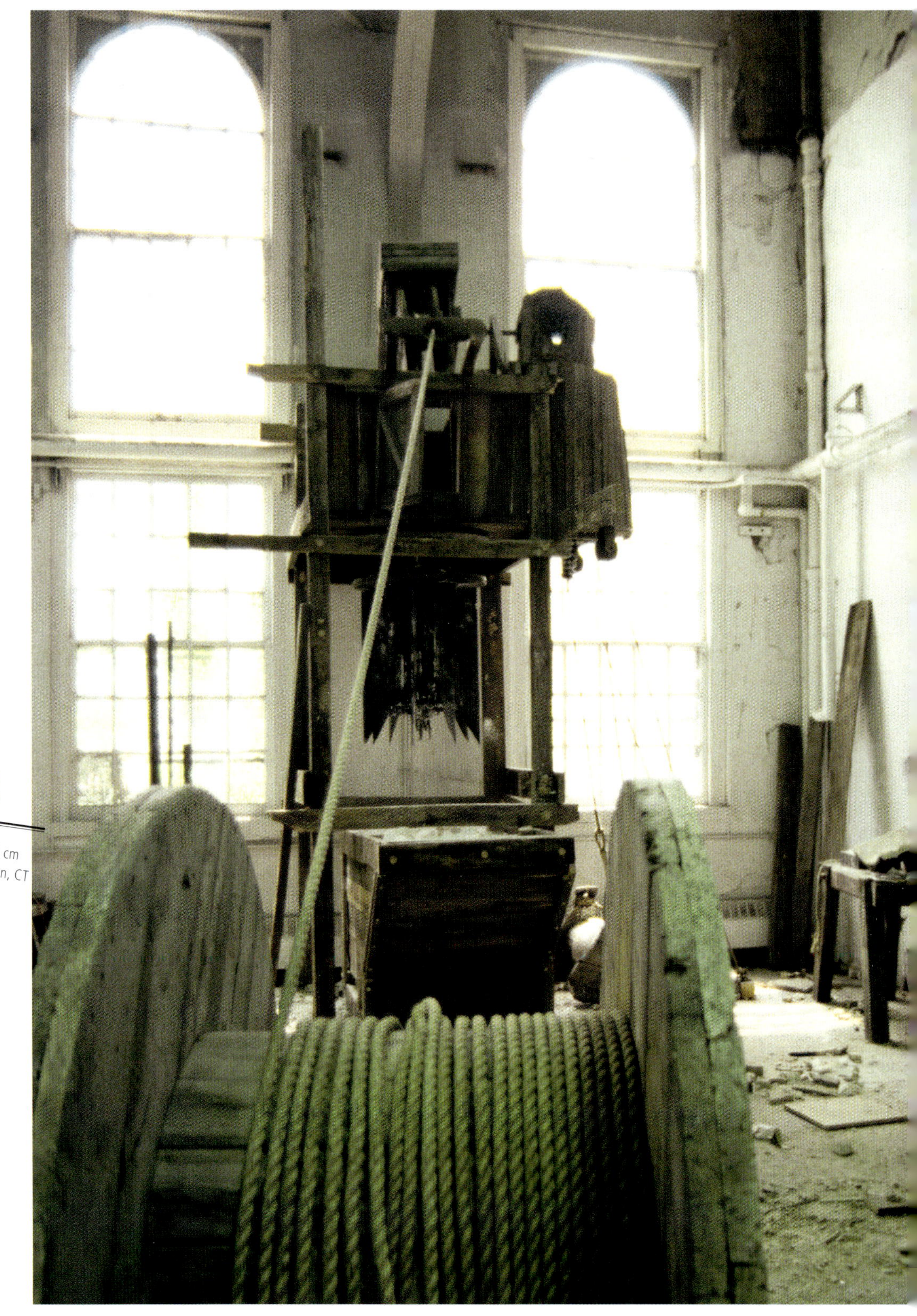

Untitled

1992 ⋆ Wood, salt, soap, flour ⋆ 518 x 366 x 640 cm
Installation view, Yale University (studio), New Haven, CT

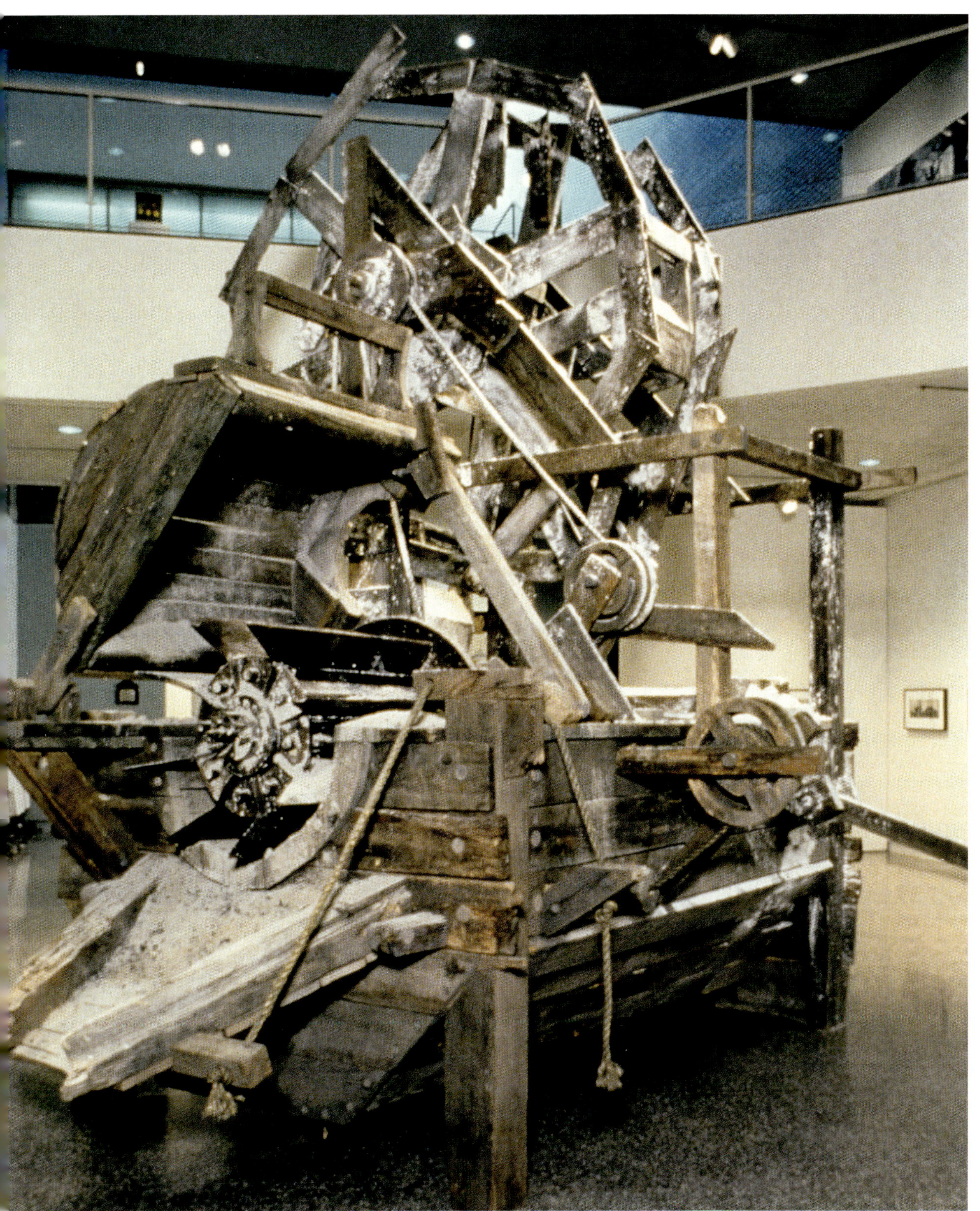

Untitled

1993 * Wood, salt, ash, soap * 580 x 366 x 275 cm
Installation view, Minneapolis College of Art and Design,
Minneapolis, MN

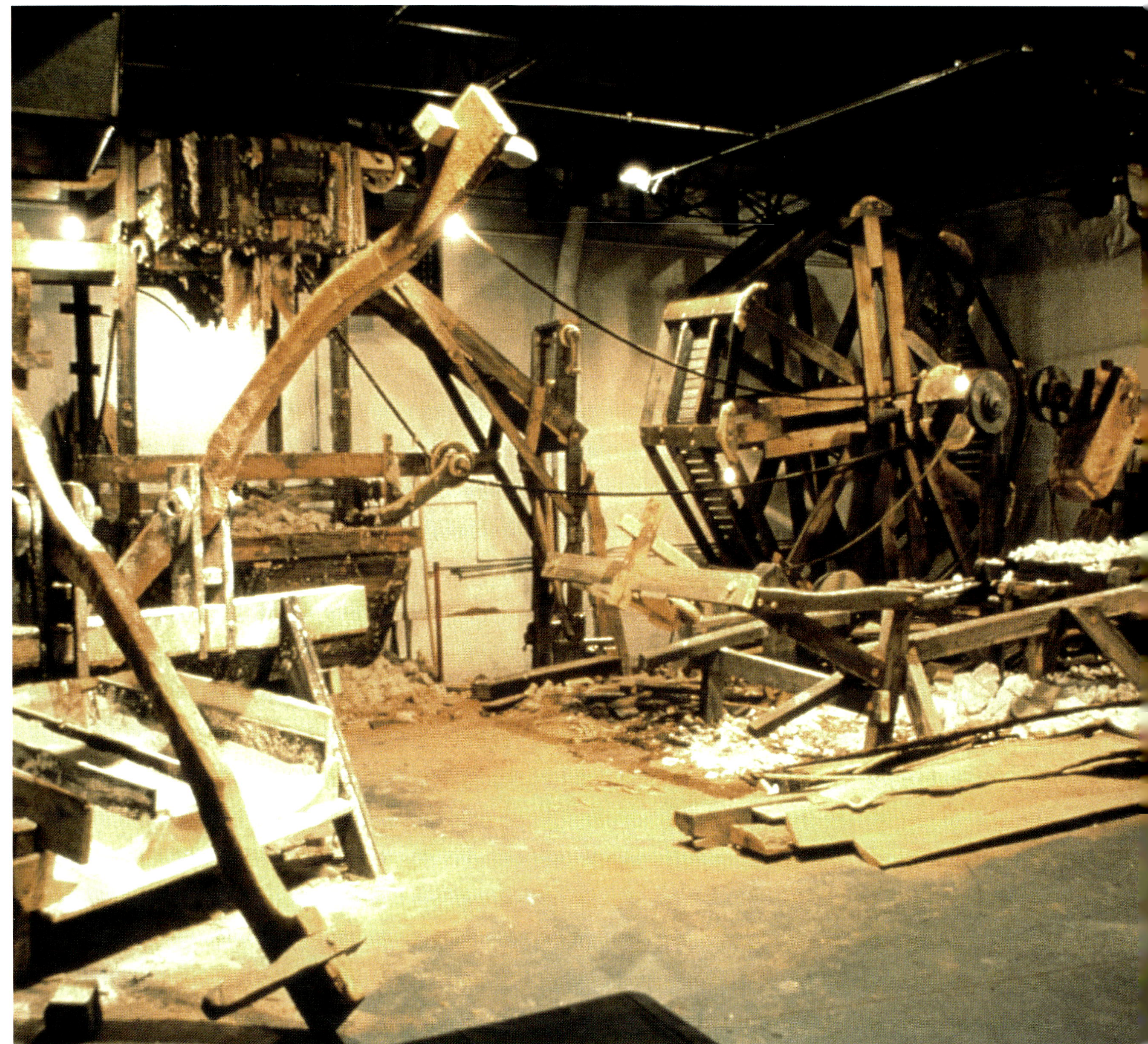

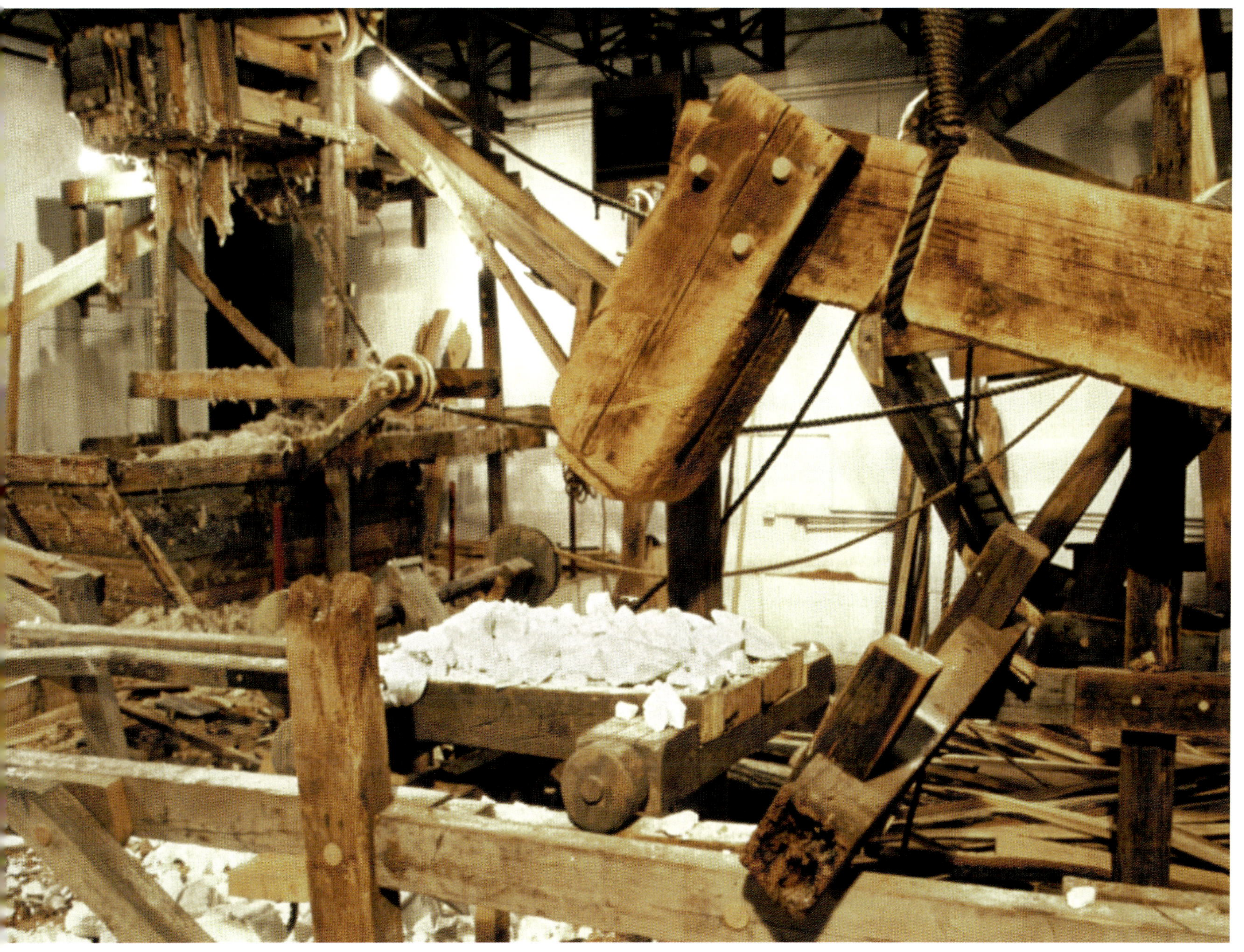

Untitled

1995 * Wood, soap, flour * 457 x 914 x 1372 cm
Installation views, Intermedia Arts, Minneapolis, MN

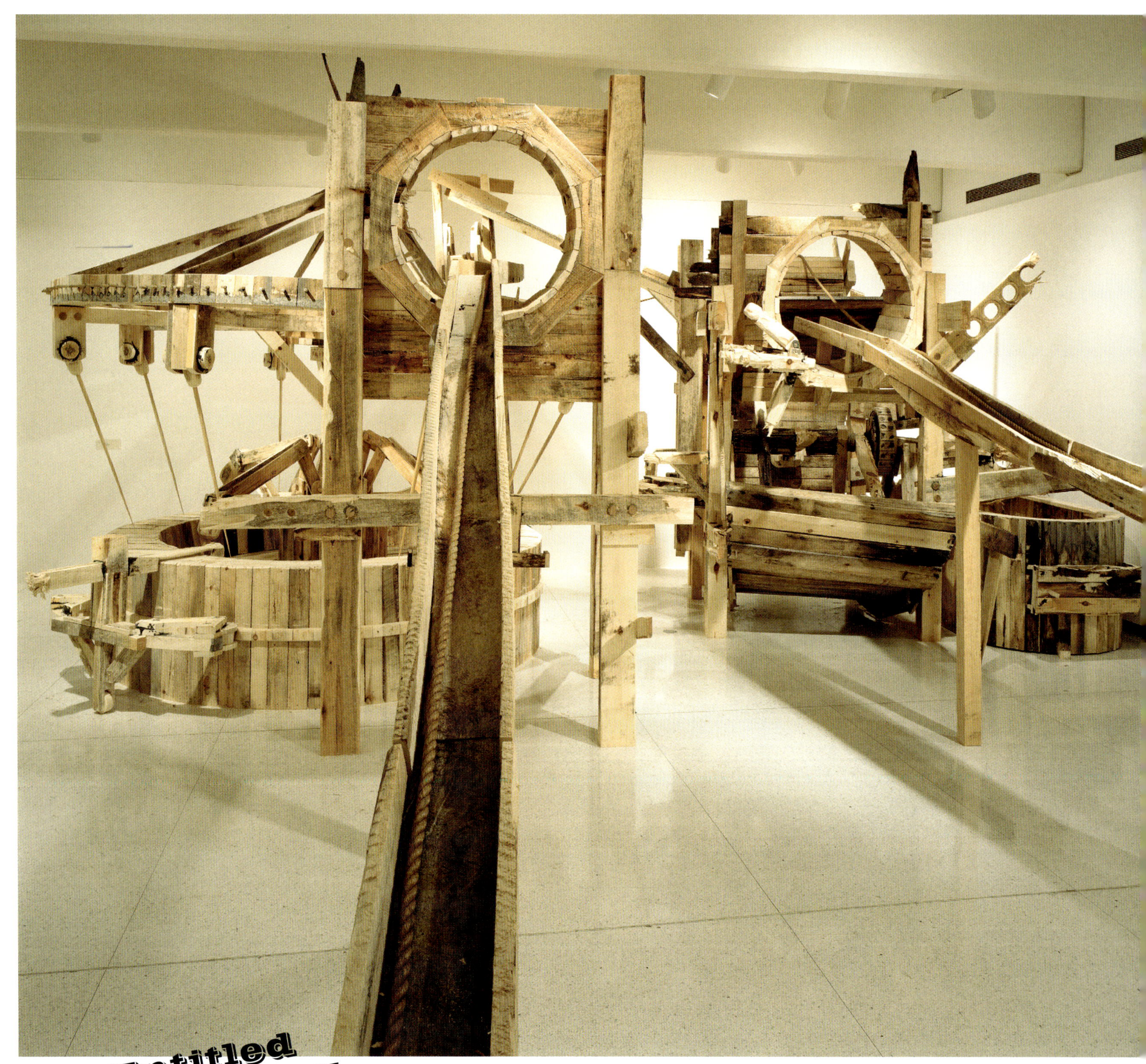

Untitled

1998 • Wood • 304 x 640 x 1067 cm
Installation views, Walker Art Center, Minneapolis, MN

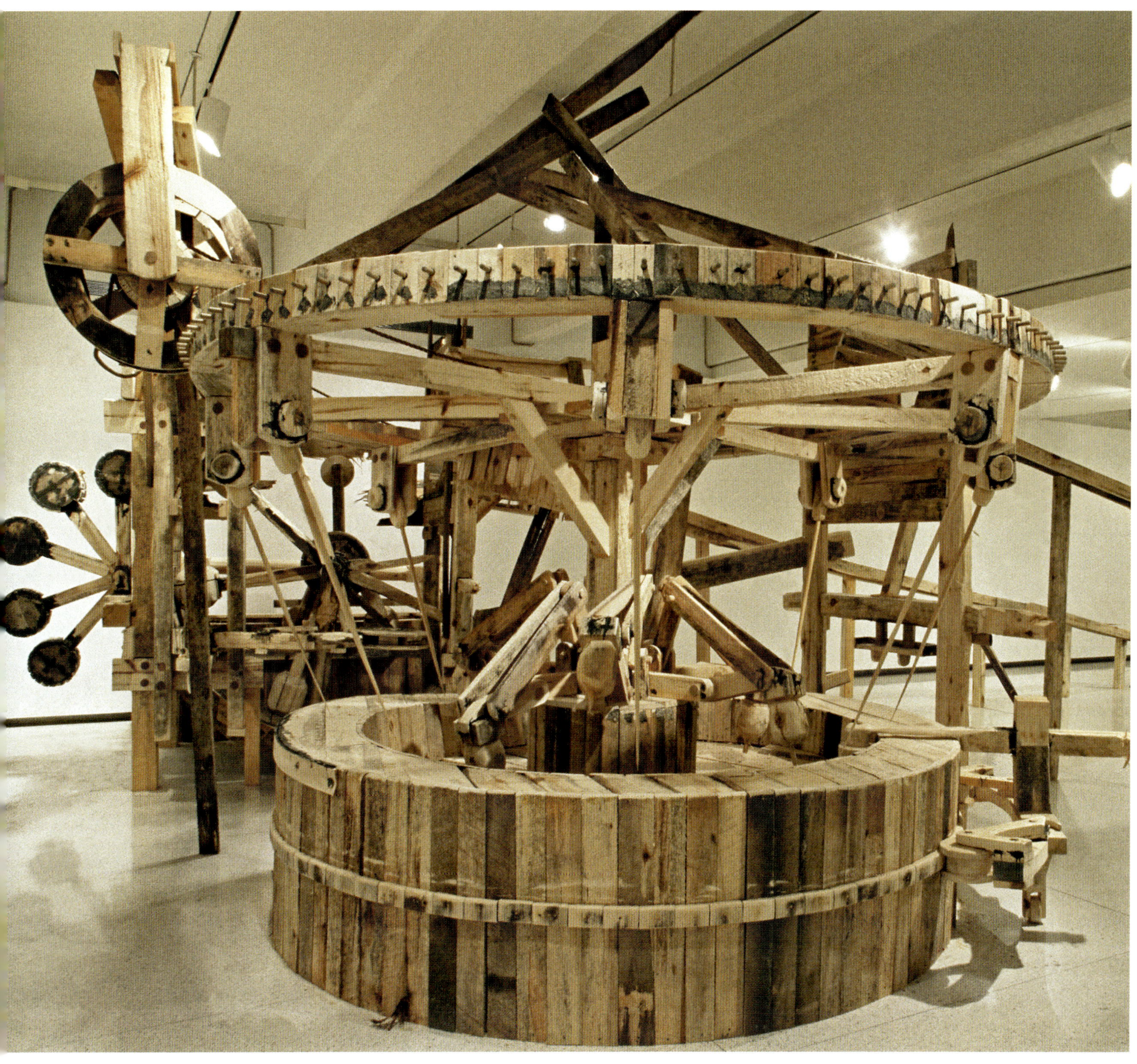

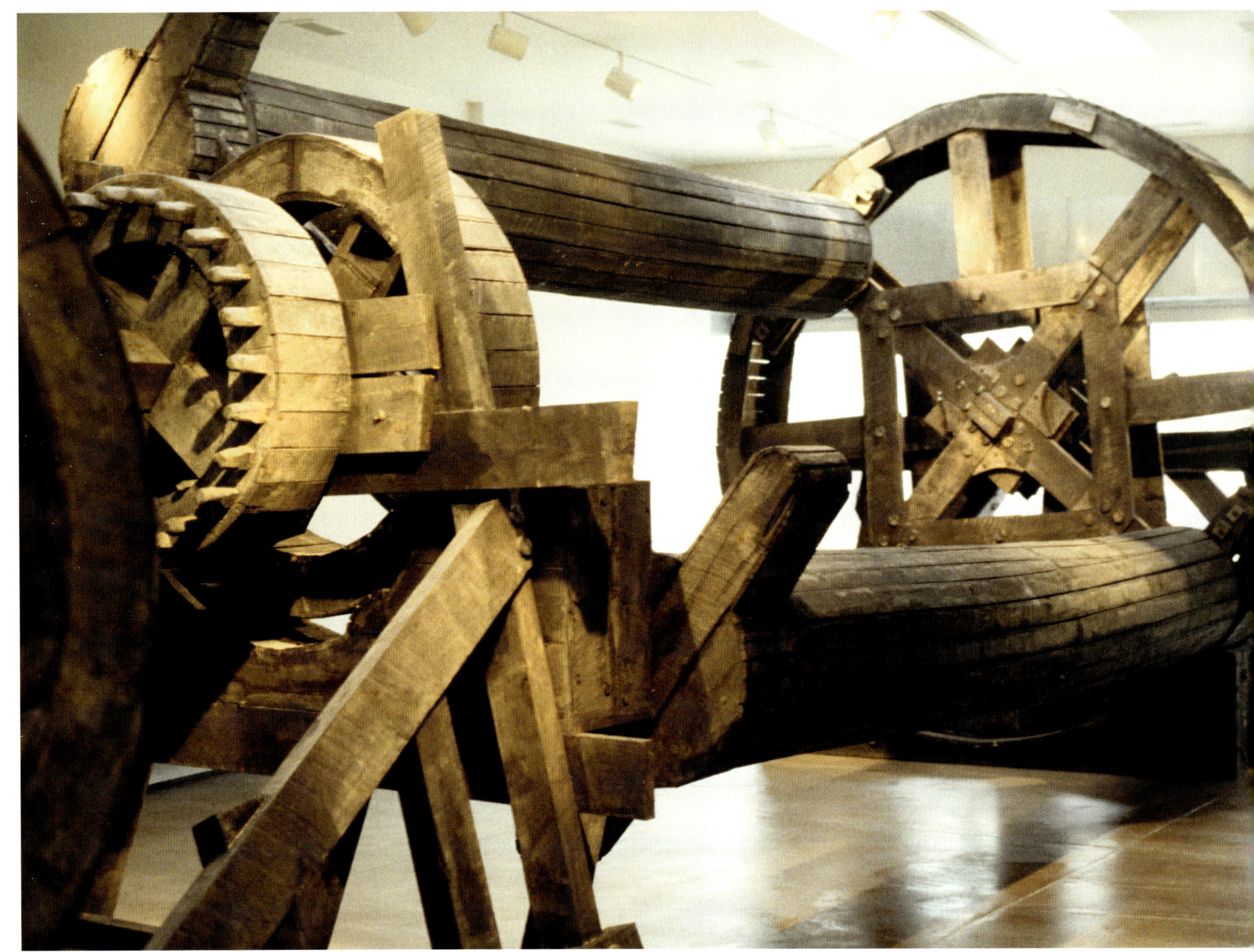

Untitled

1997 * Wood * 366 x 427 x 1036 cm
Installation views, Grand Arts, Kansas City, MS,
and Franconia Sculpture Park, Franconia, MN

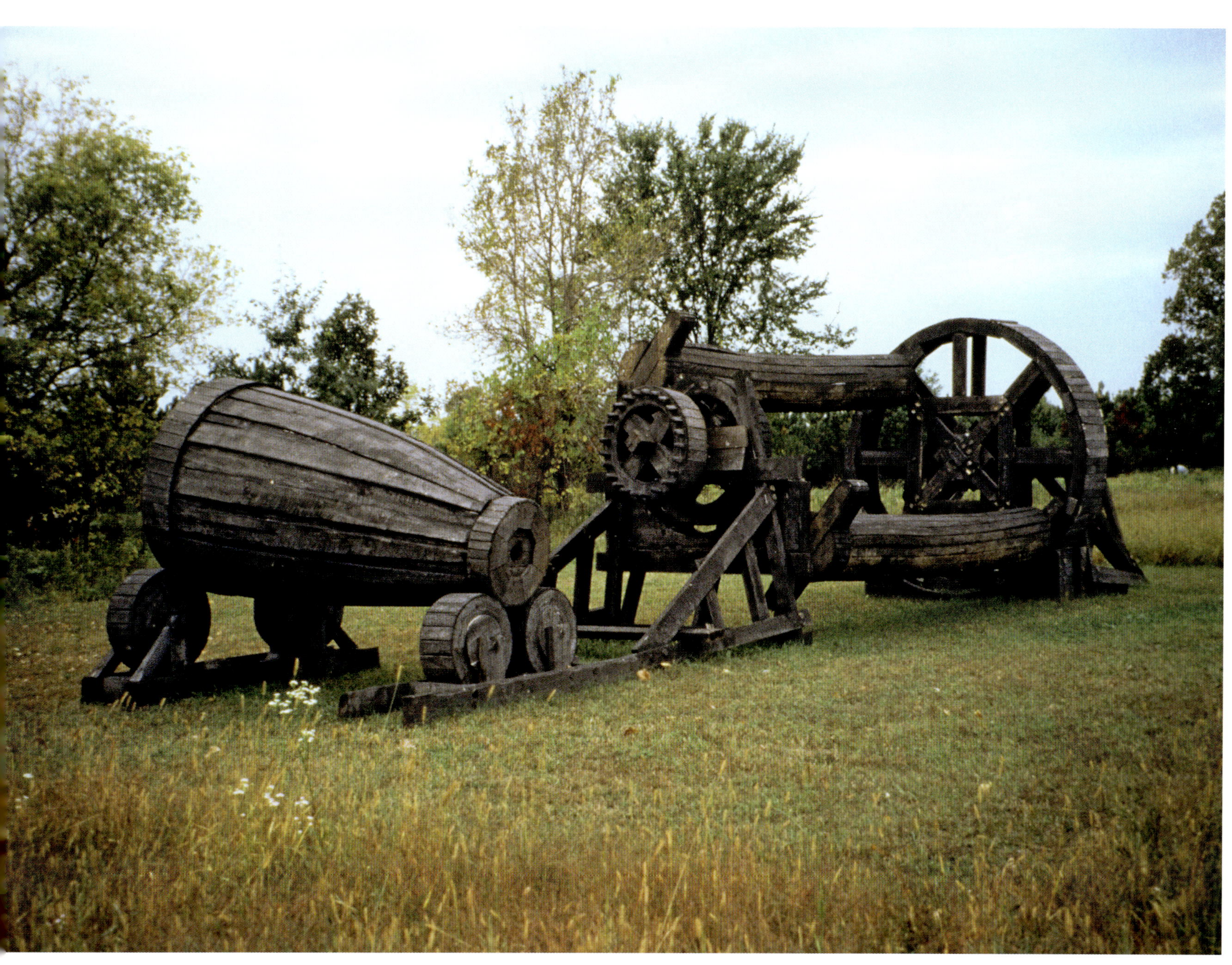

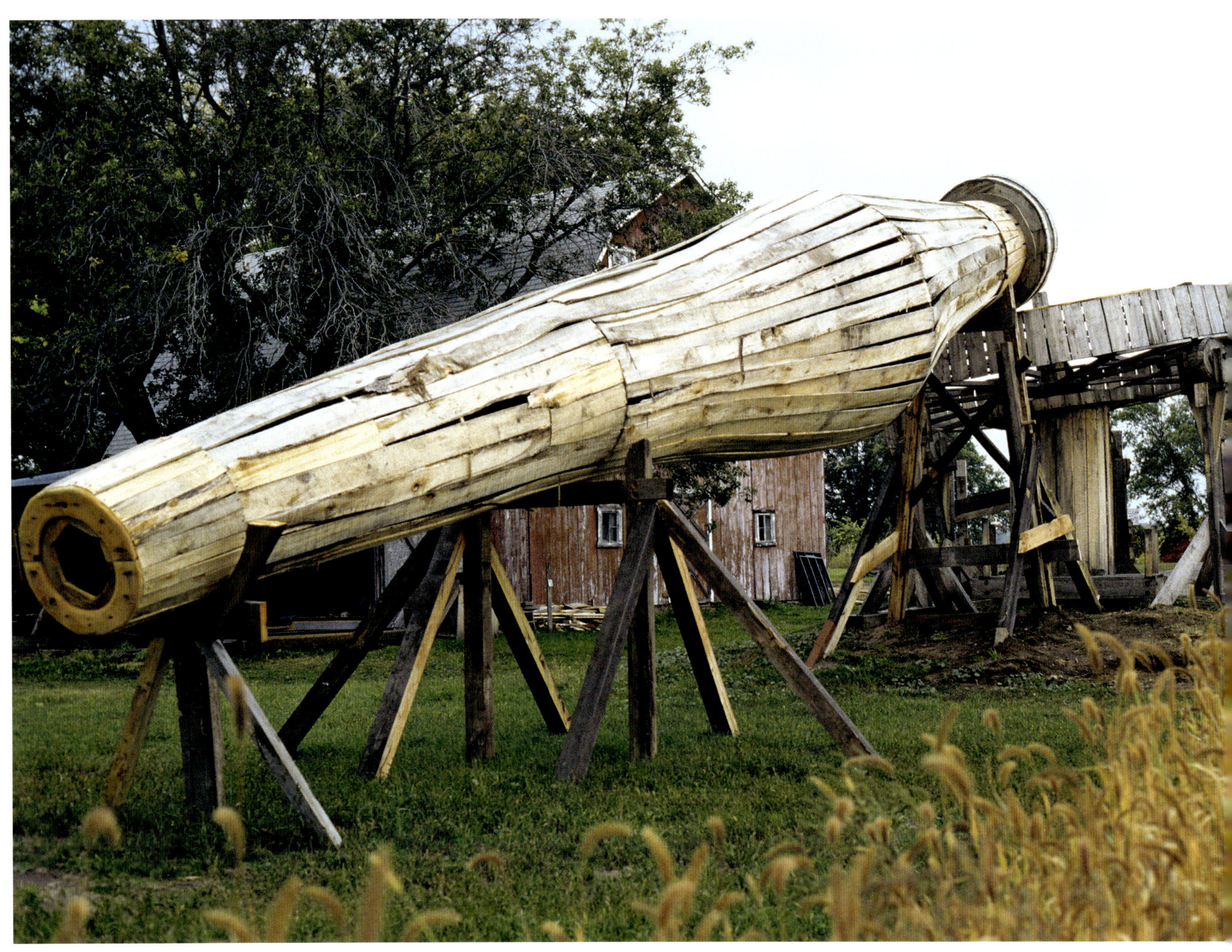

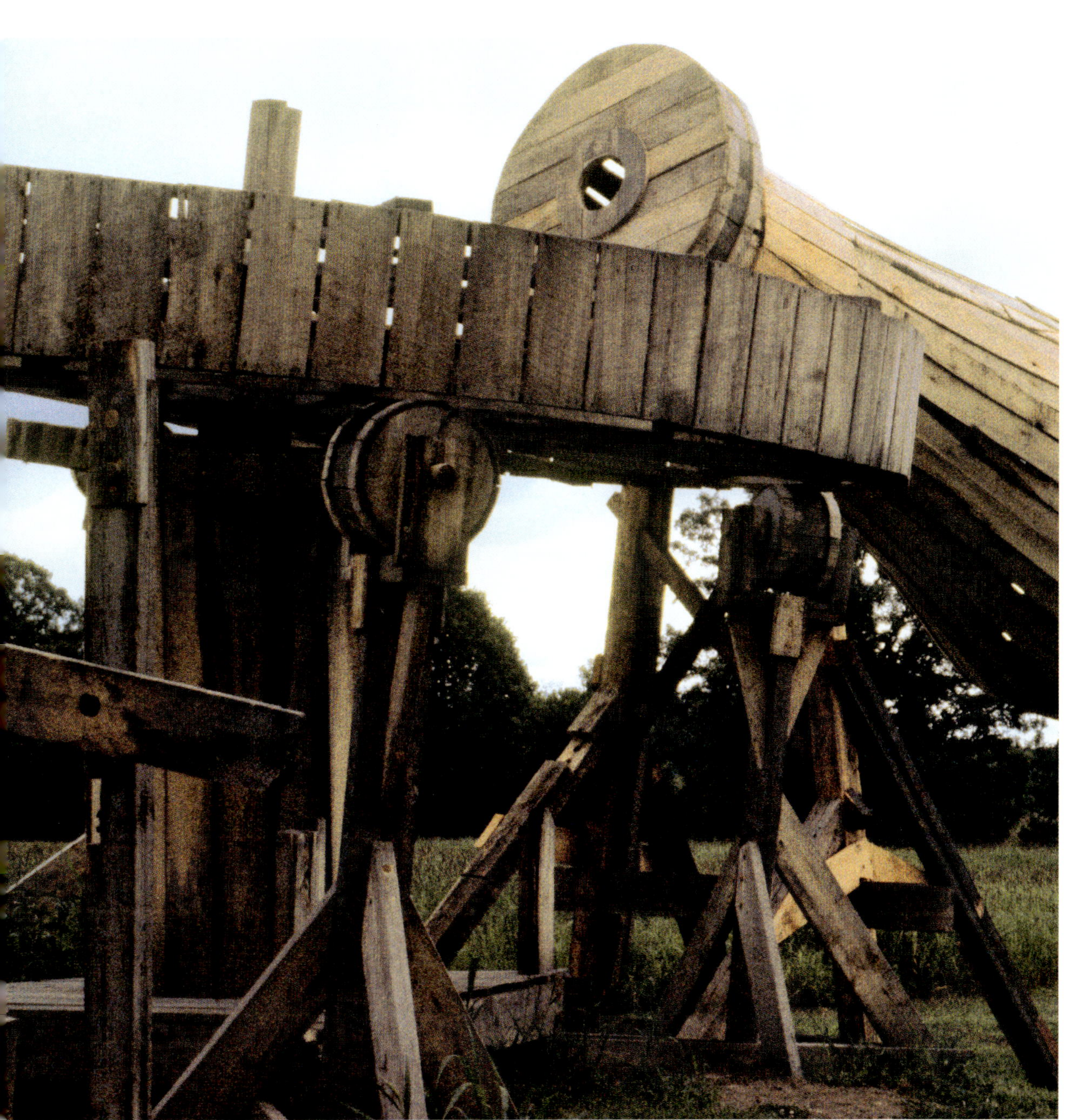

Untitled

1996 * Wood * 518 x 884 x 1128 cm
Installation views, Franconia Sculpture Park, Franconia, MN

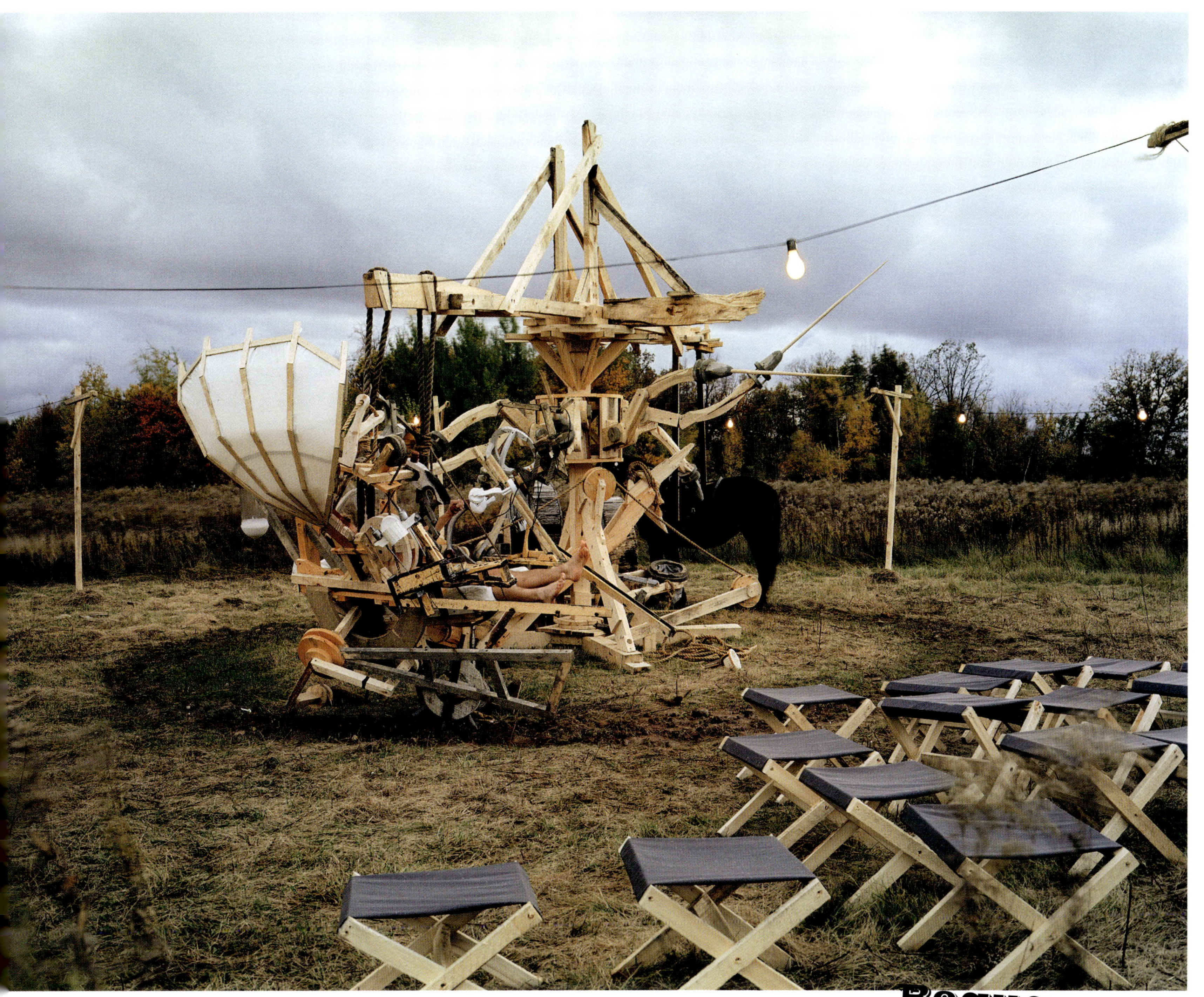

Bogus Brook Township (Machine with Horse)

2002 * C-print * 102 x 152 cm

County Line

2004 • HD video transferred to DVD
Running time: 9:21 min.
Video still

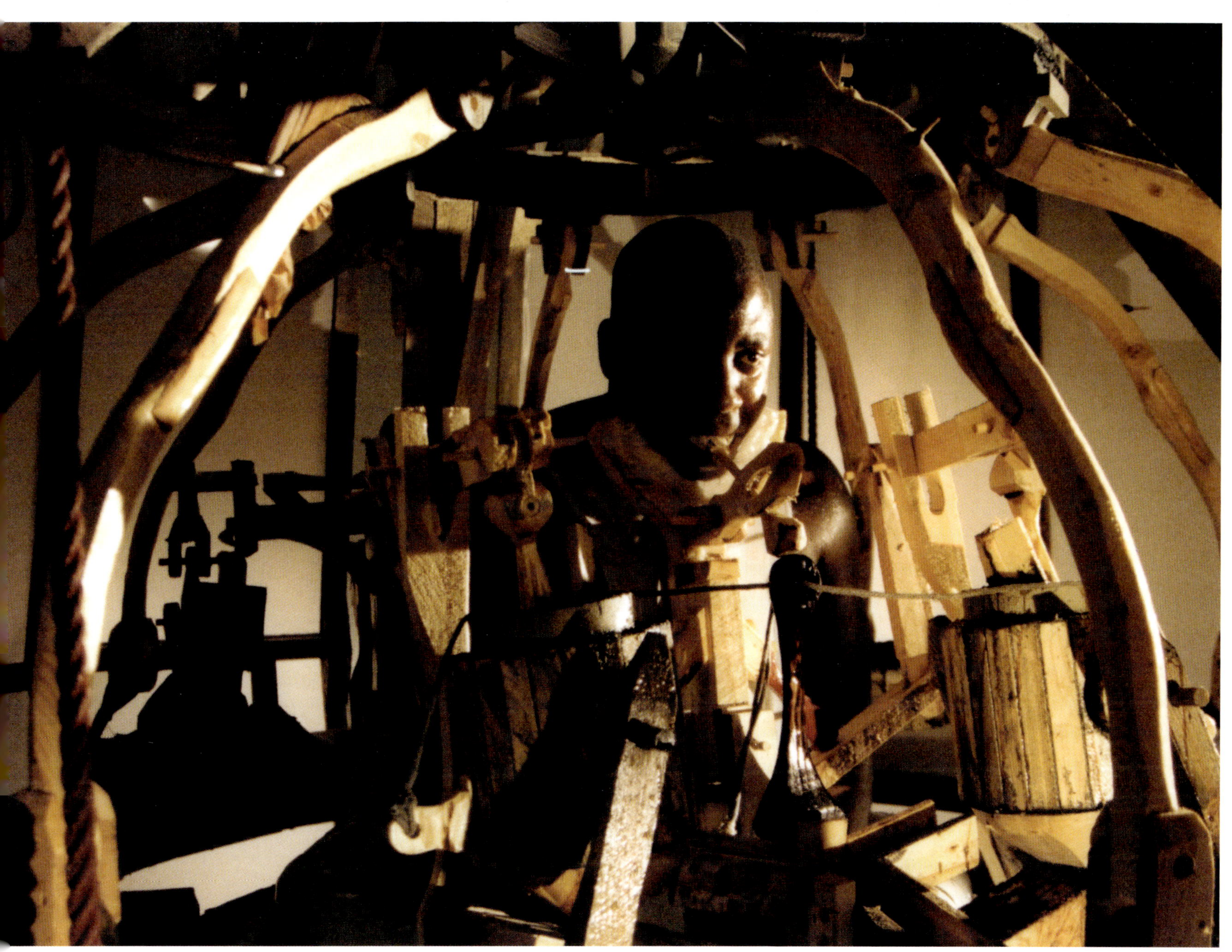

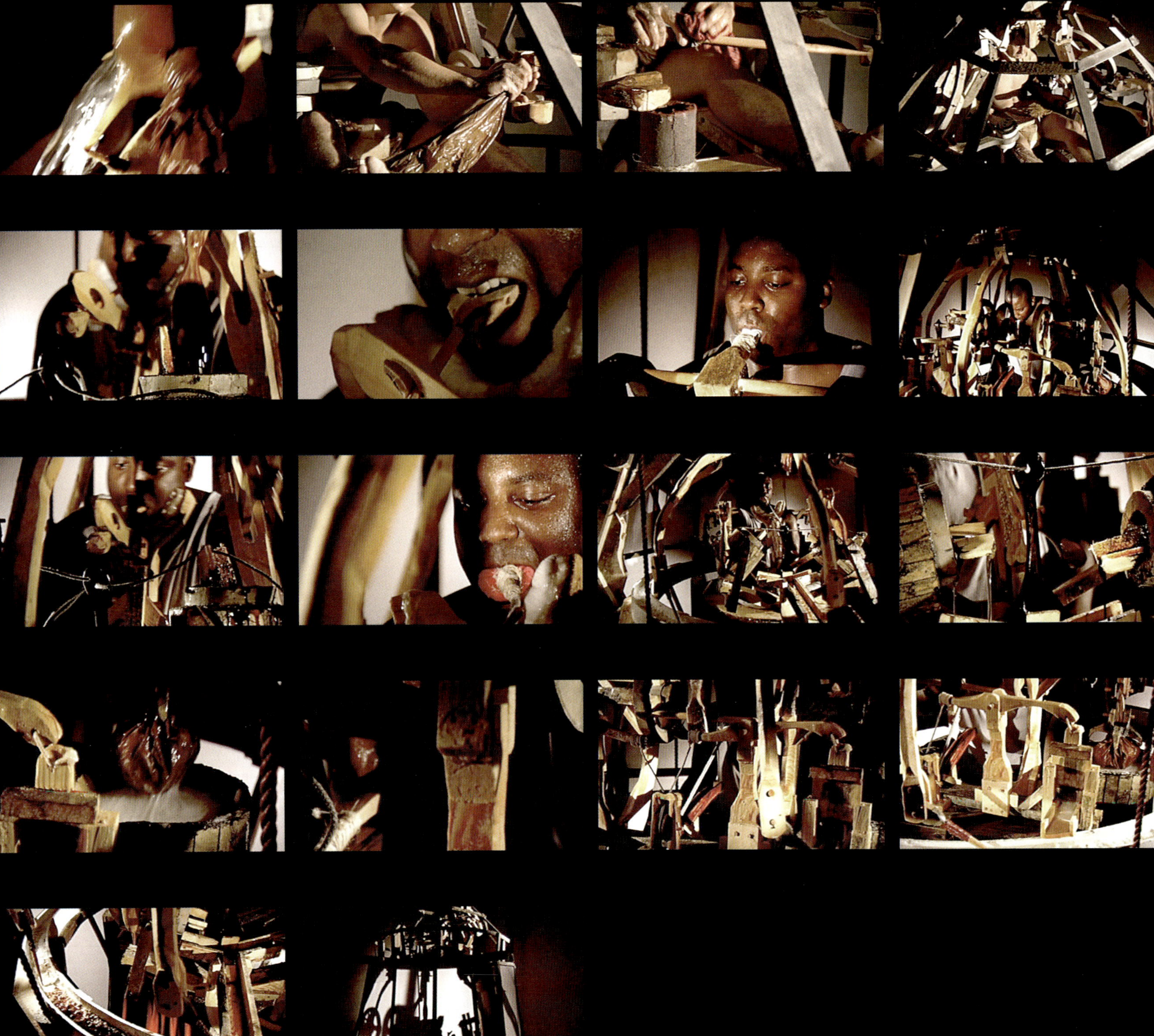

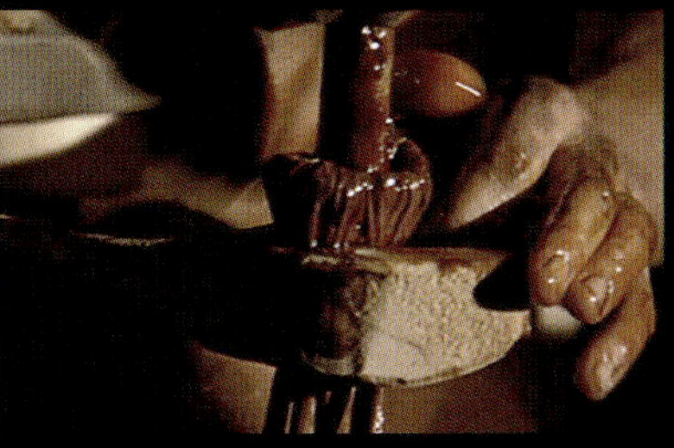
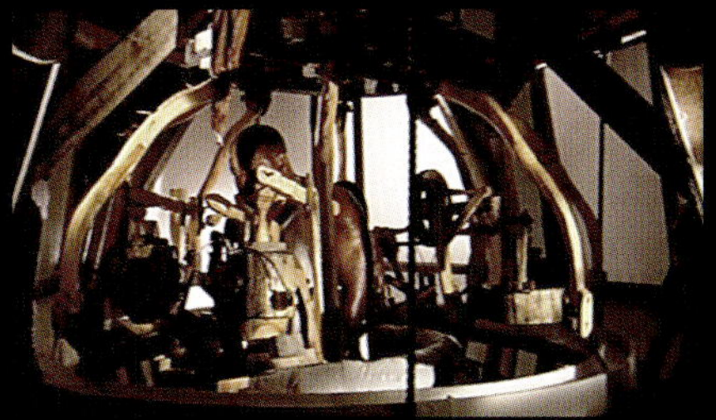
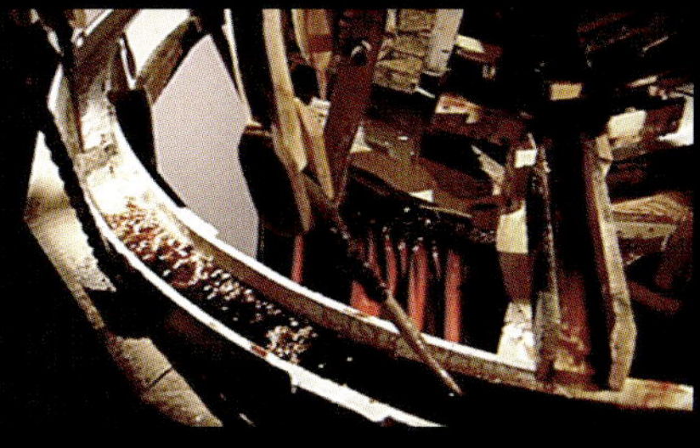
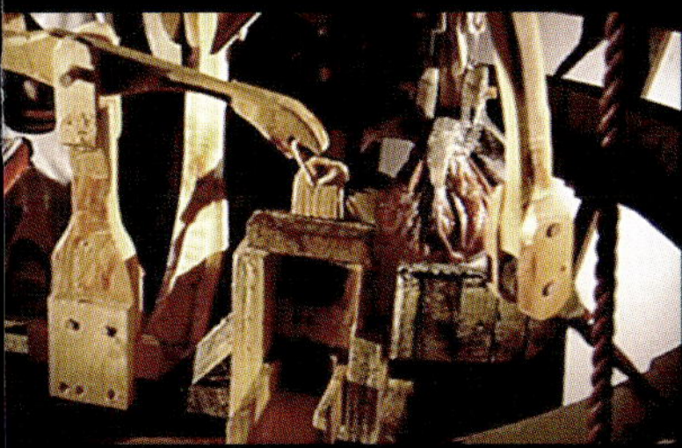
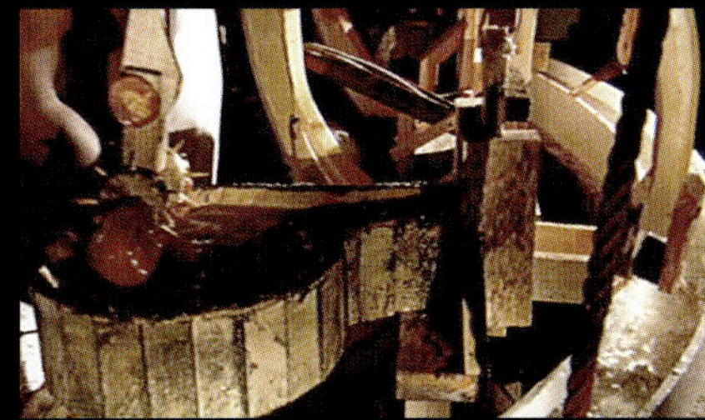
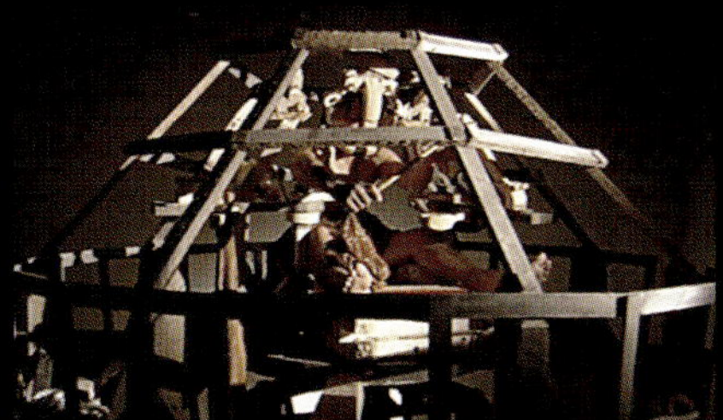
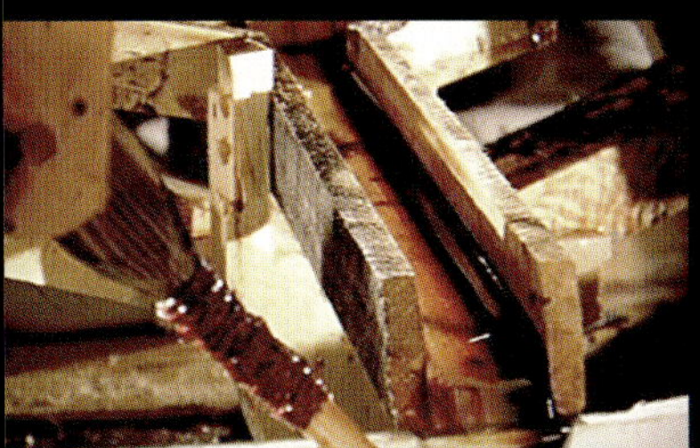
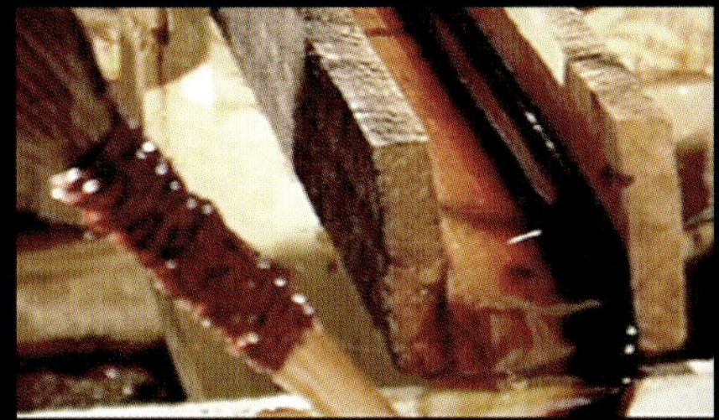
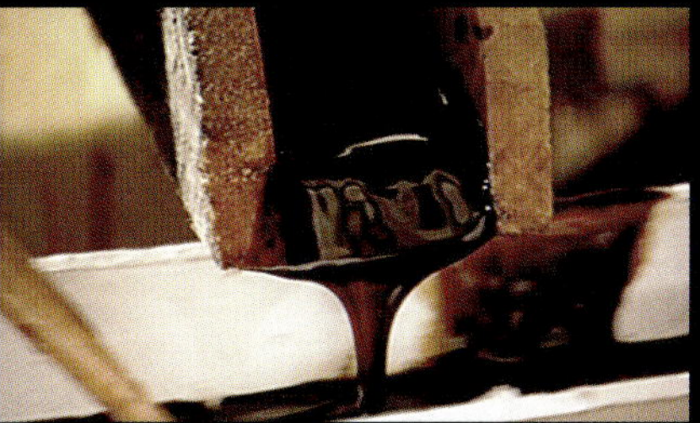
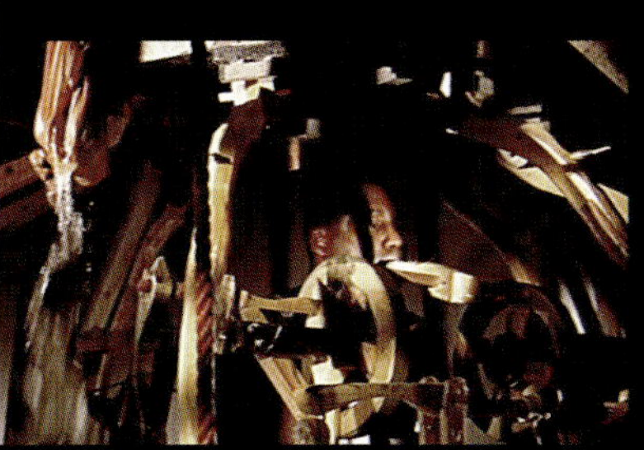
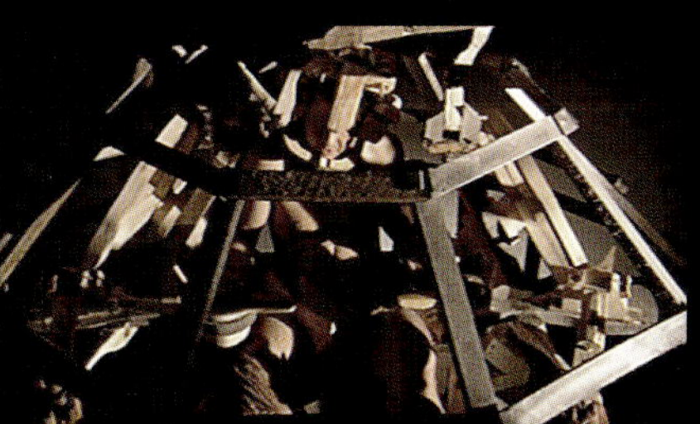
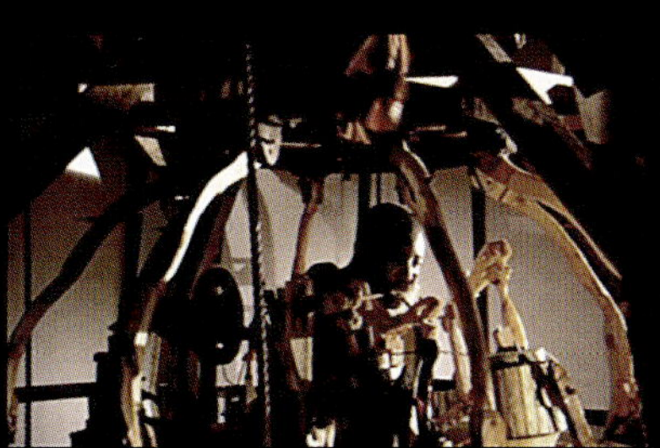

County Line

2004 * HD video transferred to DVD
Running time: 9:21 min.
Video stills

Sönke Magnus Müller: Chris, when we had your video *County Line* on view for the first time in our gallery in 2004, I felt very disturbed by this work: two men working in a wooden machine, the white man (who was you) above a black man, producing weird liquids that unify underneath them in a pot. Because of the many close-ups, I needed to view the film several times to finally get a first sense of what is going on in the film. How important is it for you to disturb people with your work?

Interview

Sönke Magnus Müller
with
Chris Larson

Chris: I can understand why you may say this. I guess I can't deny that a man working a machine with his mouth is disturbing. My initial intention is not to disturb, but to set up a situation that's real. As I build these machines the activities become normal to me, part of my visual language; I sometimes forget how unusual their tasks must seem. True, they are doing these very physical activities with their bodies. But for me it is about the work that both characters are making—together—just not in the same space.

Sönke: *County Line* provoked a lot of thoughts for me: first of all, the racism in American society. But in a weird way, the liquids of the black guy and the white guy melt together in one pot; both of them are half-naked and sweating in the machine. Their weird disposition also evokes a slight homosexual tension within the video. How much is this intended by you?

Chris: In this particular piece, I was simply interested in setting up a conversation between two different people in an odd and unusual situation. I guess I would say I was not intending to create a homosexual tension, but I can understand how one might see this in the work. I am aware of what happens when I place two sweaty, working men in a machine; these types of responses will come up. Many times people have said that I build machines of torture. I have never thought about my work as torture machines; the characters in the films never appear to be tortured, nobody is in pain. Having said that, I like the tension of what seems like torture, but isn't. I think it gives the work a certain edge that I like very much. *County Line* has that tension of torture, though I wanted to offset this by adding some human elements such as sweat and dripping fluids. This human element can point to many things; I am aware of this and of the many different feelings they evoke. This would also be true of the two racially different characters in *County Line*. The work for me was not about race, but I like that race naturally enters into the conversation—even though it is not my intention to comment on race. Does this make sense? I guess I am sometimes afraid of naming or identifying something: my fear is that if it is named, it will lose its tension.

Sönke: It often feels that the situations and activities in your films are not real. How important is fantasy in your work?

Chris: When I build these situations, they seem very real to me, but I can see why you would call them a fantasy; they do seem otherworldly. Overall, I am not interested in fantasy. Fantasy to me deals with magic and the supernatural, my work has nothing to do with these ideas. I do like placing the unusual in the commonplace. In *County Line* I built a machine that really worked, had real people operating it, and they produced real sweat from working. Maybe we could talk about this as a situation where people are performing unrealistic tasks. I perform these types of tasks in my studio all the time. I like to think of my artworks as fragments of a story or pages that were torn from the middle of a book. My works begin in the middle of an action and end in the middle of an action. Nothing is ever resolved.

Sönke: The film *County Line* was preceded by the film *American Gothic* (2001). I feel like there is a big difference between these two projects. What encouraged you to do *County Line*?

Chris: I had just finished my last project called *American Gothic (Saturday Night/Sunday Morning)*, a short film that was layered with metaphors and symbols. I was tired of making these types of connections in my work and did not want to start working on this new project with a list of "this stands for this" and "this stands for that." When I began building the sculpture for *County Line*, I started with only two concerns in mind. I wanted to build a machine that had two levels, a top and a bottom and I wanted to use two characters. In *American Gothic* I played all three characters. In this film I wanted to play one of the characters, and I wanted someone else who did not look like me to play the other. As I began building, I first built the skeleton or pod that would hold the characters and the machine. After completing the pod, I began working on the environment that I would work in. I wanted my actions to be minimal and mundane. My character's job was to exchange numerous liquid-filled bladders that had been broken over the course of the operation. The bladders hung and spilled a liquid into the space that the other character would occupy. After completing my area of the machine, I then focused on the lower level of the contraption. I decided to cast a friend, Brooklyn-based artist Rico Gatson, to run the lower level. I was interested in using Gatson for this project because he does not look anything like me. I am white and skinny, Gatson strong and black. His tasks were more complicated than mine; he would only use his mouth to operate the machine and would perform multiple movements to complete the cycle of the machine. I wanted to set up a situation in which two people were working together in the same capsule, not in direct contact with each other but with the appearance of working together. When workers are working on an assembly line, they are only responding to the work that is coming at them from down the line. They are not in physical contact with the other workers but are aware that they are part of something larger, they are all contributing to the completion of a final product, a product they usually never see or use. I have never been interested in the final product. I am interested in the emotions and questions that are created by the physical interaction with the machine and the materials that are being mixed, manipulated, and transformed.

Sönke: Chris, we have spent quite some time together, and in one of our conversations you said that you could not live anywhere else in the world than in Minnesota. What is this specific relation you have to this area and how much is it related to your work?

Chris: There is something about who I am that is dictated by this place, the Midwest. There is something about the work ethic, about making things. I grew up making things. I mean I know they make things in other places, but the motivation or the purpose of making things seems different; maybe one could say that things here are on a more human scale, or more mundane. I guess it is why I have so many references to the South in my work, because I think there is a similar ethic there. Making mundane things, for mundane purposes, by, I guess, mundane people, becomes iconic, or at least important to point out or see.

Sönke: Tell me more about your childhood then.

Chris: When I was in second grade, our family moved from St. Paul to a rural part of Minnesota. I loved walking through the woods and fields finding old obsolete farm machinery, abandoned shacks and piles of old rusted and decaying objects from the past. All these objects held a certain power for me. These mundane objects once had a specific use but no longer functioned as they once did. I loved imagining what they were used for or the people who had used them.

Sönke: Whenever I showed your work in New York, people were surprised to hear that you come originally from the Midwest. Statements like, "Oh, there is actually art in the Midwest" were common comments. How do you deal with this certain prejudice?

Chris: Do people say that? I have a hard time answering this. I can't define a style or look that's particular to the Midwest. I guess I don't think about it a whole lot. There is a lot of art created in places around the world that should have more attention. I wanted to be a part of the larger conversation so I crossed the border, took my work out of the Midwest hoping to be a part of that conversation.

Sönke: Has there been any artist you adored and any art movement you have primarily been interested in?

Chris: I love the series of photographs of Pennsylvania coalmine tipples by Bernd and Hilla Becher. Coalmine tipples are these amazing, crude wooden structures that are made roughly and quickly to illegally extract coal out of the earth. I love the immediacy of this type of building. I can't imagine that the bootleg miners made drawings of the structure before they started building. I also love the short stories by the Southern writer Flannery O'Connor and the writings of Franz Kafka. They both have an amazing ability to make the extraordinary seem commonplace. They also have a great way of developing their characters not by who they are but by what they do. I still am fascinated with the Surrealist sculptures of the 1930s, such as Giacometti's *Suspended Ball* or *Hands Holding the Void*

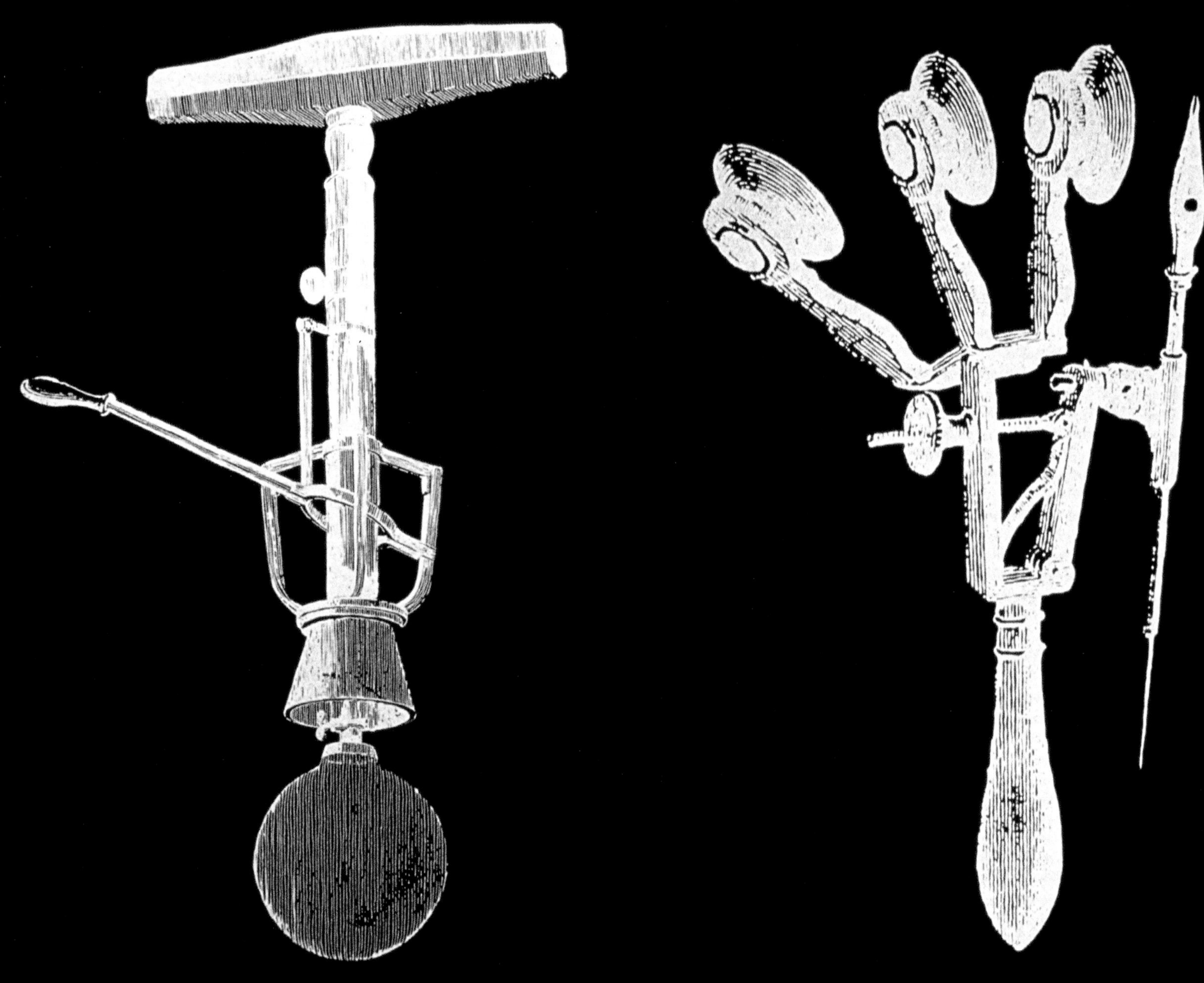

Untitled
1997 * Silver ink on black papers * Each 110 x 90 cm

(*Invisible Object*), which I discovered as an MFA student at Yale University. I would regularly visit this sculpture in the gallery, it was the plaster version, beautiful. Lately, I have been looking at the work of Paul Tech again. I wish I could have seen some of his installations. Amazing.

Sönke: As you know, as a gallerist I am basically interested in artists that work in a multidisciplinary way. But few of the artists that I am working with do it in such a wide range as you do. I know that your film production takes a lot of your time, but still you are doing a lot of performing, sculpting, photography, and drawings. How do you see this all together, and what is the evidence of this different media in the body of your work?

Chris: I began my career as a sculptor, but it seemed necessary or expedient to use these other mediums. I don't tend to separate my work out between mediums; mediums feel like tools to me. I find it exciting when a new body of my work begins to have a life of its own. I don't have to push hard anymore, it grows on its own, starts to live and breath in whatever media it wants to.

Sönke: When did you start making art?

Chris: I was attending college in Chicago, studying literature. Toward the end of the semester, I got a call from a friend who was taking art classes at a college in St. Paul, Minnesota. He began telling me about all the things he had been making in the studio. It sounded exciting to be making things. At the end of the semester, I moved back to Minnesota and enrolled. I started taking the basic art classes, beginning drawing, printmaking, and painting. I quickly discovered that working two-dimensionally was not enough. I wanted to make things that felt like they could have existed in the world or that could be mistaken for something real, non-art. Straight-up painting felt too removed. I started attaching objects to the surface of the painting hoping to make it something other than a painting. Someone showed me Rauschenberg's bed painting, and I loved it. One night while making a stretcher for a new painting in the woodshop (a place that was new to me, as I had never taken any woodshop classes in high school nor did we have any tools around the house), I picked up a large chunk of wood from the scrap bin and started cutting it with the band saw. It was amazing. I cut and shaped that piece of wood for hours. I made an odd hand tool with a hook on the end.

Sönke: Certain works, especially your sculptures, appear in a rather rough way, since you basically build them yourself. How important is the means of execution of the sculptures for you?

Chris: It is very important. I like the way wood can feel clumsy, not precise. Machines are suppose be made of metal and work smoothly. When I build a machine out of wood, it is already set up to fail or function in an unproductive manner. I also use rough wood so I can work very fast and not worry about finishing the surfaces. This allows me not to be troubled with the next decision. Unfinished wood, rough wood, is odd, peculiar. I like it very much. It is like the way farmers fix things: they just use the wood they have to prop up a wall or mend something. They don't necessarily fix it or replace it with what was there before, but just with something that works. I do not draw my sculptures out before I begin. I react to the needs of the last thing I did on a piece.

Sönke: Yes, tell me more about how you invent these complex sculptures. Are they just coming out of your mind on the spot? Hard to believe.

Chris: I get asked this question often, and I sometimes feel uncomfortable saying that I just start building and something comes out. But this is very important to my working process. This is the way I have come to understand how my work develops. I will go back to the first object I made in the woodshop. I knew I wanted to make something that could be used in my hand, and I wanted it to look sinister. Is this way of thinking or building hard to believe? When I began working on the set for the ice house film, *Deep North*, I knew I wanted to build a shotgun shack; I was interested in the idea of this particular type of Southern architecture. The term "shotgun house" comes from the saying that one could fire a shotgun through the front door and have the bullet go out again through the back. I was intrigued by the idea of a force passing in through the kitchen and out the back through the bedroom. I knew I wanted to fully furnish the house, and I also wanted to install a machine inside as though it had grown up out of the house. Ultimately, what the machine did or looked like, I did not know. As I began building the machine, I slowly started to understand its function. It was to carry ice tubes from the front of the house to the back of the house. It is all based on needs. How do you move an ice tube from one end of the house to the other? These machines do not exist, so I invent as I go along, adding dysfunctional, absurd, odd ways of transferring an object or liquids from one place to another. This is a task that could easily be done by picking the thing up and carrying it to the other side, but the characters in this house do not work this way. They labor, performing mundane tasks with rapidly fading preindustrial machines. This is how they work, this is what they do, and they know no other or have forgotten other ways of how to do things.

Sönke: Objects like musical instruments, pianos for example, appear often in your work. Could you tell me more about your relationship with these objects? What content do the instruments symbolize and how important is music in general for you?

Chris: I have played music as long as I have made art. I like to think about musical instruments as tools or weapons or machines—the smashing of a punk rocker's guitar, or how Fats Domino would bump his piano across the stage with his belly while he played, or how Woody Guthrie painted on his guitar "this machine kills fascists." There is something about the way you interact with an instrument or wield it that transforms it into a tool of another kind, something beyond the music. I love the piano as an object in a room. I like the way you approach this object and then sit down in front of it as if you were sitting down at a table for a meal or at a workbench ready to build something. A wooden piano on rockers was the first object I made as I began working on the film *Crush Collision*. In the film you find a house floating on the water, a family sitting around a table praying before they eat, while upstairs, a man sits in front of a piano as if he were sitting down at a table waiting for something to happen. As the family starts to sing, the man starts to play the piano, not in the usual way but with his foot on the pedal, rocking the piano back and forth, following a rhythm, keeping time or trying to make an attempt to understand something he once knew. A piano is an object that is still, heavy, and hard to move. I wanted to alter this reality.

Sönke: Beside musical objects, music itself also plays an important role in your films and performances.

Chris: In my live performance *Shotgun Shack* at Creative Electric, I used music to dictate the actions of the three characters. The set for the perfomance was a large shattered wooden shack; inside the shack were a piano, three working stations, and a small stage. The music that played throughout the performance was loud punk rock music. I liked the dichotomy of something new mixing with something old. In that collision—sometimes literal—I played and then smashed the piano and guitar underneath the abrasive sounds of the music; a collision happened and out of this collision of the old and new, something new was created. Music was my entrance into art. As a teenager I was blown away when I picked up the record *London Calling* by the Clash and realized they had borrowed the look for their album cover from an early Elvis Presley record I had as a kid. The Clash swapped out the image of Elvis singing with an acoustic guitar with a photo of their bass player in motion to smash his guitar on the stage. There was much more than music going on here, and I wanted be a part of that conversation.

Sönke: For me as a European, I see actually certain American stereotypes and parts of American culture in your work. How much would you interpret your work as being American? How much distance do you feel yourself to this question of having the identity of an American?

Chris: Everything I do is a result of being an American. The way I think or see things, the way I build, or the tools I use. It is like when I first picked up a gun, not to go hunting or whatever, but when I picked up a shotgun as a tool for making art. It is in some ways the quintessential American tool. A gun is a farm implement; it is necessary to have one around to eat or put down a sick cow, but it is also a tool, the tool that made the conquest of this large country, or manifest destiny, possible.

Sönke: What is intriguing in your work is this junction of the high-tech world you produce your work in and then, on the other side, the odd and rough way you produce your sculptures and dress the people that play in your films.

Chris: I guess you could think of the machines I make as a kind of crude technology. In the new ice house film, the rough machine grows out of a home, a large waterwheel in the living room next to the stereo and TV. The machine is just as real as the appliances in the house—maybe more real. Perhaps I am commenting on the technological world that I live in and make my work in. I might be talking about current technology, but it is necessary for me to use mechanical technology—like a wheel or a hand crank or even a piano—as opposed to electronic technology, because you can see it working or not working, you can see how it is supposed to or could work. When I look at an iPod, it is hard to see it working: Does it move? Is it supposed to? Can you tell if it is broken by looking at it? Sometimes when people look at my sculptures, they ask me, "Does it work?" It is funny; no one ever asks if a painting "works." I like getting asked that question.

Sönke: Some of your machines and drawings appear like they've been inspired by Leonardo da Vinci. What fascinates you about Leonardo?

Chris: I love his drawings of the flying machines that never really worked, but in a way they did work. He had an amazing ability to make things in his head. They worked in his head and maybe seemed to work on paper, and that was more important than whether or not you could build an operational helicopter from the drawings.

Sönke: In *Crush Collision* a black family sits in a very old-fashioned, conservative way at their dining table in your floating house singing a gospel song. How important is religion for yourself and your work?

Chris: In a way, it is like when you asked me how important it is to be an American. Religion, the Christian religion, is just a part of who I am, how I was raised, the world I was born to. Whether or not I agree with every impulse or tenet of being an American or a Christian doesn't matter. These are foundational stories for me. It is hard for me to think outside of them or around them, especially if I am trying to talk about the beautiful mundanity of humanity—religion is just a core part of that vocabulary.

Sönke: In your films you often depict black and white people in opposite functions. How much do you refer to a black and white conflict in your work?

Chris: I understand why you may say this, and I guess I don't mind that race enters into the conversation of the work; my hope is that it does not dominate the conversation. When I was shooting *County Line* with Rico, after the filming Rico said, "Be careful Chris, your work is quickly moving from grey into black and white." I didn't understand at the time, but I am slowly starting to understand what he meant. I don't use black and white people in my work to talk about a conflict, but I am aware of the ways this could be read. I guess I use the people I use in order to talk about a conversation or collision that is or is not happening between my characters. They have a relationship with each other, just not in the way we think of relationships. I think, maybe, if there is any way that I think about it, it is that I am looking for people who are different from me. Race, of course, is a very real issue, but I am not thinking about it in any global way; I am thinking about characters and people in a personal way. The people in my work—black people or women—are people who are physically different from me, people whose life experience is different from mine—but they are people with whom I have formed relationships, and that is the kind of collision I don't understand but am really interested in.

Sönke: A lot of times, sculptures you created get destroyed or shot. Even though it is a very destructive act, it never appears violent to me. What is this fascination of yours with destruction?

Chris: You are right, it is not violence. I am not thinking of violent destruction—I am thinking about collisions, like conversations, juxtapositions, that inevitably change both things. Like when I collide a machine with a house, something new comes out of that.

Sönke: Even though lots of things get destroyed in your films, it never looks like there is no hope. Does mankind have a chance to survive in this evil world?

Chris: Do I think we have a chance to survive in this evil world? No. Is there hope in my work? Yes, I think so. The hope comes from the collisions. Like, if there is just that house, a frozen ice house or a house floating on the water, adrift, there is no hope there—they need a collision, something to crash into them, then there is hope, possibility.

Sönke: You are one of the few contemporary artists who are part of the famous German Surrealist collection, the Sammlung Scharf-Gerstenberg housed by the National Gallery in Berlin. How important is Surrealism in your work? What is your fascination with this bizarre world and with a turning away from real life?

Chris: Surrealism, for me, was never about what is not real. It is about what is most real, manipulating reality so as to heighten or recontextualize something that is very real: emotional responses. Like with Meret Oppenheim's fur-lined teacup or Giacometti's suspended ball: the emotions they evoke are so much stronger, the desire so much more intense, than what you might feel simply observing the ordinary or the so-called real.

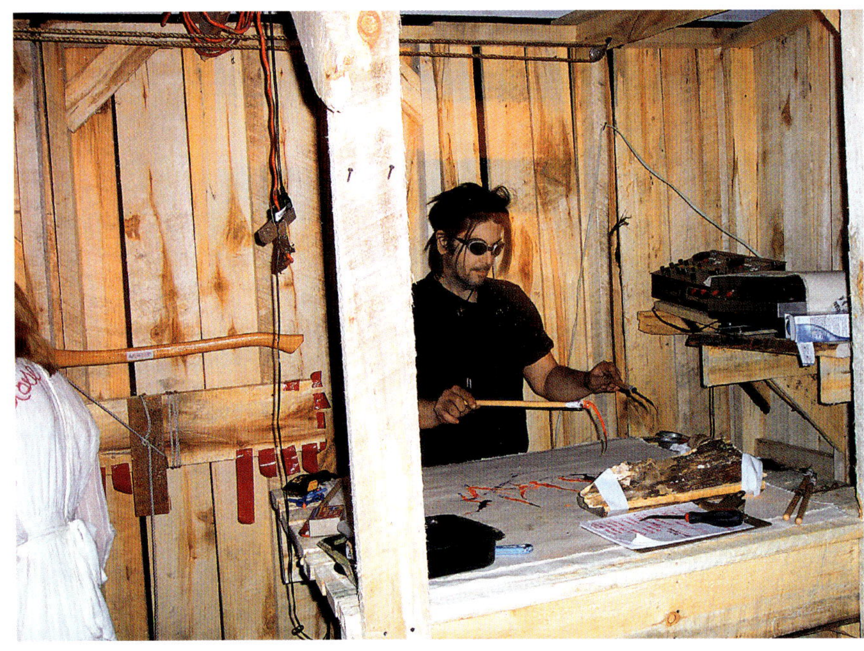

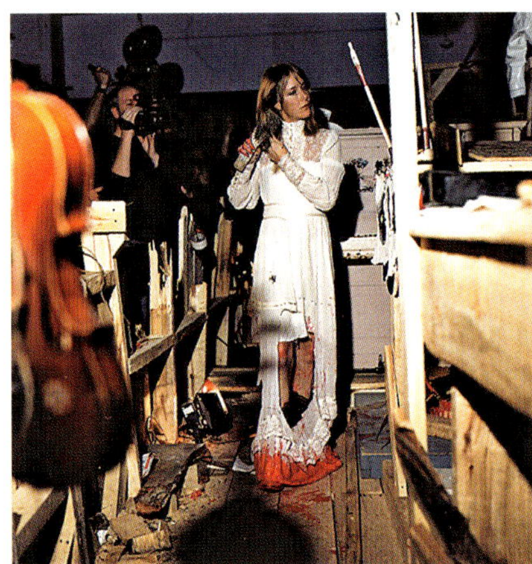

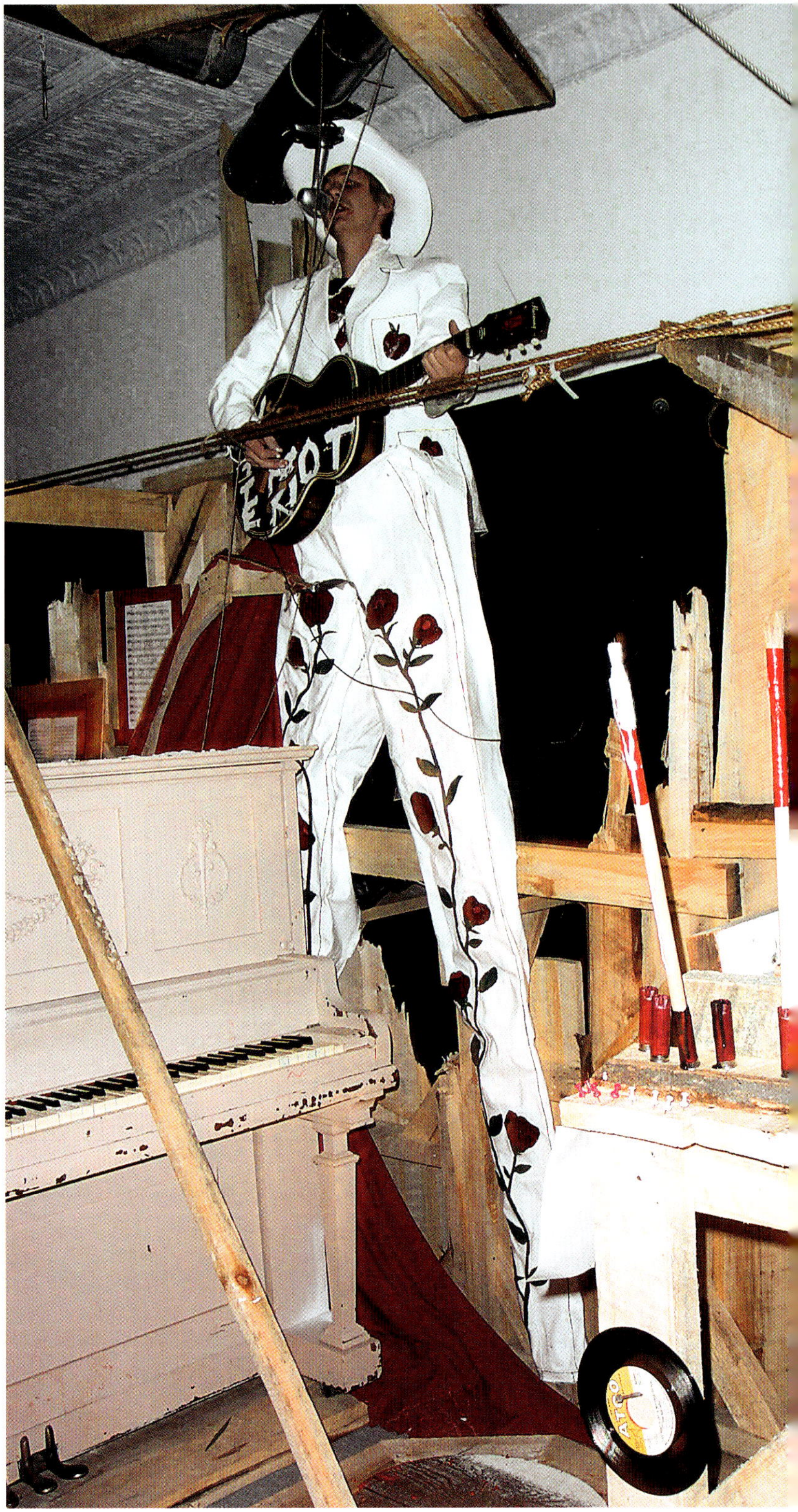

Shotgun Shack

2006 * Installation, performance, and video at Creative Electric, Minneapolis, MN
Performance with Grant Hart and Britta Hallin
Running time: 9:00 min.

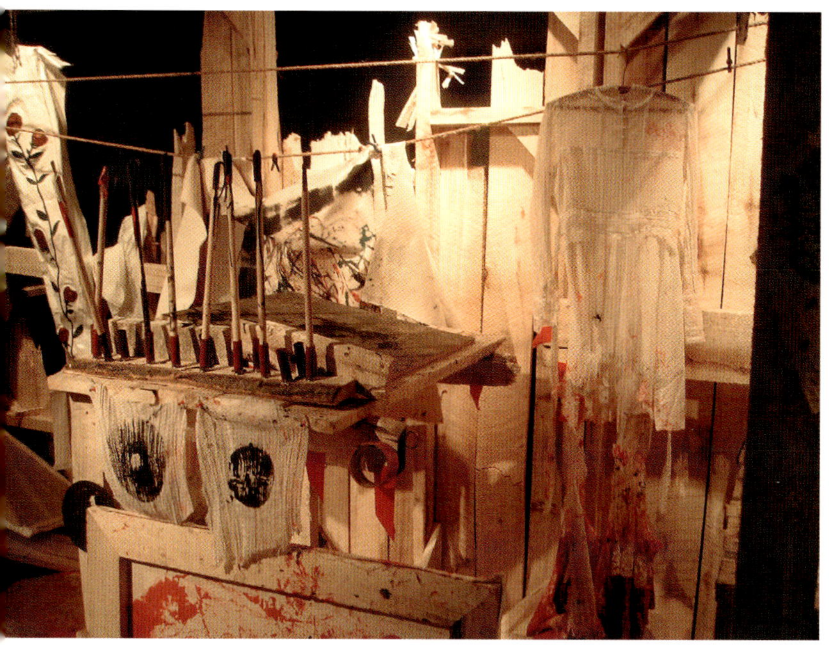

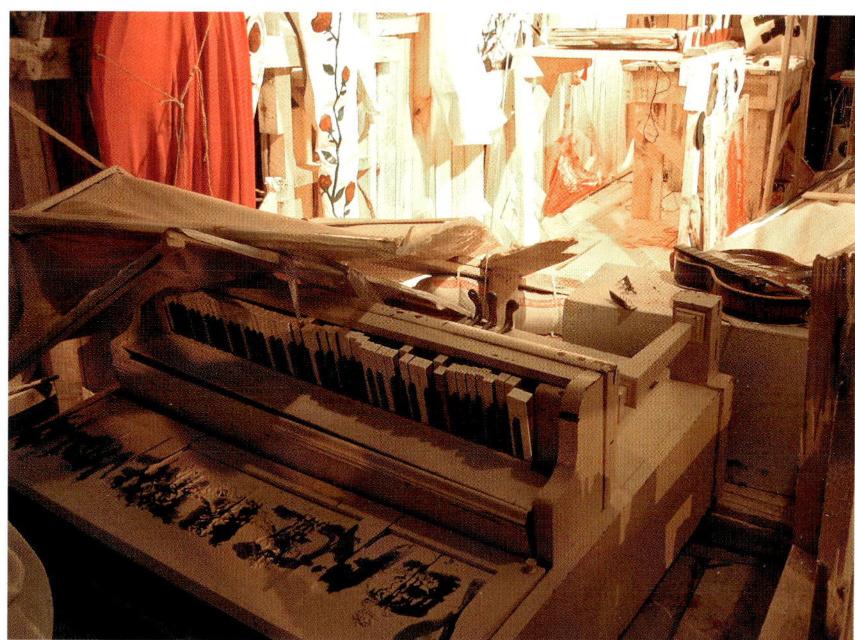

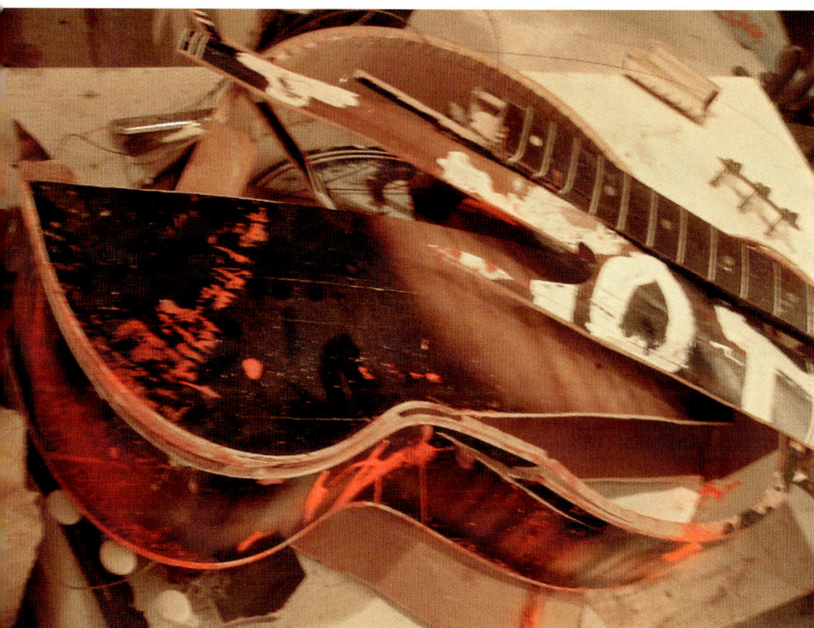

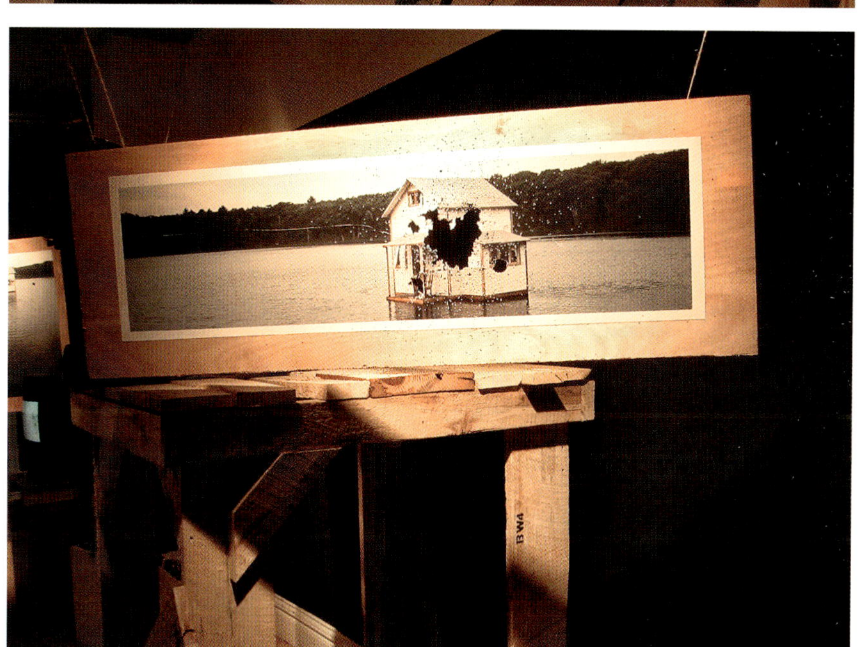

Drawings

Page 65
Untitled • 2006 • Pencil on vellum • 63 x 48 cm

Page 66
Untitled • 2006 • Pencil on vellum • 63 x 48 cm

Page 67
Untitled • 2006 • Pencil on vellum • 55 x 49 cm

Page 68
Spaceship Crash • 2006 • Pencil on vellum • 63 x 63 cm

Page 69
Drawing #4, Under Nova • 2007 • Pencil on vellum
79 x 79 cm

Page 70
Untitled • 2006 • Pencil on vellum • 63 x 63 cm

Page 71
Untitled • 2007 • Pencil on vellum • 51 x 63 cm

Page 72
Untitled • 2006 • Pencil on vellum • 63 x 51 cm

Page 73
Rural Explosion • 2007 • Pencil on vellum • 63 x 51 cm

Page 74
Drawing #1 (Revolving Blue (h)) • 2007 • Pencil on vellum
64 x 51 cm

Page 75
Untitled • 2006 • Pencil on vellum • 54 x 49 cm

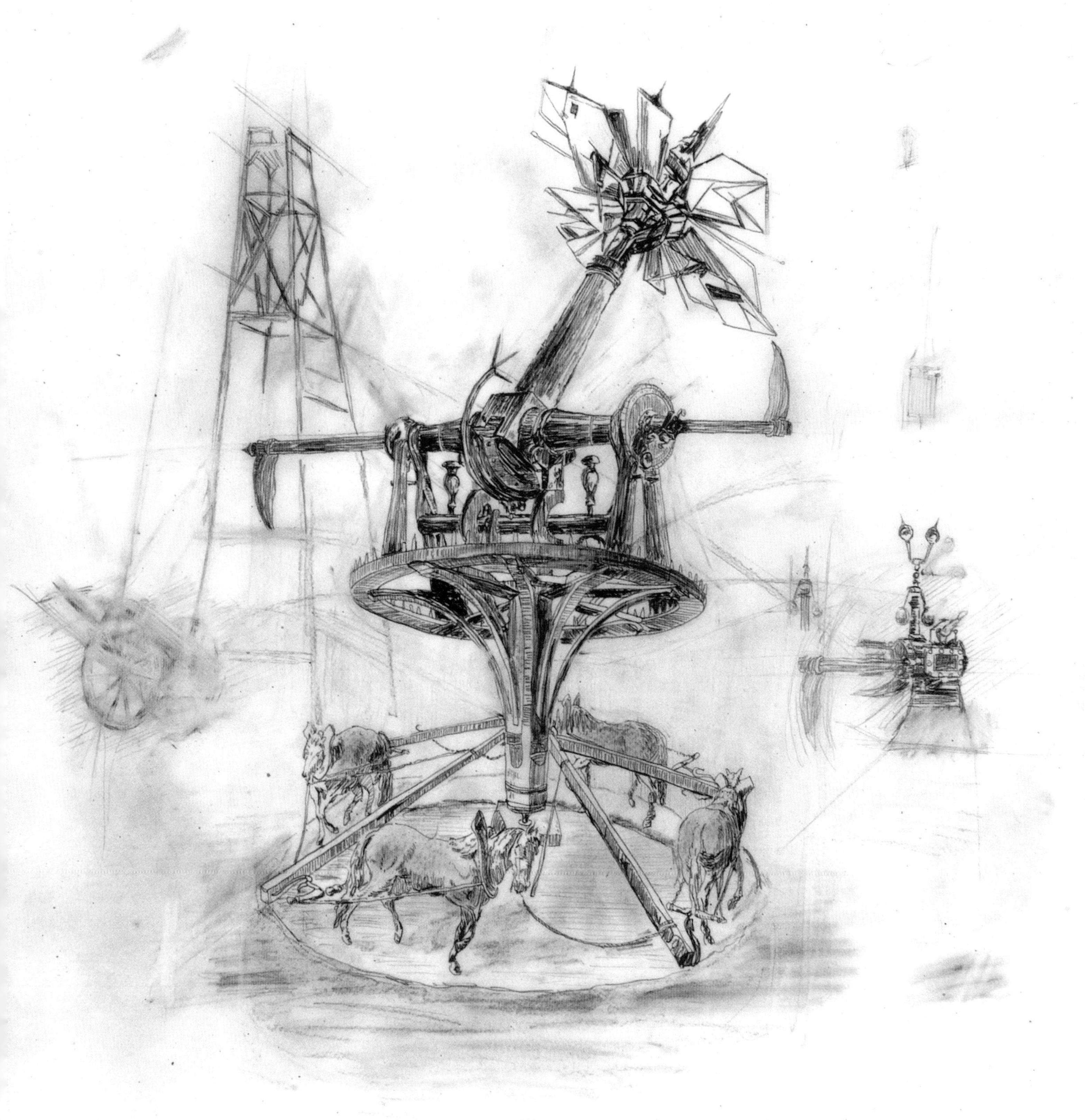

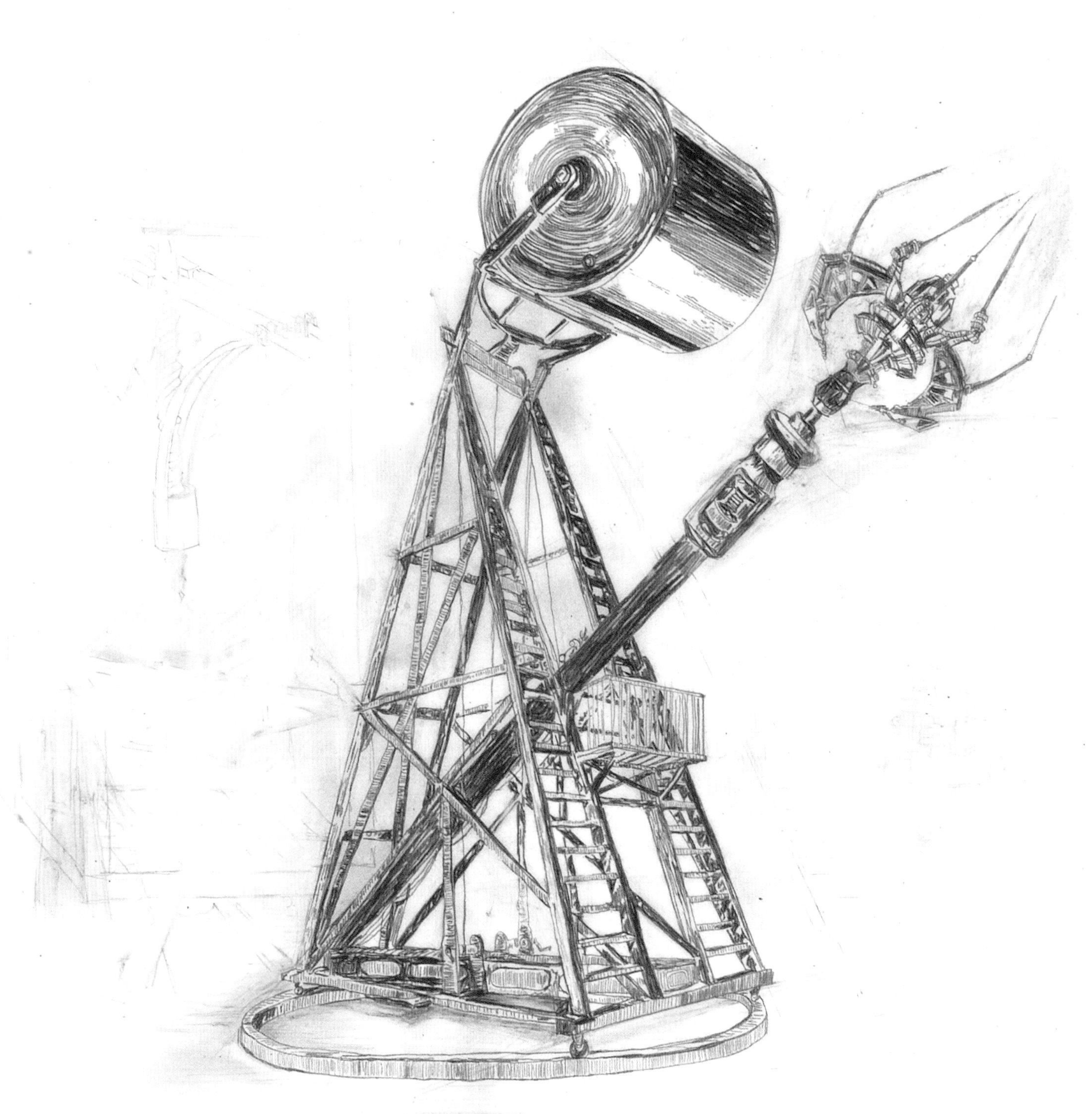
6/24

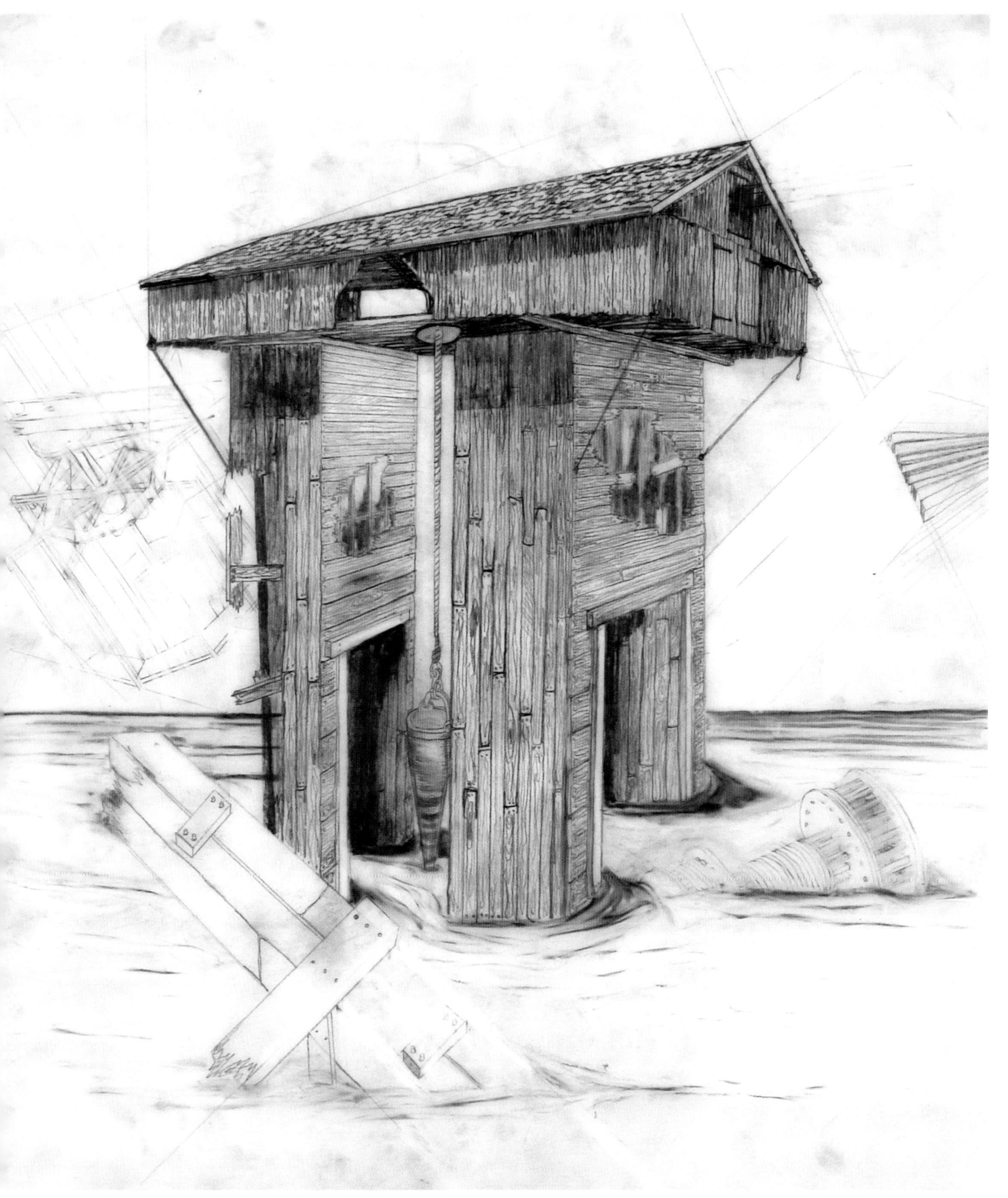

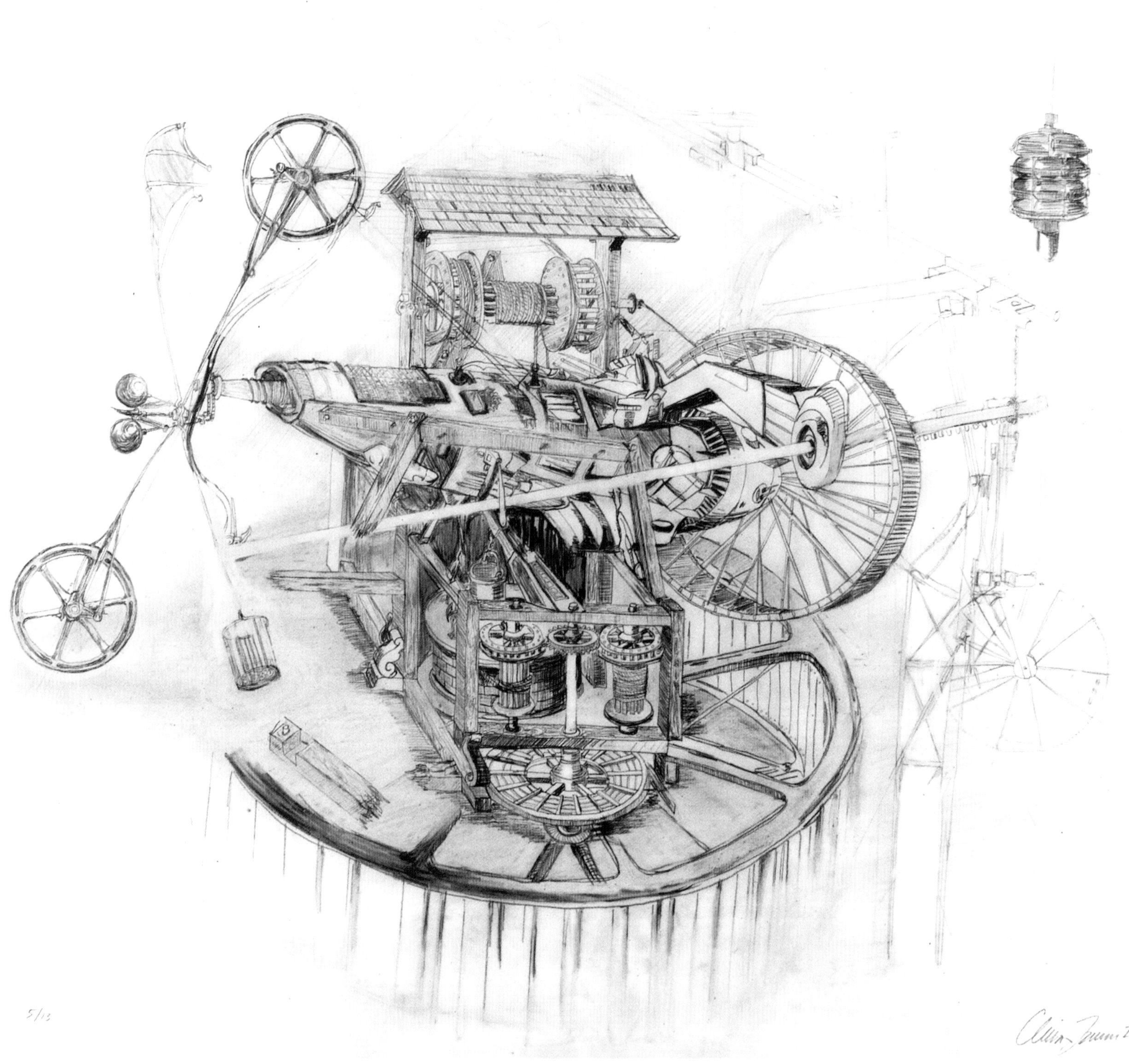

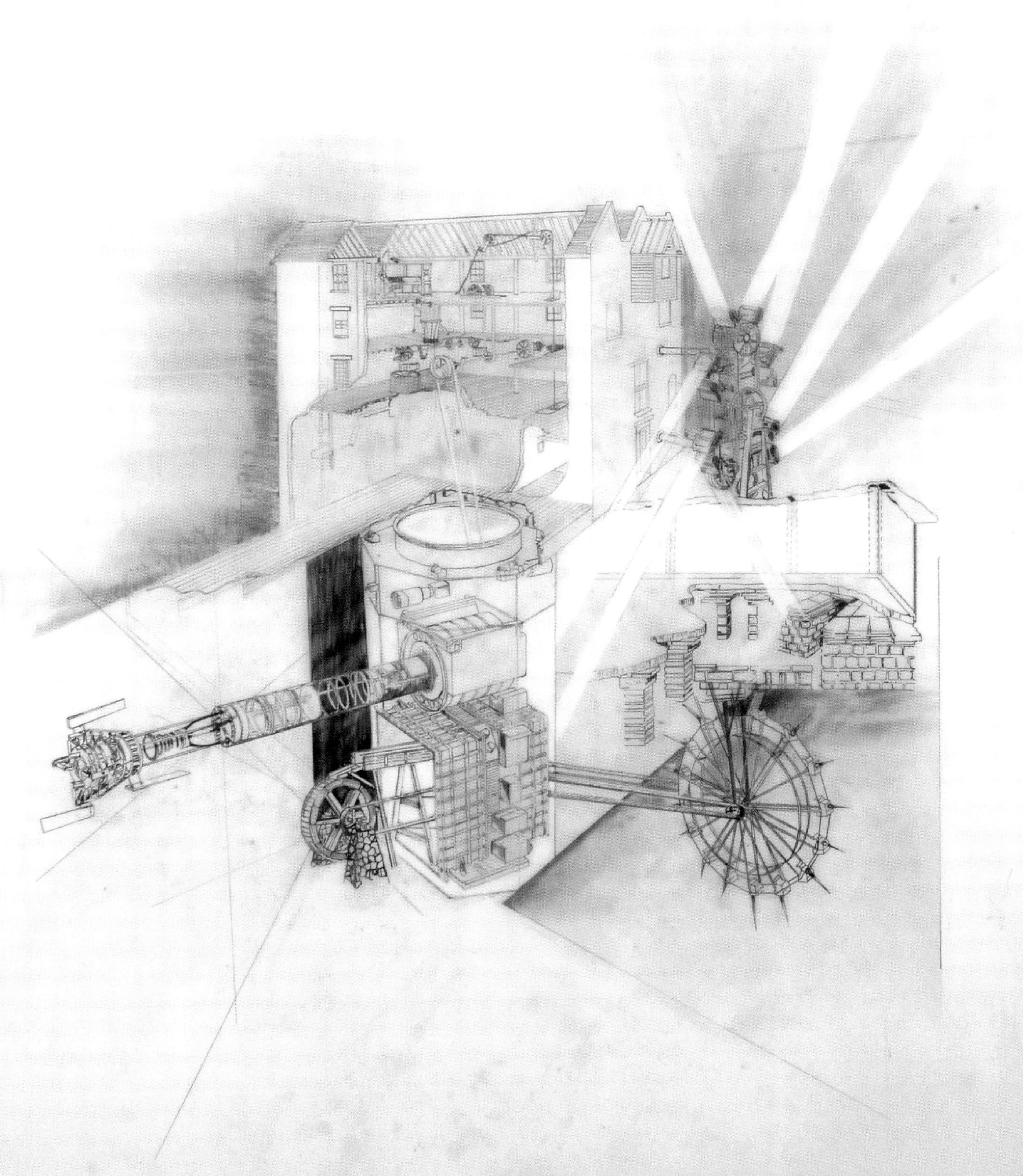

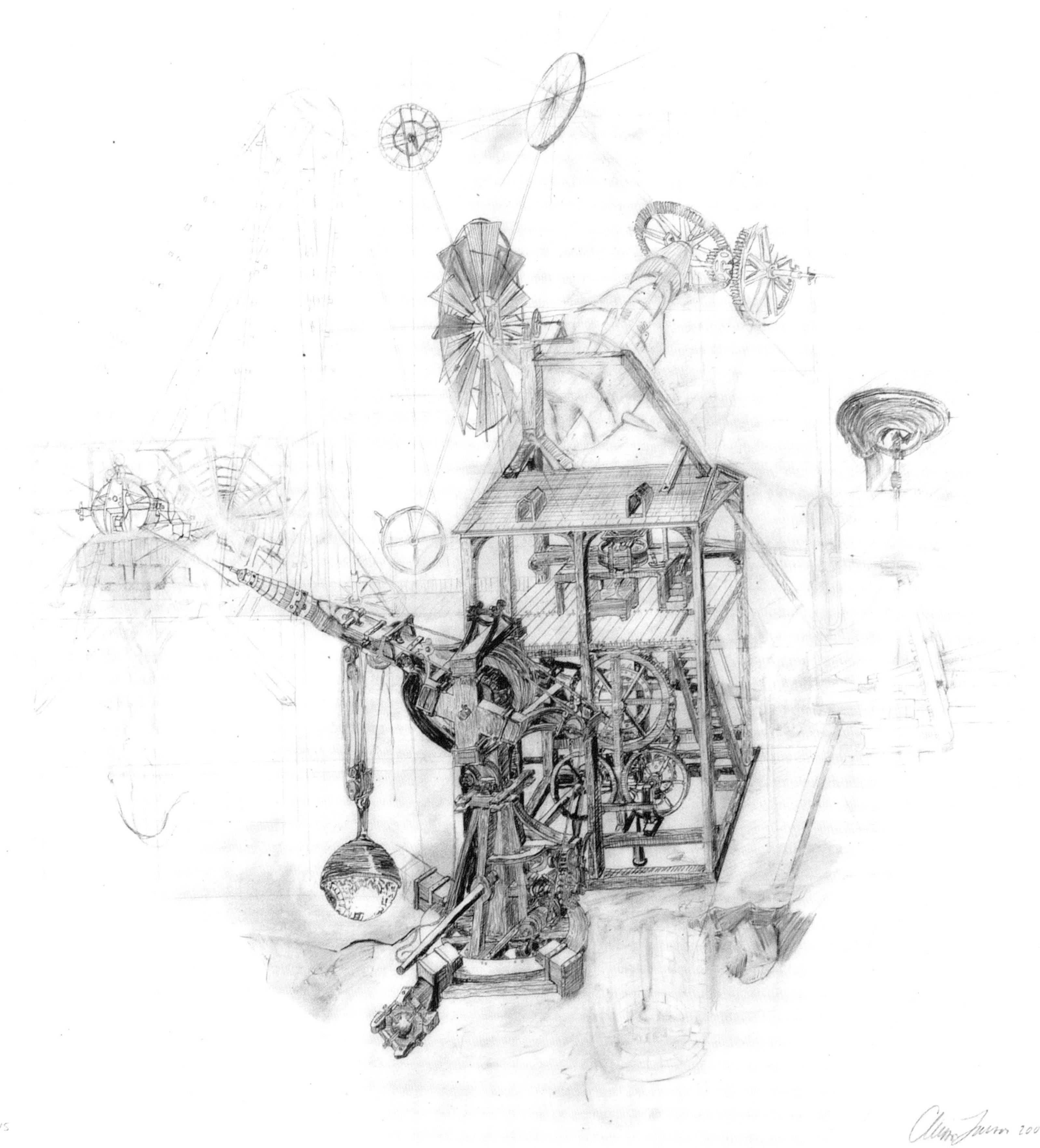

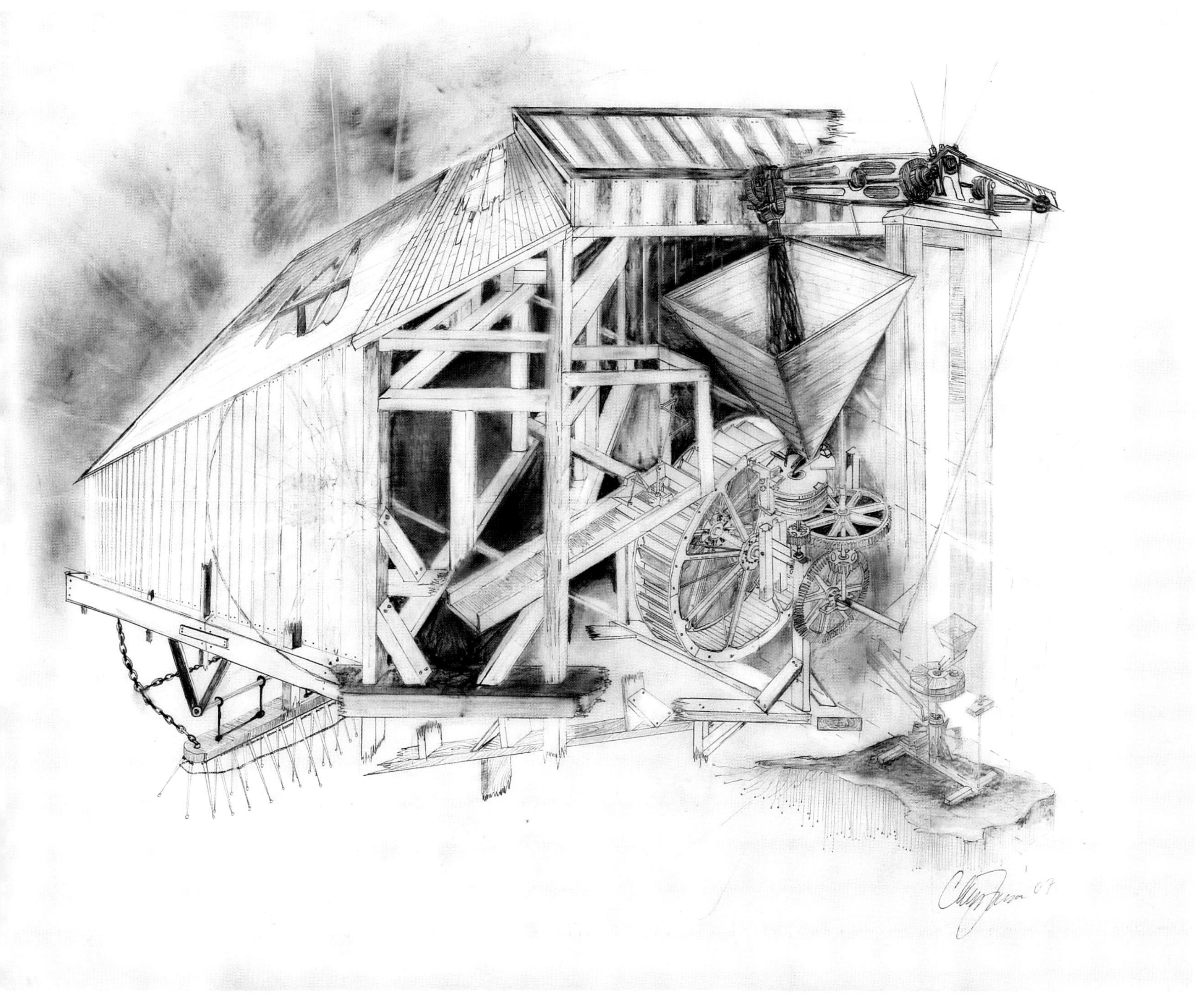

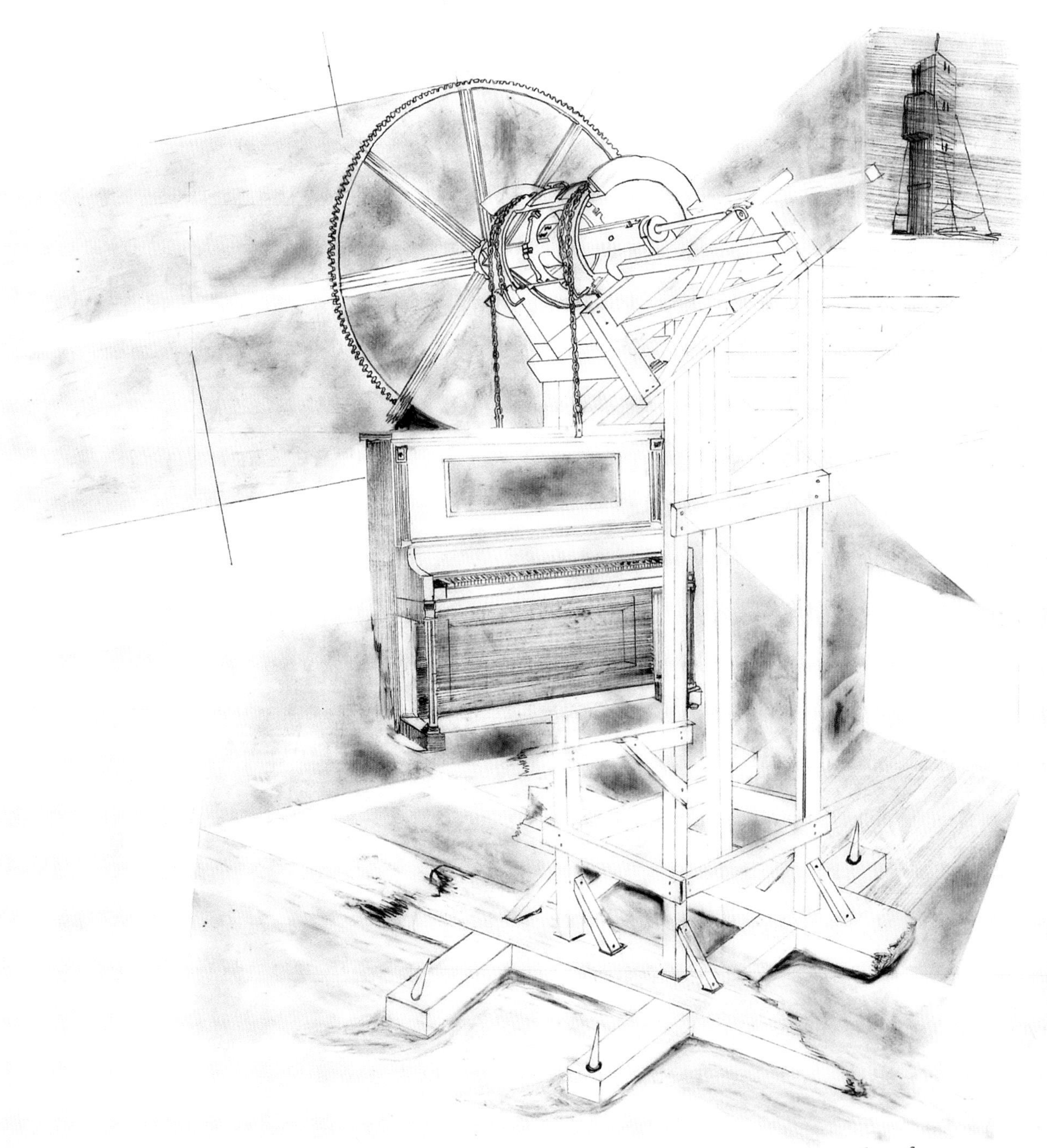

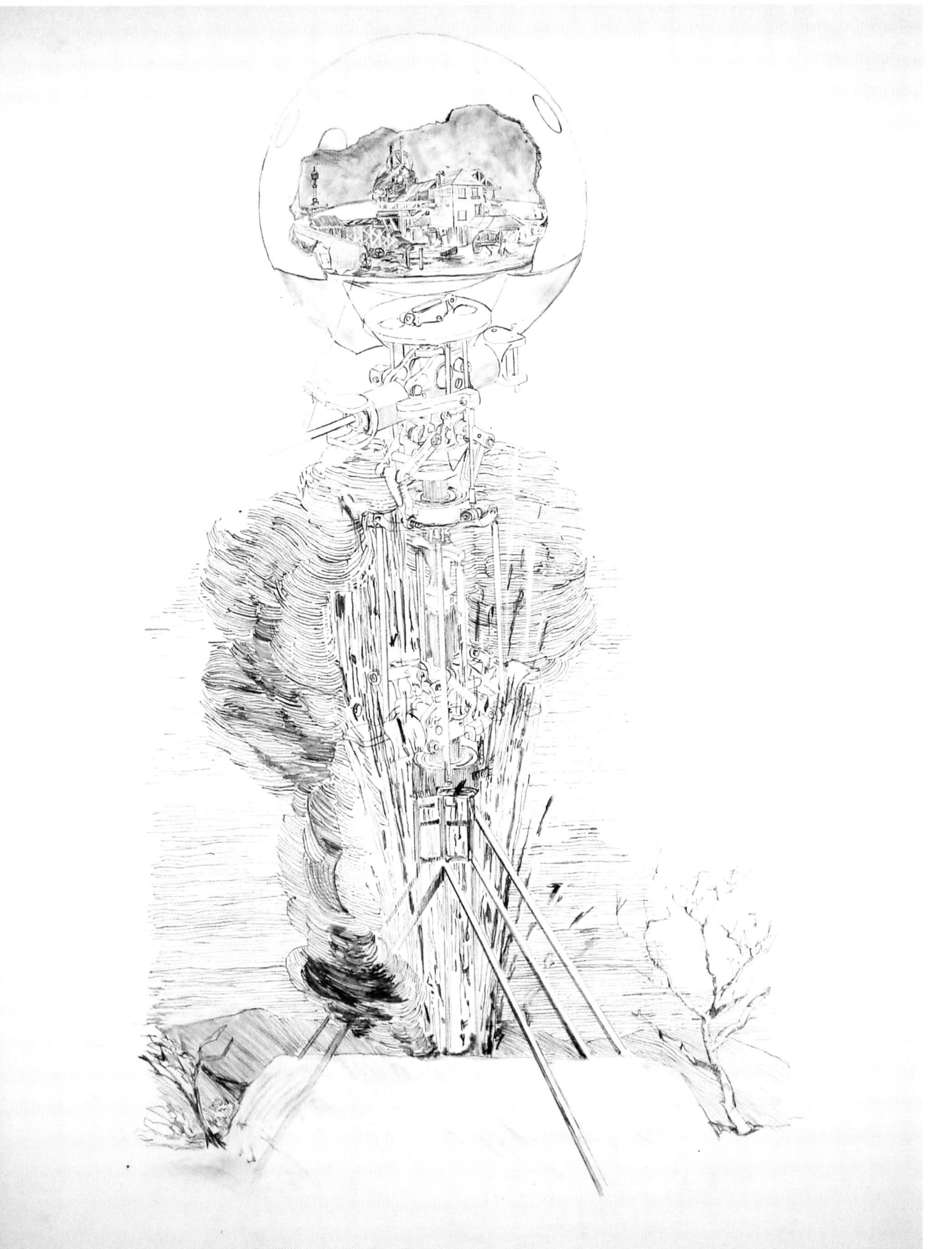

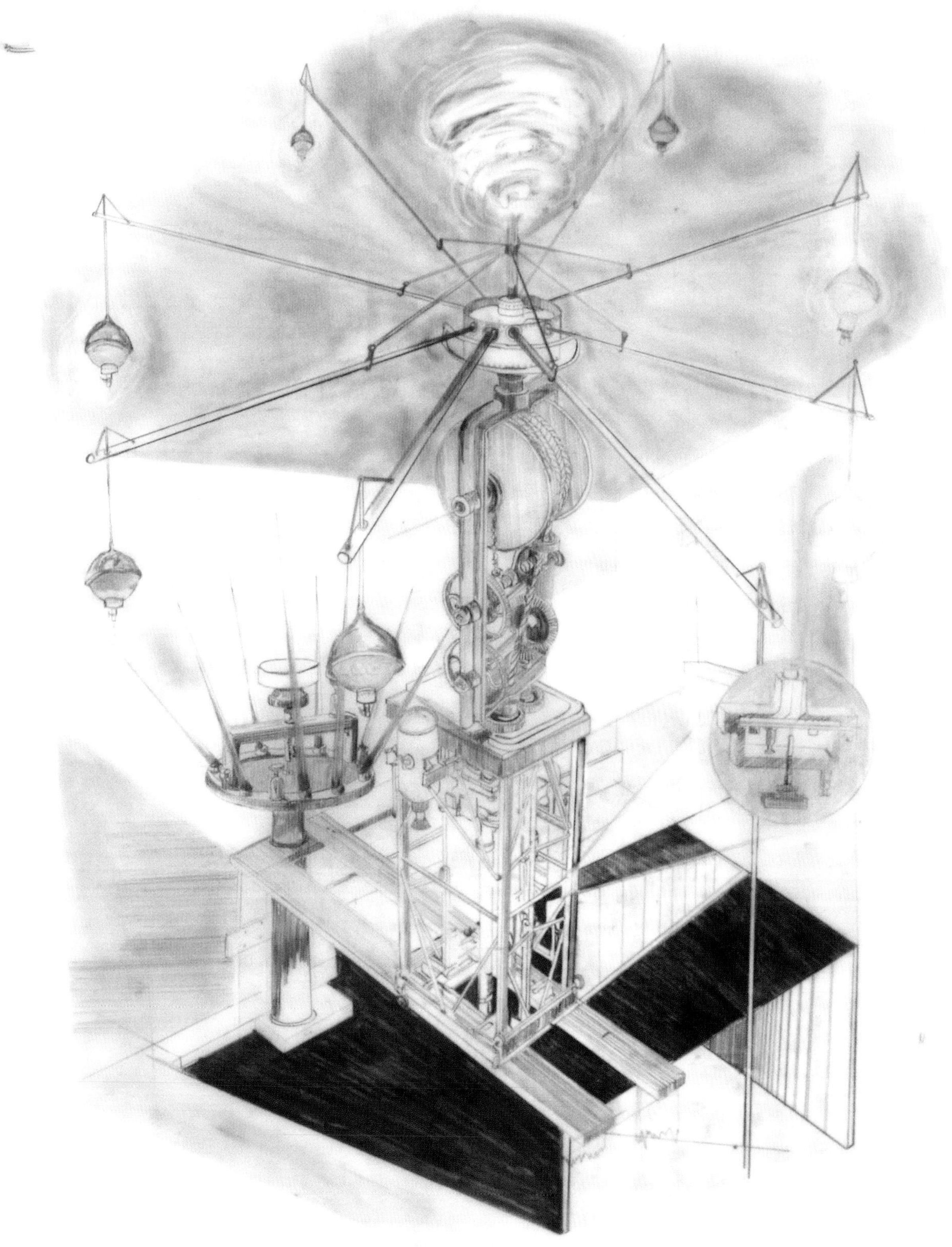

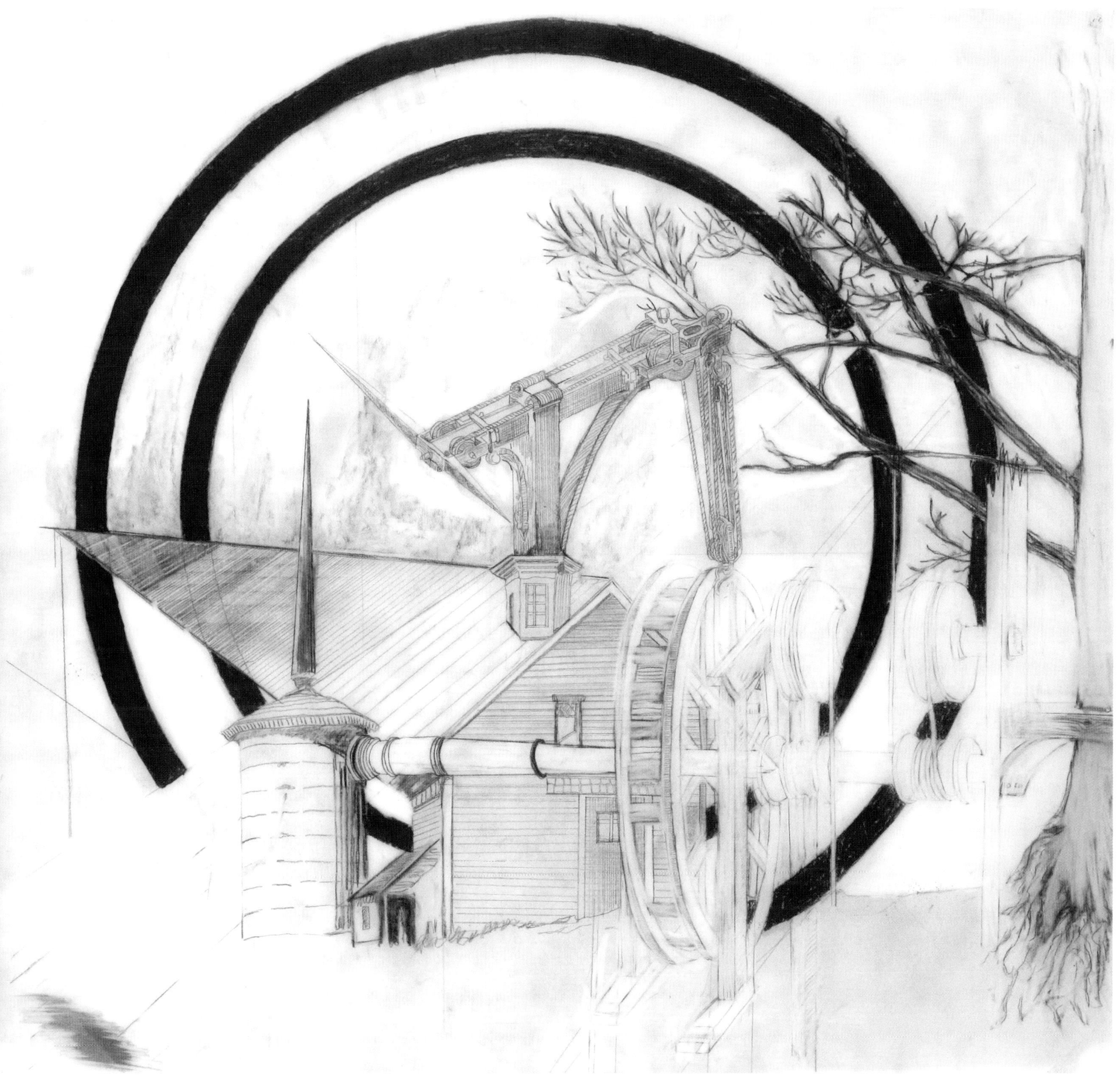

Crush Collision

Tamatha Sopinski Perlman

On September 15, 1896, a reported 30,000 spectators gathered in a short-lived town just north of Waco called Crush, Texas, to witness a staged public-relations spectacle. The brainchild of William George Crush, a passenger agent for the Missouri, Kansas and Texas Railway (the Katy), this fund-raiser promised ticket-holders a head-on collision of two 32-ton unmanned locomotives, each pulling seven boxcars. People from Texas and surrounding states had spent two dollars apiece on the round-trip ticket to Crush to observe the drama.

Spectators spent the festive day eating, playing games, and enjoying traveling medicine shows, as they eagerly awaited the main attraction. At 5 p.m., the freshly painted engines gently touched noses at the center of a four-mile-long track. Then, slowly, they backed up to their starting points, one to the north, the other to the south. At ten minutes after five, William Crush appeared on the tracks astride a white horse. He threw down his hat. The trains, whistles wailing, careered toward each other, reaching a combined speed of 120 miles per hour. The crowd cheered wildly when the engines crashed in a thunderous climax before settling in a silent heap.

Suddenly, both engines' boilers exploded simultaneously. Chunks of metal, large and small, flew through the air, killing and injuring some of the spectators. Regardless, the Crush Collision was deemed a financial and public-relations success. By day's end, the rubble had been cleared, spectators had returned home, and Crush, Texas, was no longer a town.

Ragtime music composer Scott Joplin was among the spectators that day. Inspired, the twenty-eight-year-old composed *The Great Crush Collision March*, commemorating the event.

Like William Crush, the man behind that memorable collision of 1896, Minnesota artist Chris Larson has been staging his own collisions. His crashes, expressed in art installations, are collisions between cultures, beliefs, religions, and the art of people from disparate worlds. With the unassuming demeanor of a well-seasoned storyteller, Larson creates films and large-scale sculptures that deliver tales in a rich, iconographic language he has developed during the past fifteen years.

Larson's film *Crush Collision* (2006) begins with a man in worn work clothes coming out of a floating house (ills. pp. 84–85). He steps into a boat and rows off into the night. We hear the music of local percussionist Michael Bland (formerly with Prince and The New Power Generation and Soul Asylum), establishing a mood. The man, played by Grant Hart (formerly of the bands Hüsker Dü and Nova Mob), and a woman, played by performance artist Britta Hallin, begin to operate an elaborate machine that creates an endless circle of clay. Working on two levels, the actors are a study in contrasts. Hart's dark hair and world-weary appearance complement Hallin's angelic face and white dress. She passes lumps of clay to Hart, who feeds them into the machine to be repeatedly beaten and smoothed.

As Hart works, a reverie transports him to another life lived in that house—that of a family, portrayed by the Knight Family, a Minneapolis gospel quartet, who are gathered around a supper table saying grace. As the family sings, Hart finds himself on the house's upper level playing a silver piano, not by striking its keys, but by rhythmically rocking it back and forth.

Hart and the Knights represent stories from different times running parallel in the same location. The film is Larson's fourth with producer Jason Spafford and sound designer Alex Oana. It's a meditative study of dark and light, of the physical and spiritual.

The actual two-story house that served as the film's set spent the winter frozen in a northern Wisconsin lake and was installed in the gallery of the Minneapolis Institute of Arts as part of Larson's exhibition there in 2006 (ills. pp. 80–83). Weathered and worn, it stood as a testament to the events that occurred within its walls. As such, it blurred the lines between fiction and reality.

The sculptures in the exhibition's adjoining gallery were constructed destruction. Filling most of the space was a house, while along the back wall sat a piano. Larson built the house on its side and painted it flat black as if charred by fire or weathered with age. The staged scene contrasted with the natural decay of the house from the film. This one is a prop, telling a story of its ruin rather than of the life it once held. Suspended in time, it tells a story—past or future—of destruction and decay.

The pianos (in the film and in the installation) play a role in this ambiguous place and time. The keys on the pianos are painted together, the wires and hammers removed, rockers are attached to the bottom. The instruments are common enough, but their repurposing takes away the comfort of their ordinariness. This constant displacement leads to disorientation, to a realm where the familiar is also unfamiliar.

Larson creates the essence of a time and place not just visually but with an assault on the senses: the earthy smell of wood; the sharp, sometimes dangerous-looking parts of the machines; the soundtracks. His scenarios resonate because they are steeped in history.

Larson grew up in Lake Elmo, Minnesota, and he remembers finding old farm implements in a barn. "I love finding old things and wondering what happened there," he said. "I love concocting things in my head."

Larson began building machines in 1991 when he was a graduate student at Yale University. While researching the town where his work was on display, he discovered that Norfolk, Connecticut, was once a booming mill town. Intrigued, Larson built a large mill of rough wood and labeled its pieces as if assembled from a kit. He studied books on old German farm tools, specifically seeking those written in German (a language he couldn't read), thereby preserving each tool's mystery. Taking away the original function of the object, in essence, creates a new object—an object that, in Surrealist fashion, requires an alternate perspective when one looks for its new function. This function is often felt on an instinctual level rather than a rational one. The object's new potential plays an elemental role in Larson's interests as an artist.

Larson's curiosity about this potential brought him to filmmaking. He wanted to film his moving sculptures—elaborate constructs of wood requiring their operators to use arms, legs, heads, and even mouths to set them in motion. However, while every movement is carefully recorded, these films are not necessarily about the machines. They are, Larson said, "vehicles to talk about the dualities of life."

Larson's vehicles are loaded with metaphor, but the artist prefers to refrain from scripted messages. He lets the images develop naturally. "I don't like to connect the dots," Larson said. "I like to put the dots out there." This approach enables his work to be lyrical and poetic. For *Crush Collision*, he said, "I knew I wanted a spinning piano to come down around Grant Hart."

The piano would deliver Hart to the Knight family, who agreed to re-enact the scene from the cover of Mahalia Jackson's 1950s gospel album, *Bless This House*. During a break in filming, Larson asked Alberta Knight to sing. Her version of "Old Ship of Zion" was so powerful that Larson recorded it for the film.

Most recently, Larson has been capturing the moment of impact in his rough-wood sculptures. A spaceship smashes into a barn in an untitled work of 2004. Ted Kaczynski's cabin explodes as the *General Lee* crashes through its roof in *Pause (The Dukes of Hazzard '69 Charger and Ted Kaczynski's Montana Refuge)*, of 2004. The stories these works tell are filled with larger-than-life heroes and antiheroes of American culture.

Explosive scenes become metaphors for the duality of human nature. Everything is "… a collision of good and evil, sin and redemption," Larson stated. "It's not a choice between these things. You have both." His works become thoughtful reflections as concepts and people collide in an ever-more-complicated world.

Larson tells strange and fantastic stories, like the folktales that influence him. His stories deal with the very different lives of contemporaneous people, their struggles, and the duality of human nature.

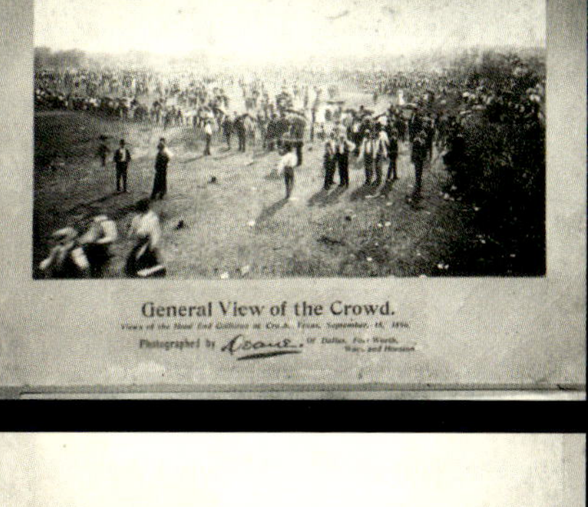

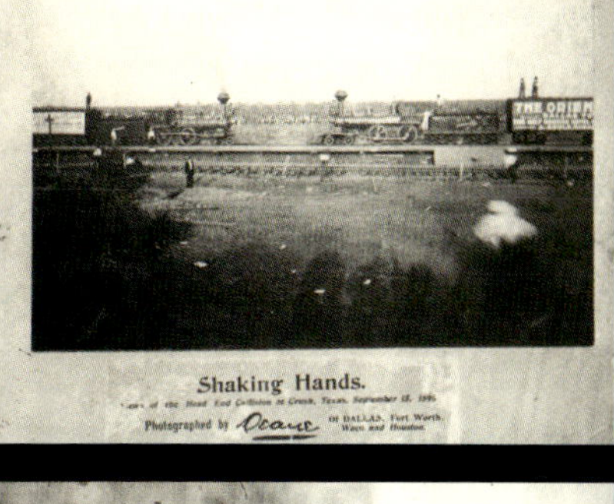

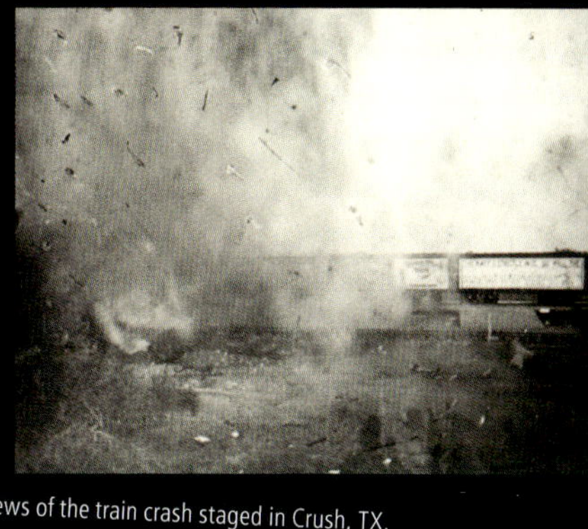

Views of the train crash staged in Crush, TX, September 15, 1896

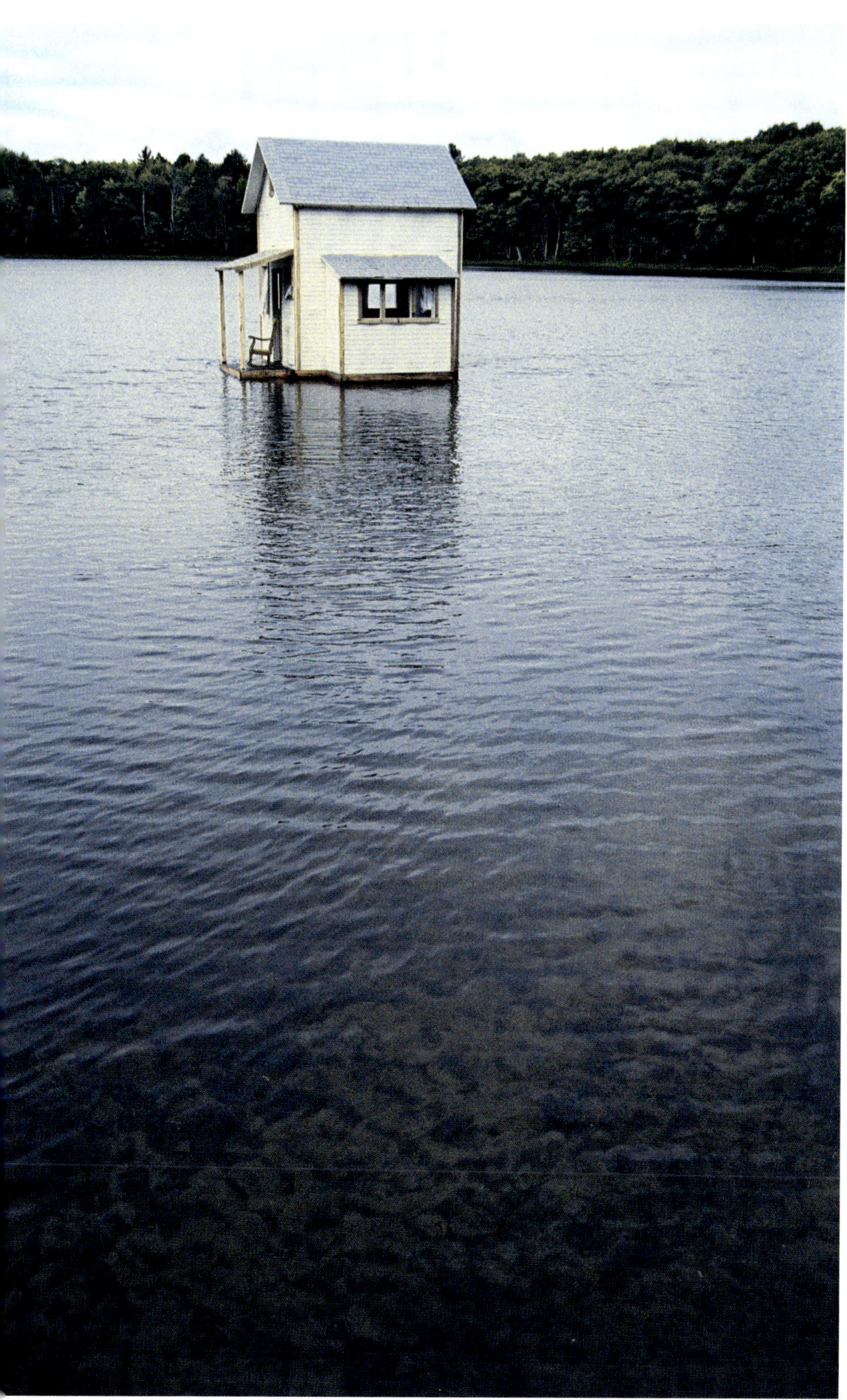

Crush Collision

2006 * C-print * 100 x 76 cm

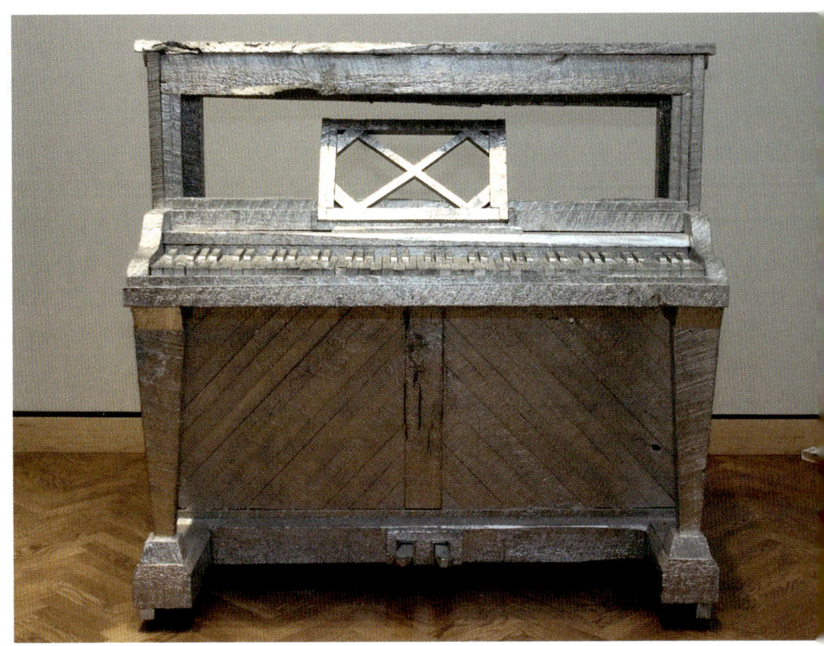

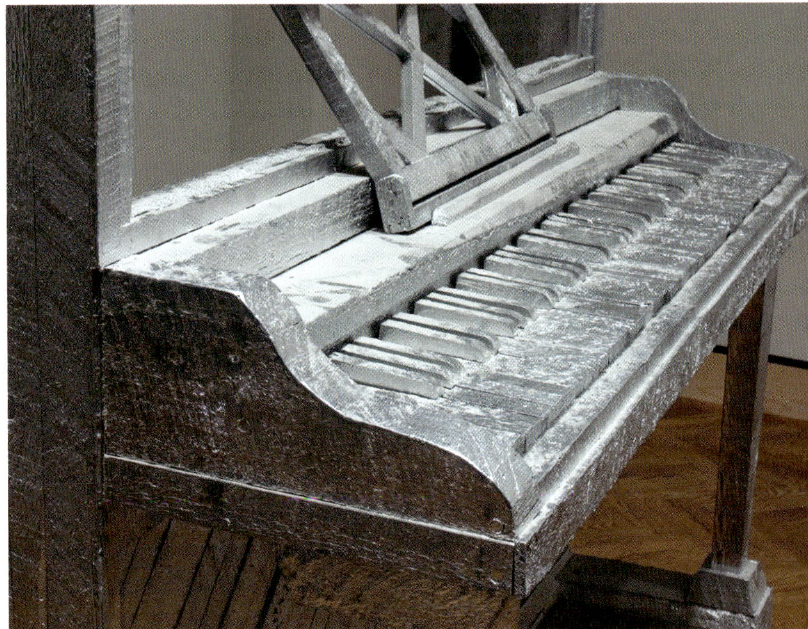

Crush Collision

2006 • Piano and house (set) • Installation views
Minneapolis Institute of Arts, Minneapolis, MN

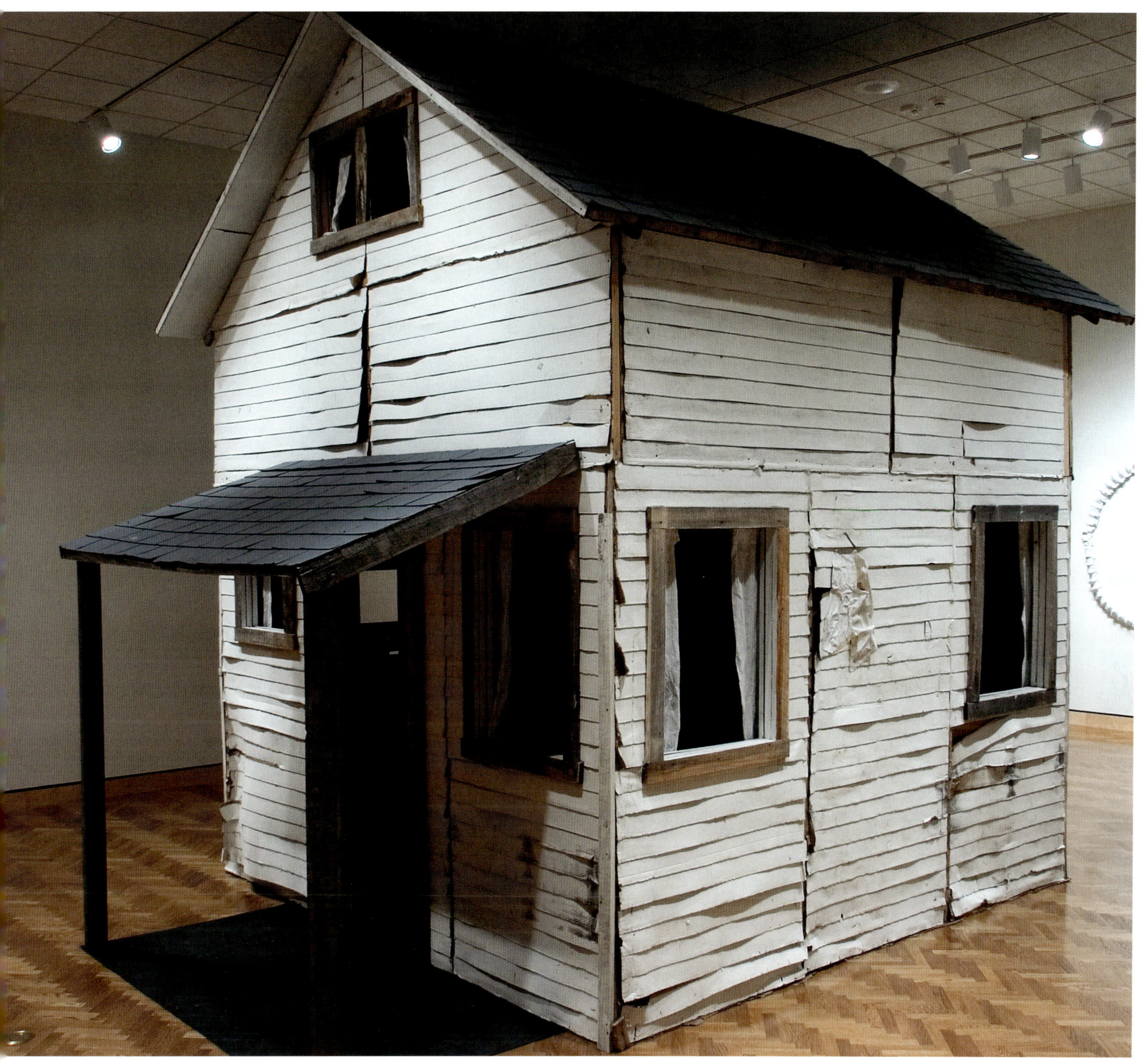

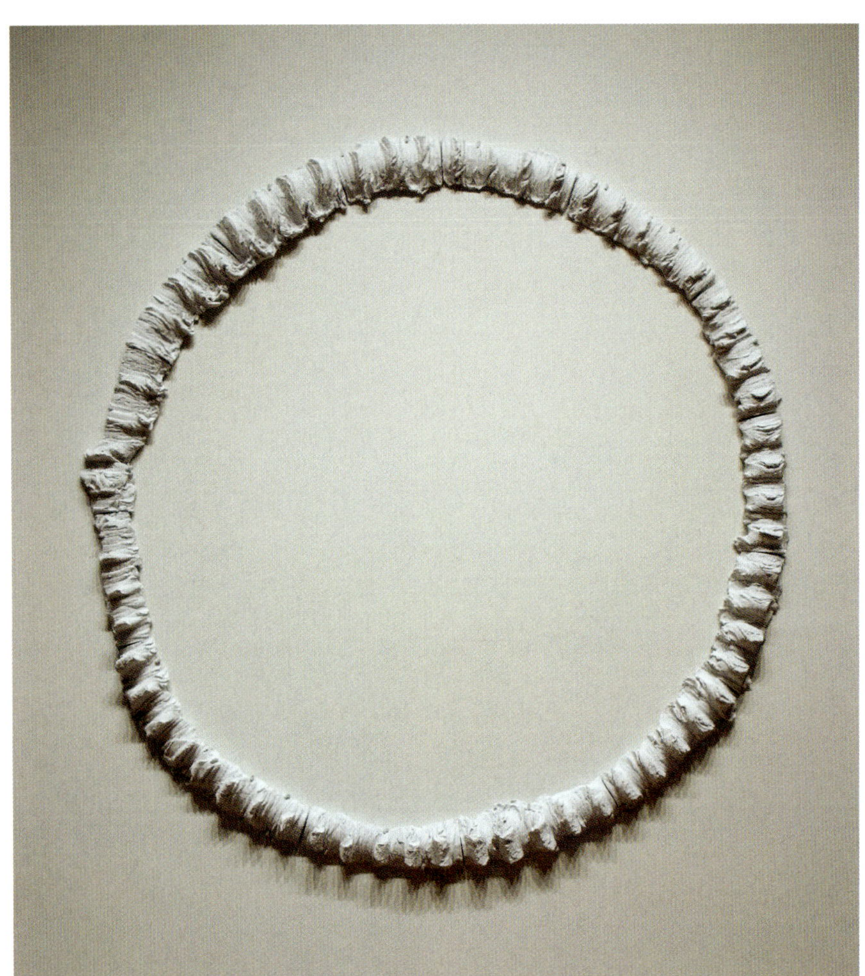

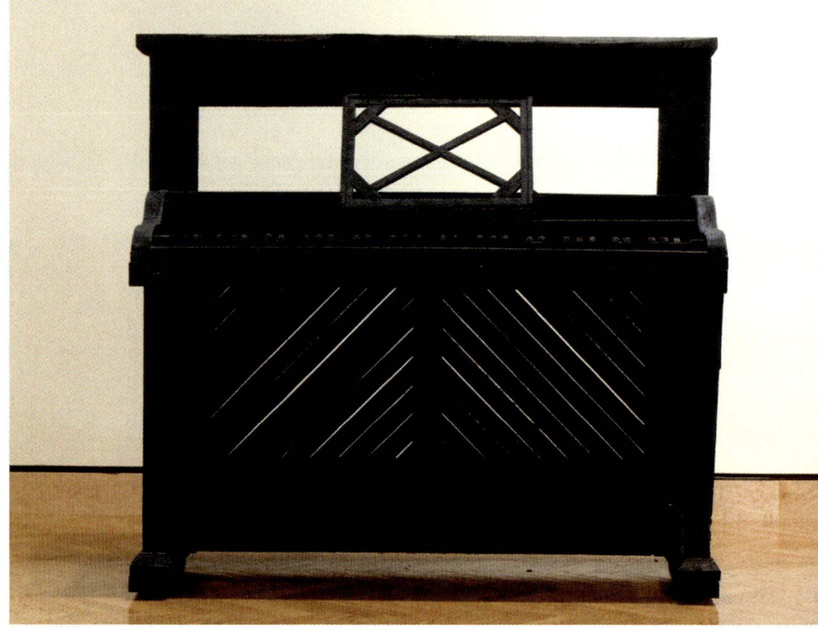

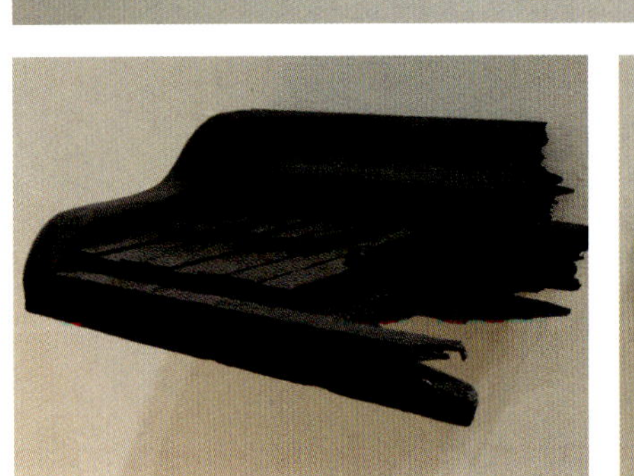

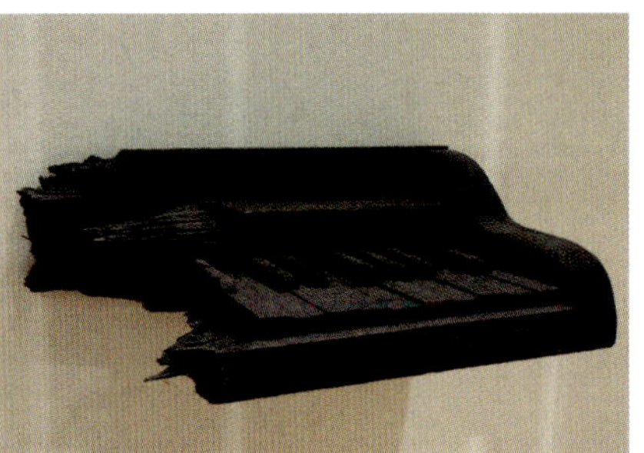

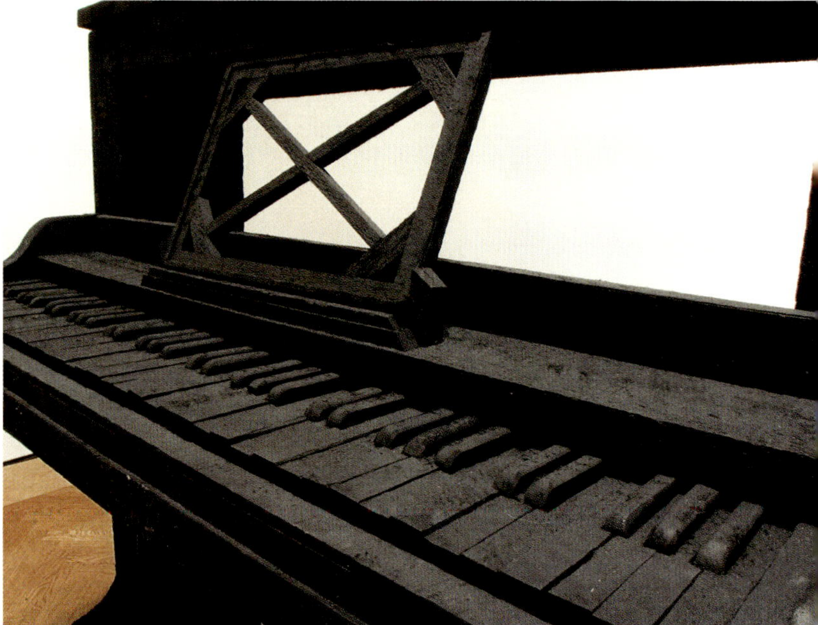

Crush Collision

2006 * Installation views
Minneapolis Institute of Arts, Minneapolis, MN

White ring * 2006 * Porcelain * 182 x 182 x 10 cm

Black Piano Keys * 2006 * Wood, black paint
Each 30 x 70 x 30 cm

Black Piano * 2006 * Wood, black paint
172 x 148 x 112 cm

Black House * 2006 * Wood, black paint
488 x 488 x 600 cm

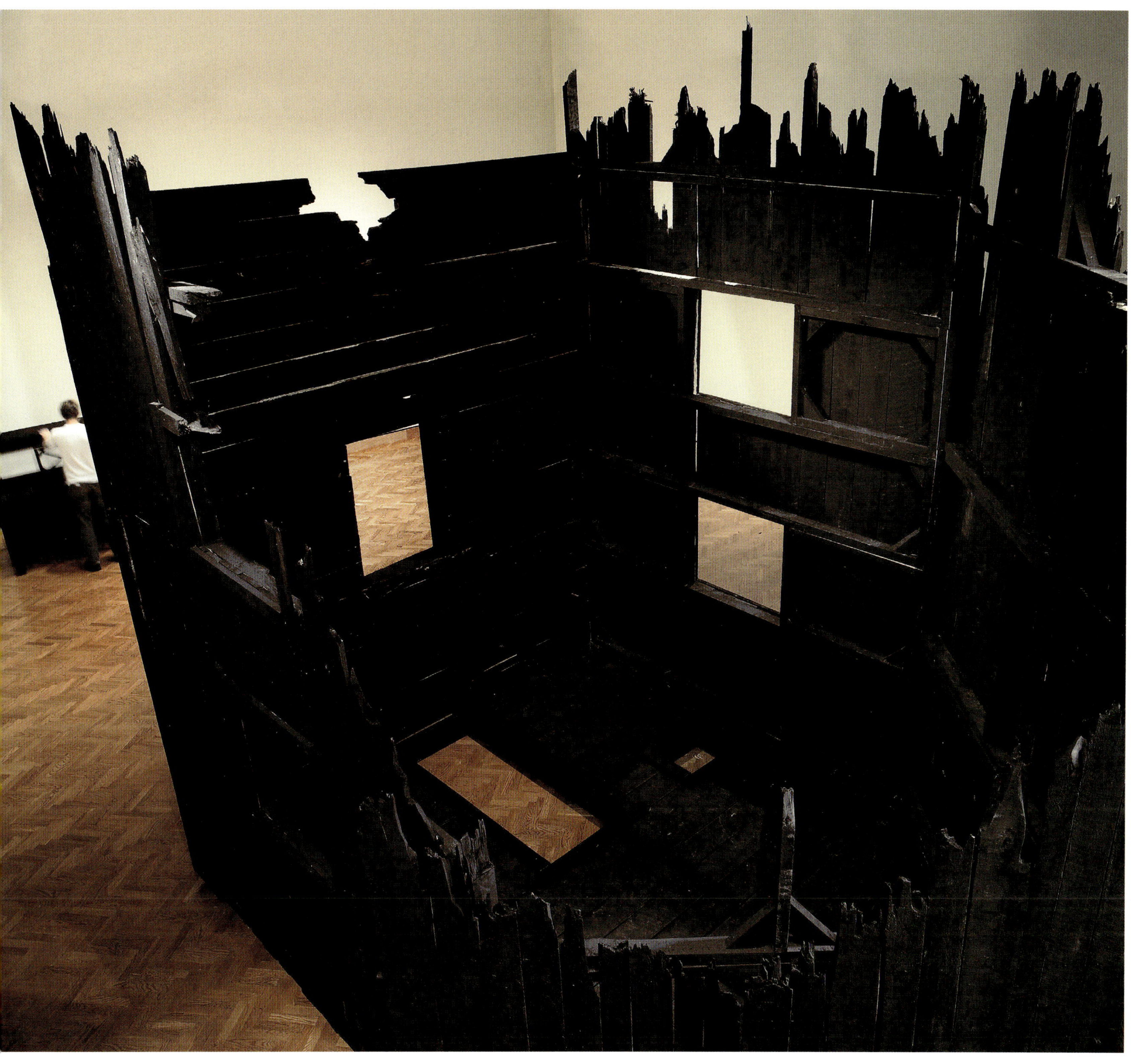

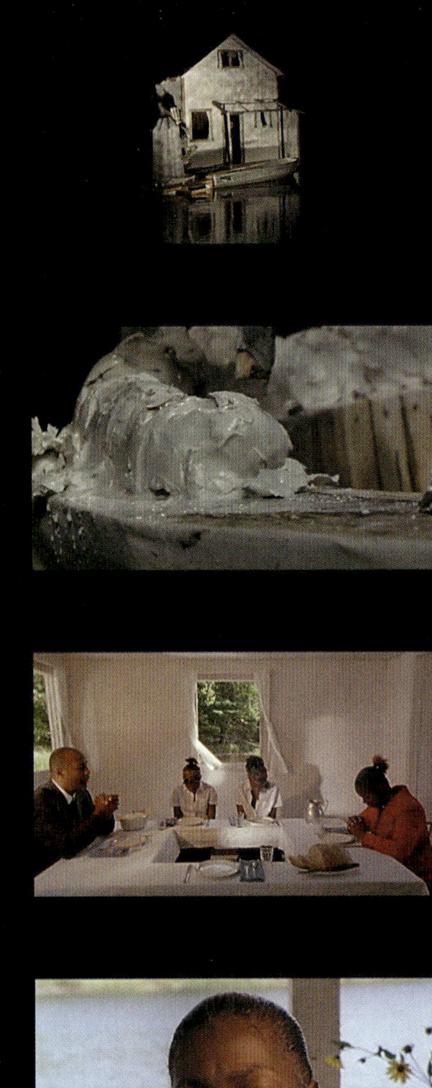
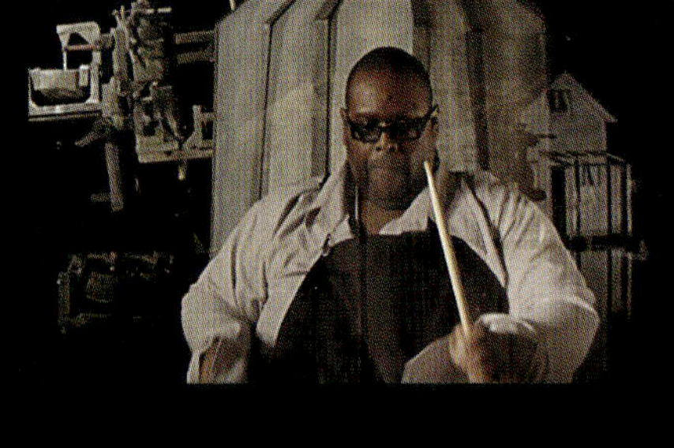
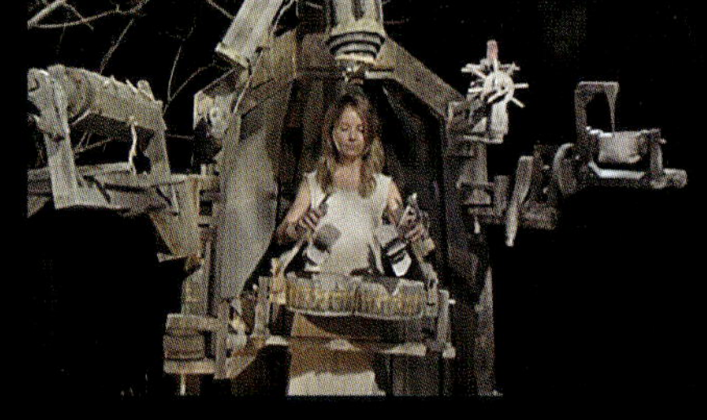
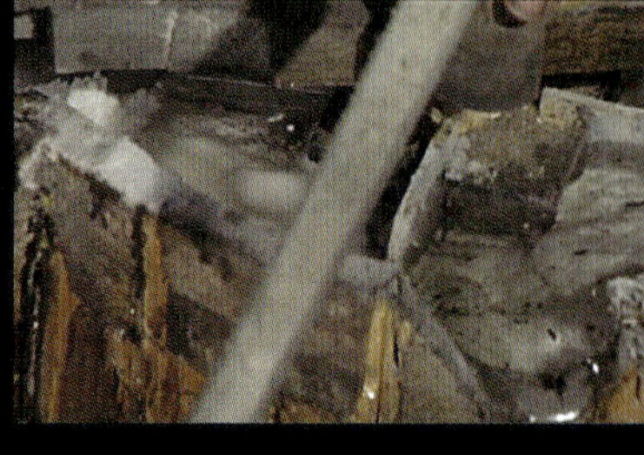
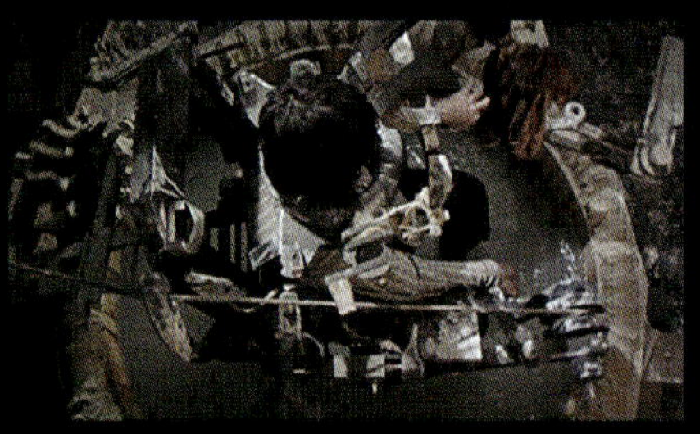
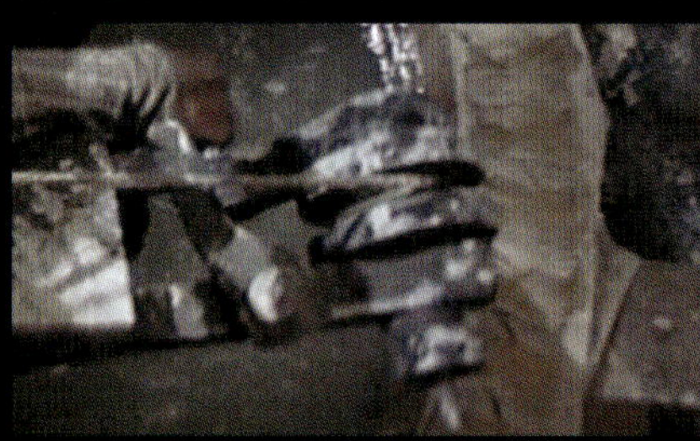
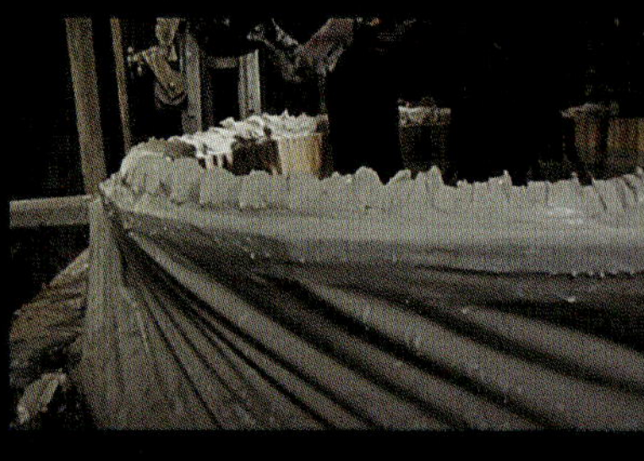
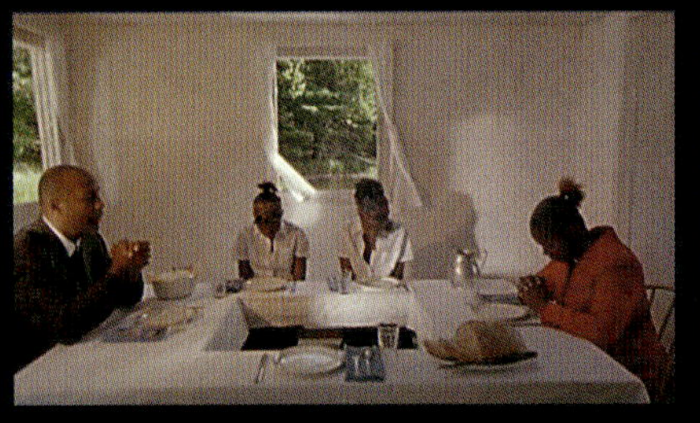
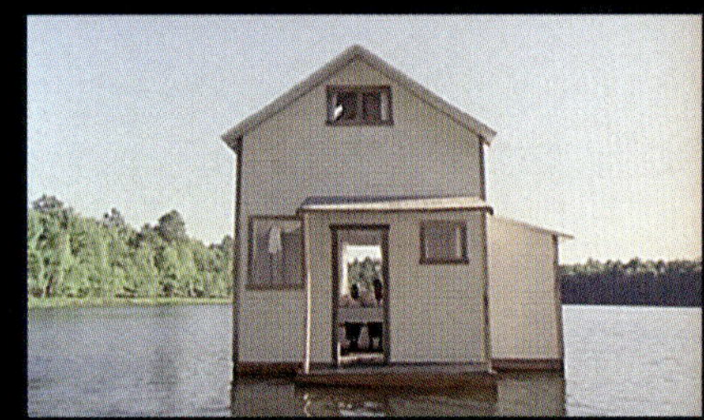
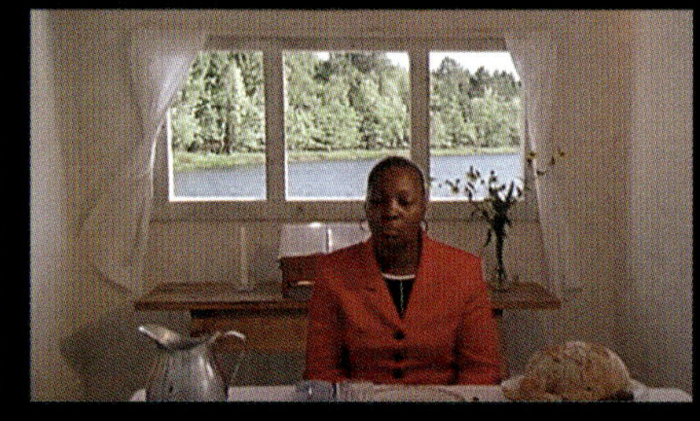
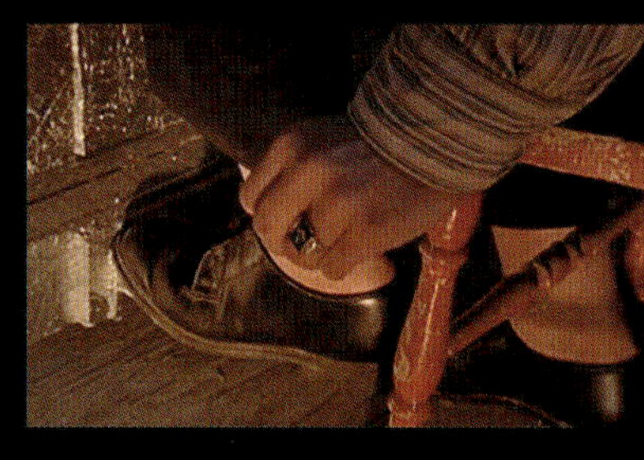
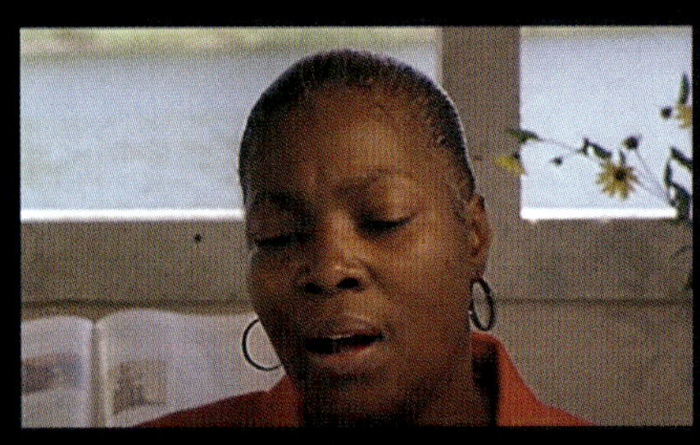
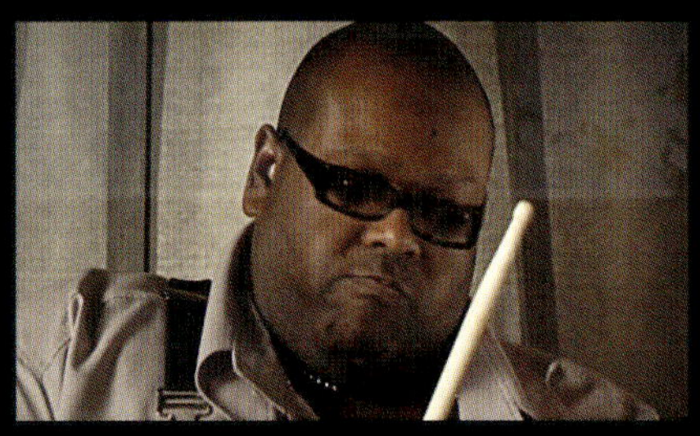
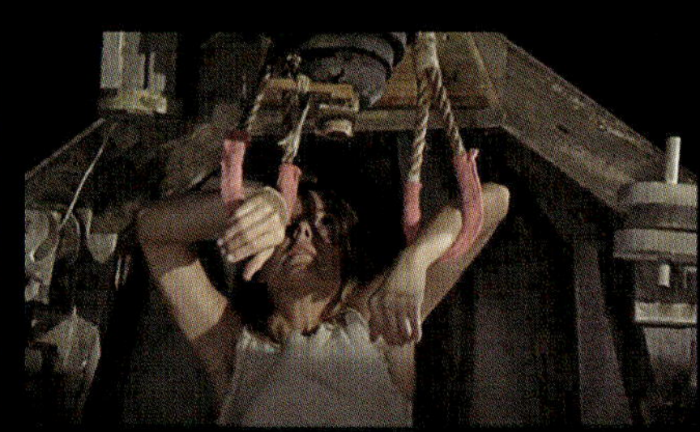
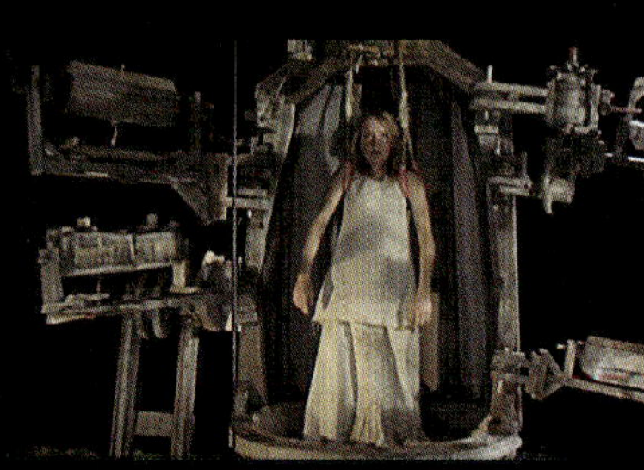
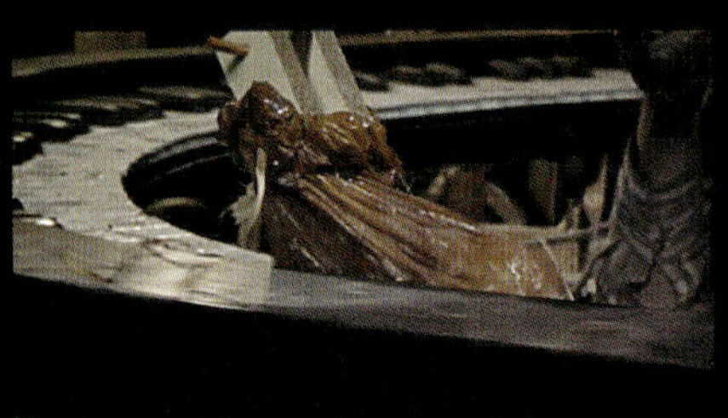
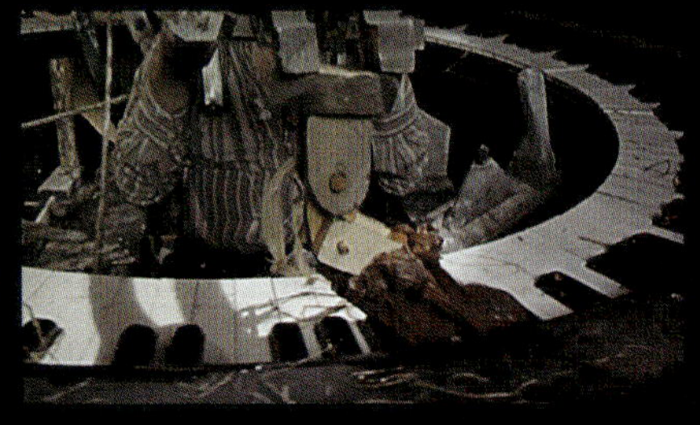

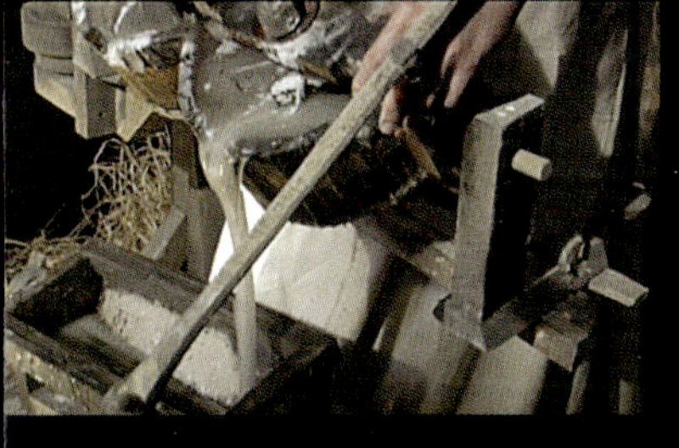
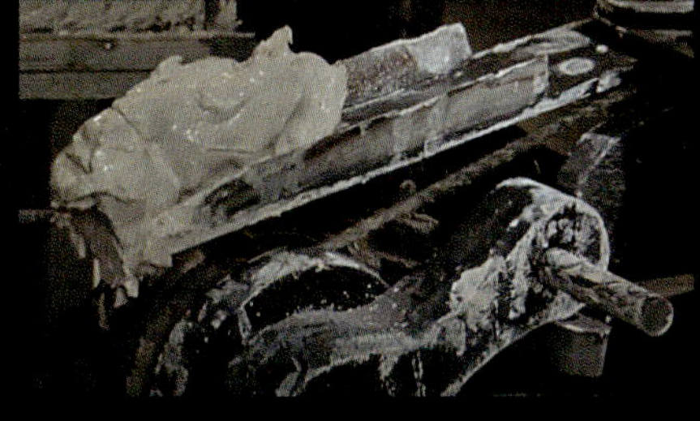
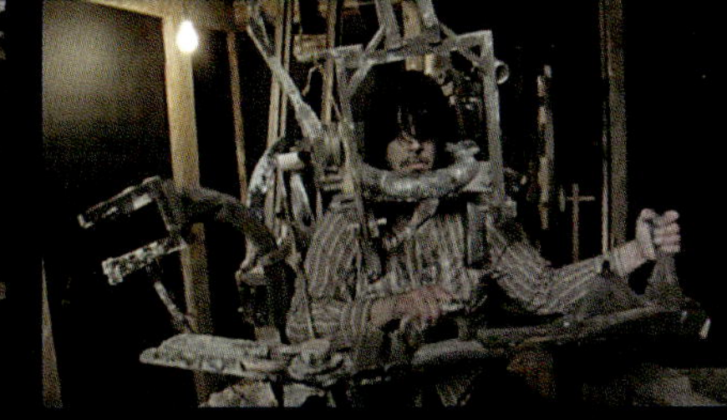
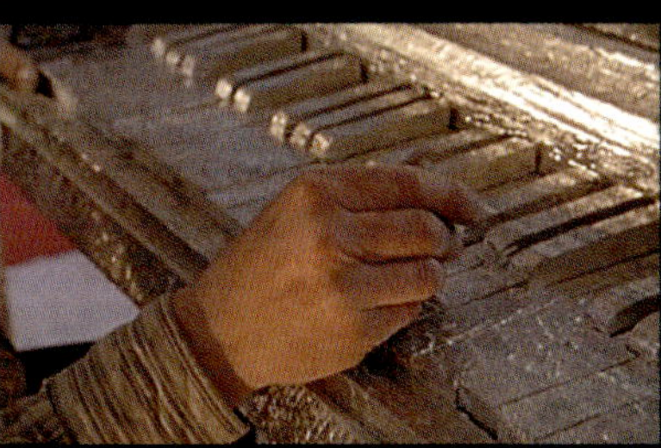
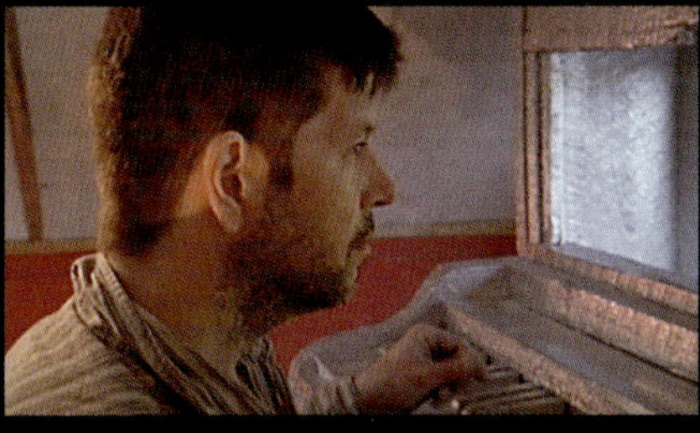
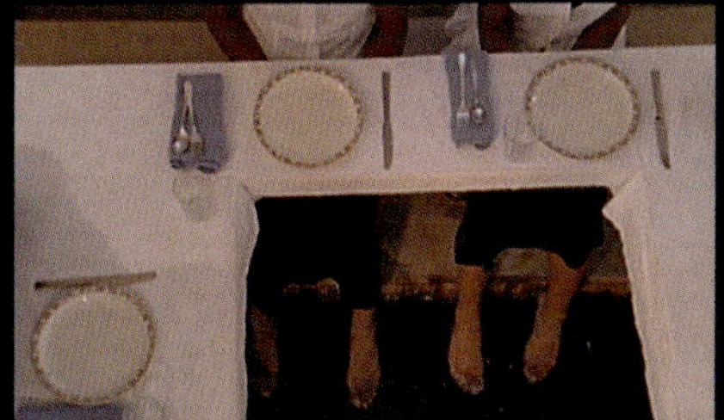
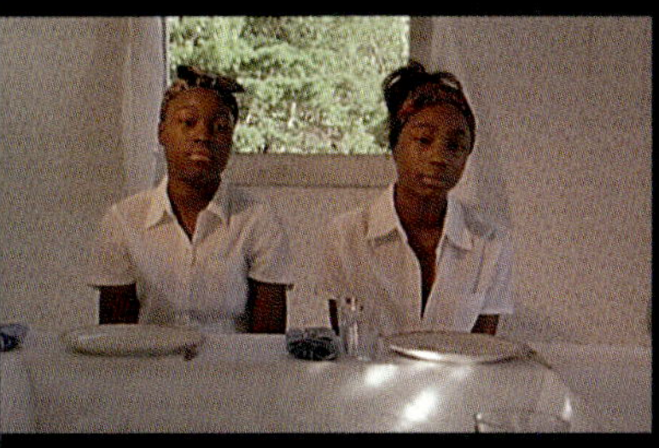
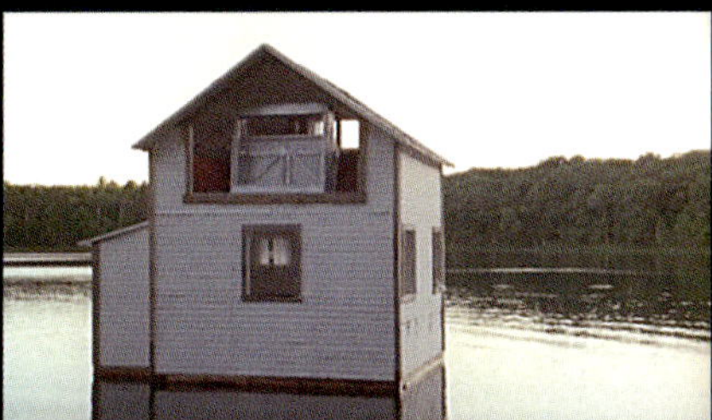
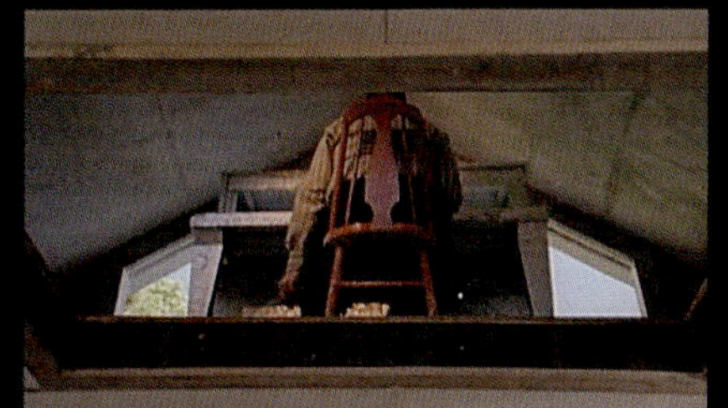
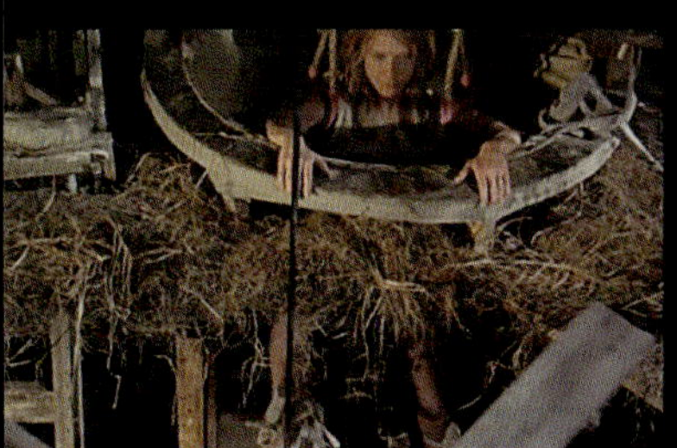
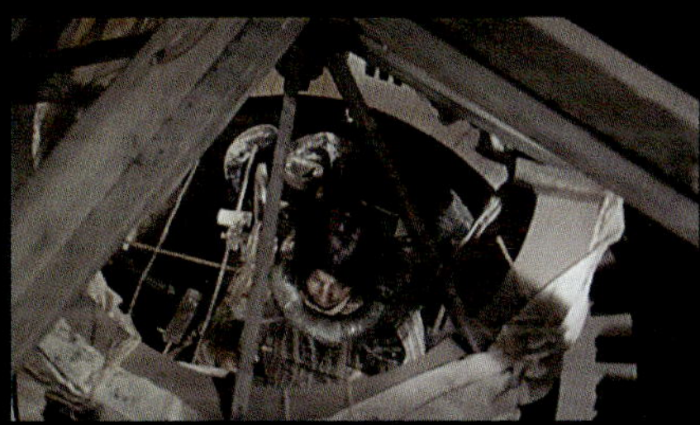
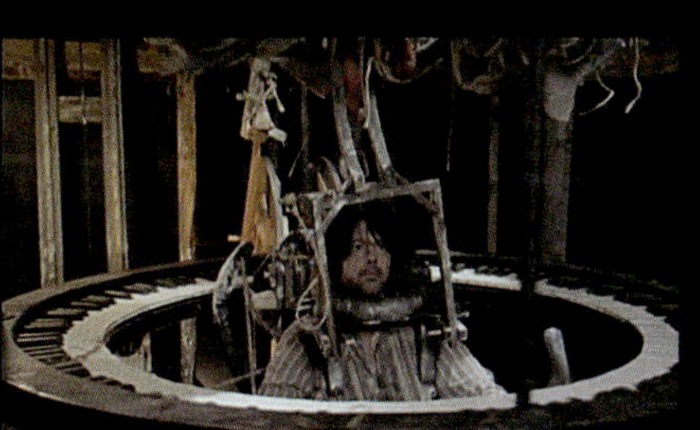

Crush Collison

2006 ⋆ Super 16 mm color film and HD video transferred to DVD ⋆ Running time: 12:10 min.
Video stills

Deep North

Pages 87–93
Deep North ⋆ 2008 ⋆ C-prints ⋆ Each 90 x 90 cm

Pages 94–95
Deep North ⋆ 2008 ⋆ HD video transferred to DVD
Running time: 5:59 min.
Photographs of set

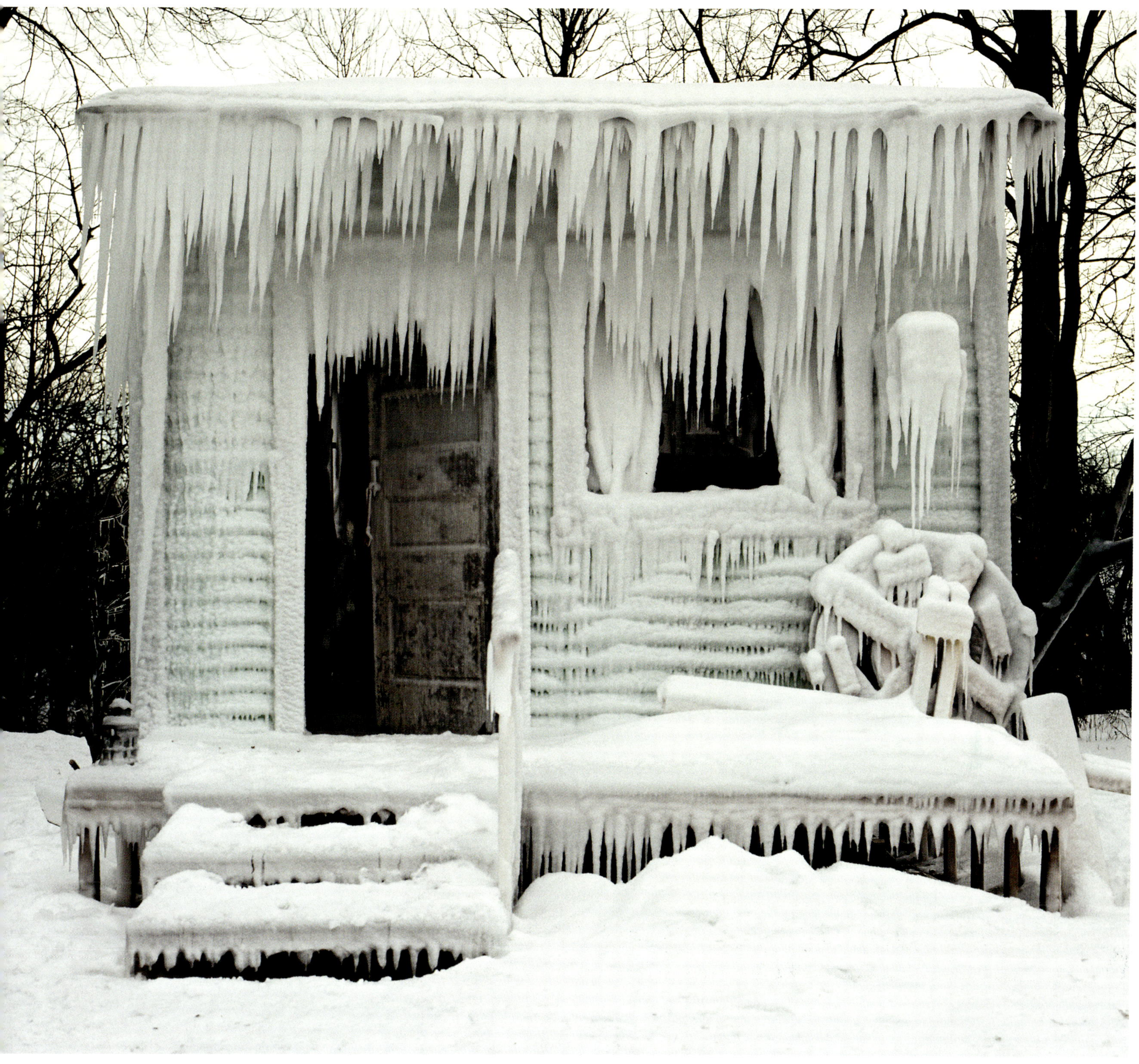

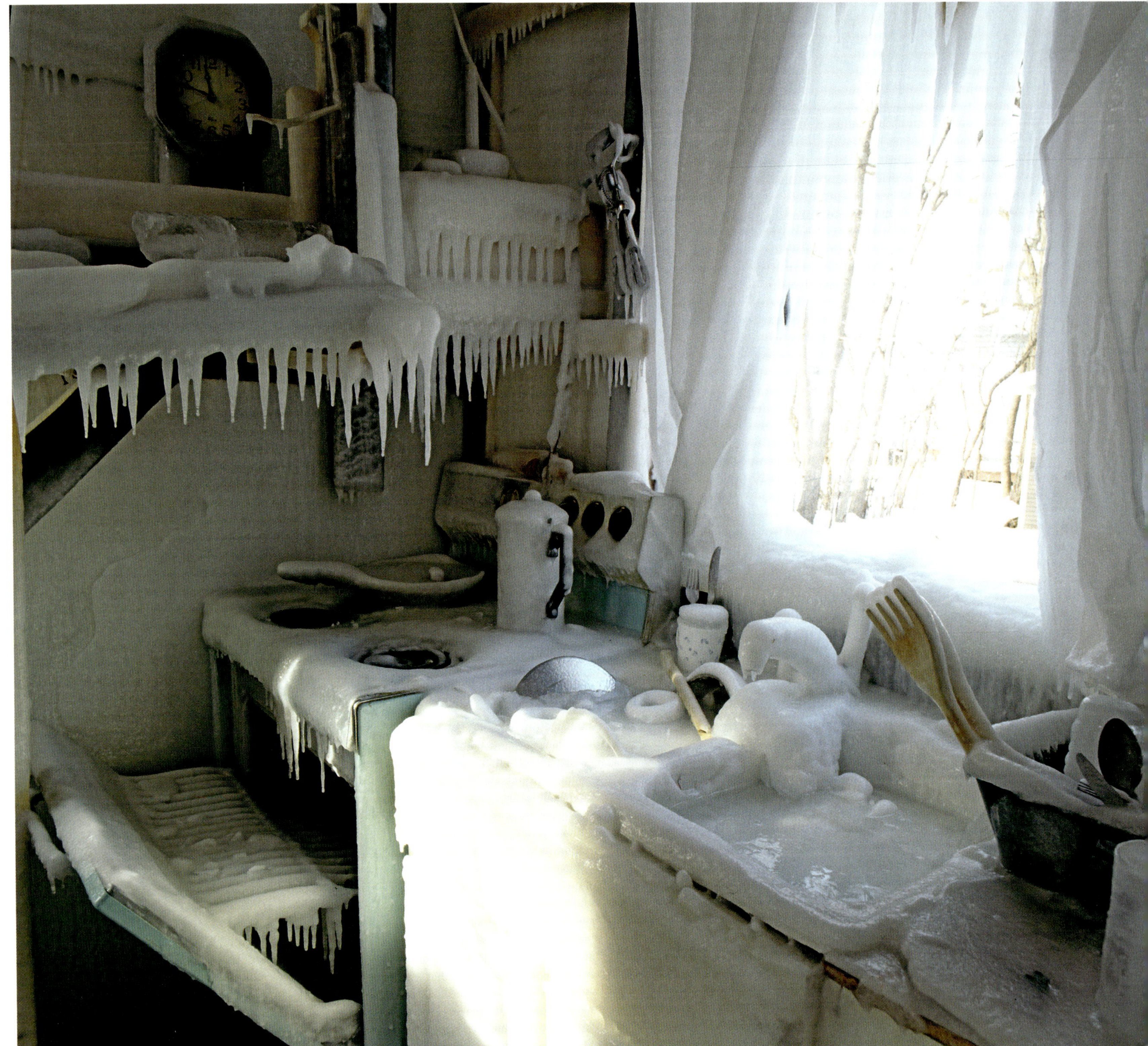

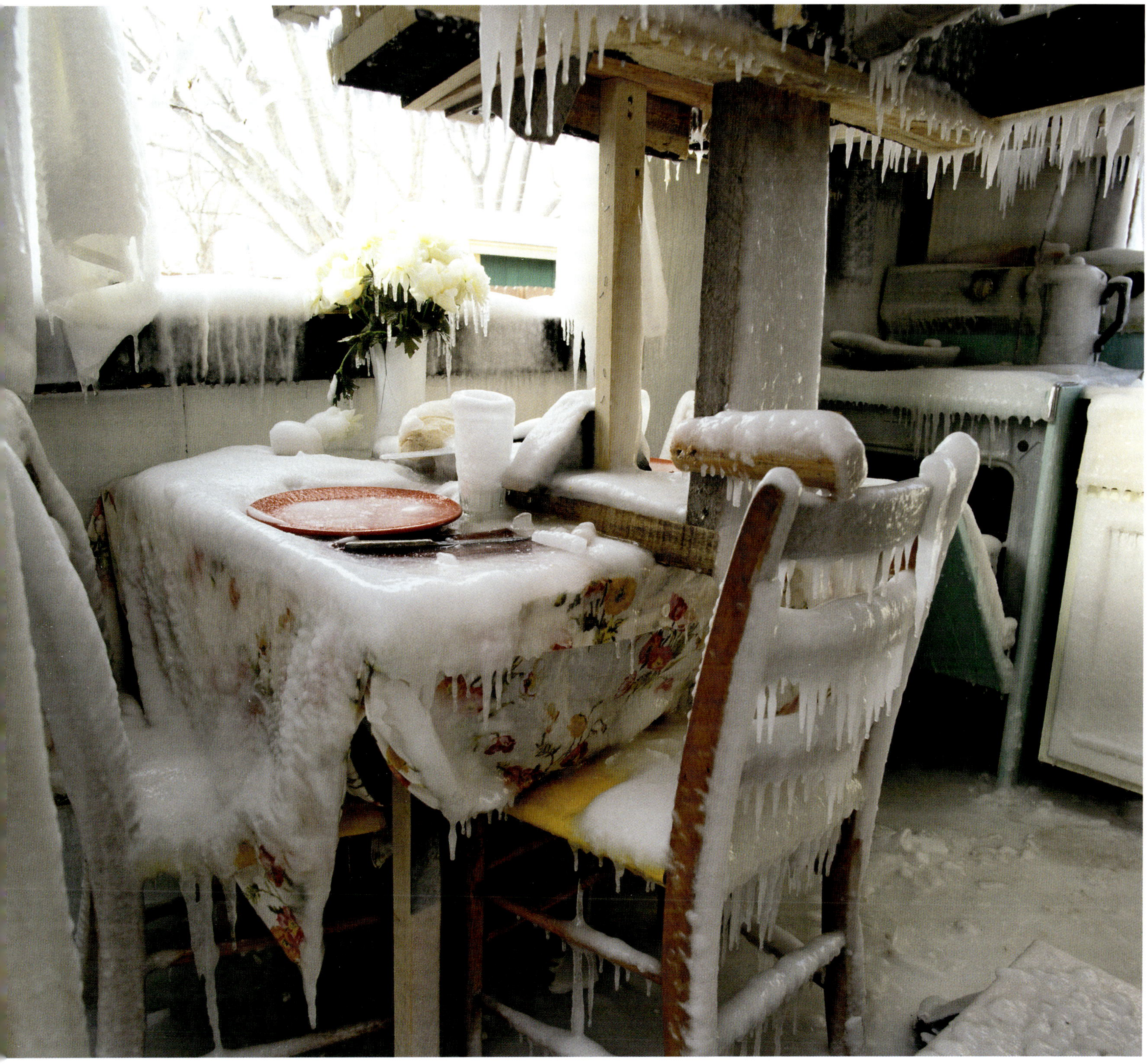

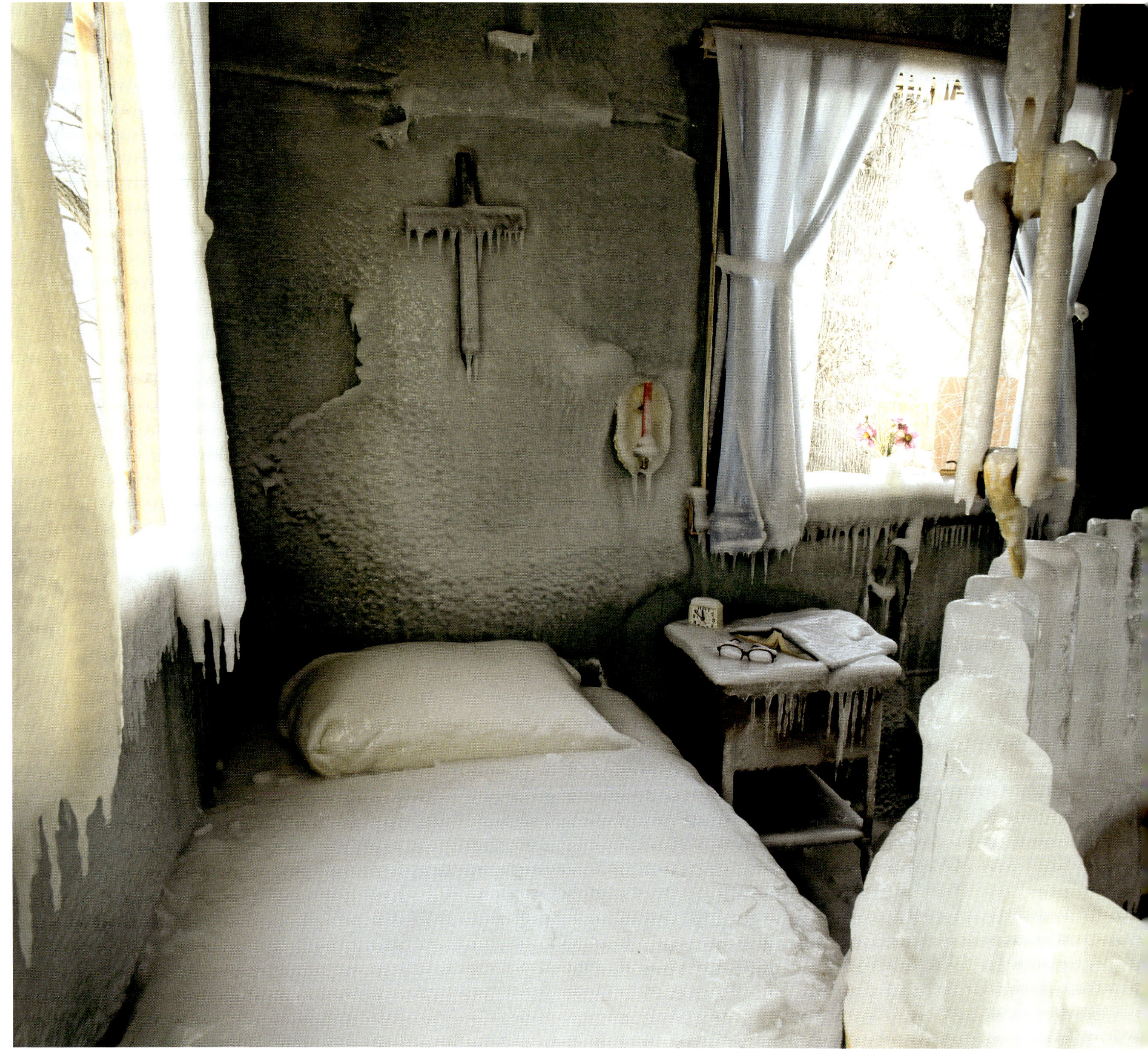

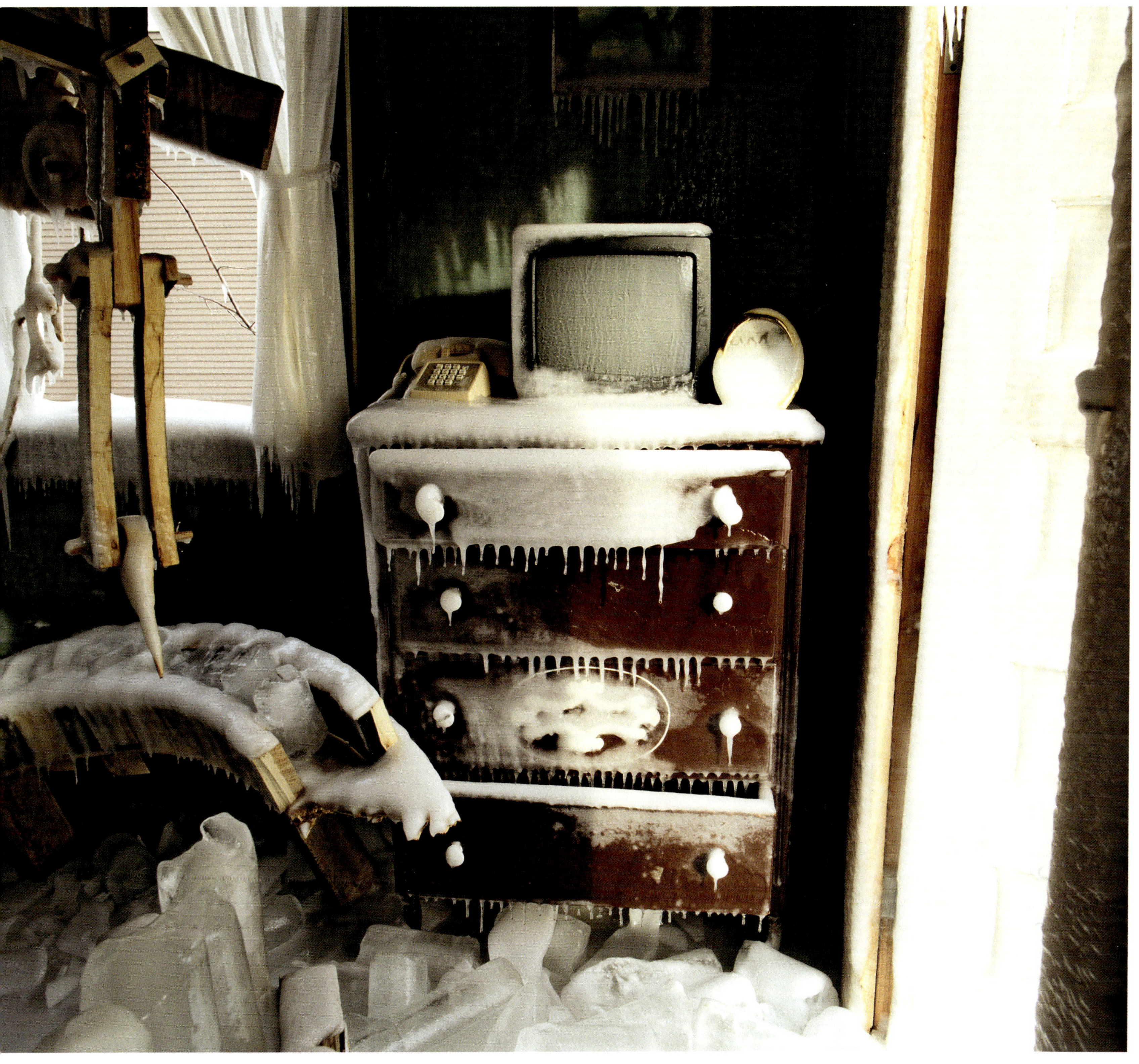

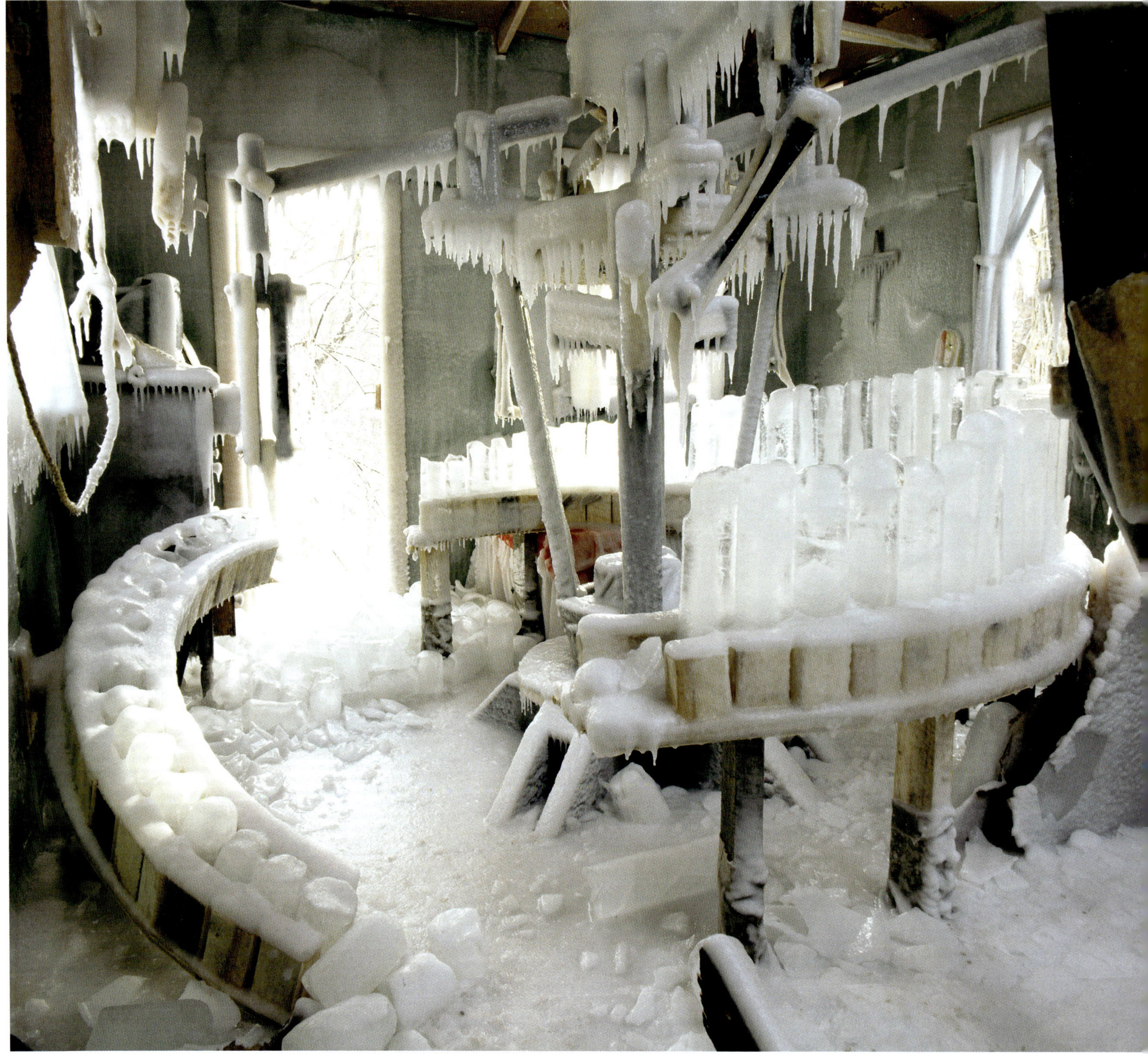

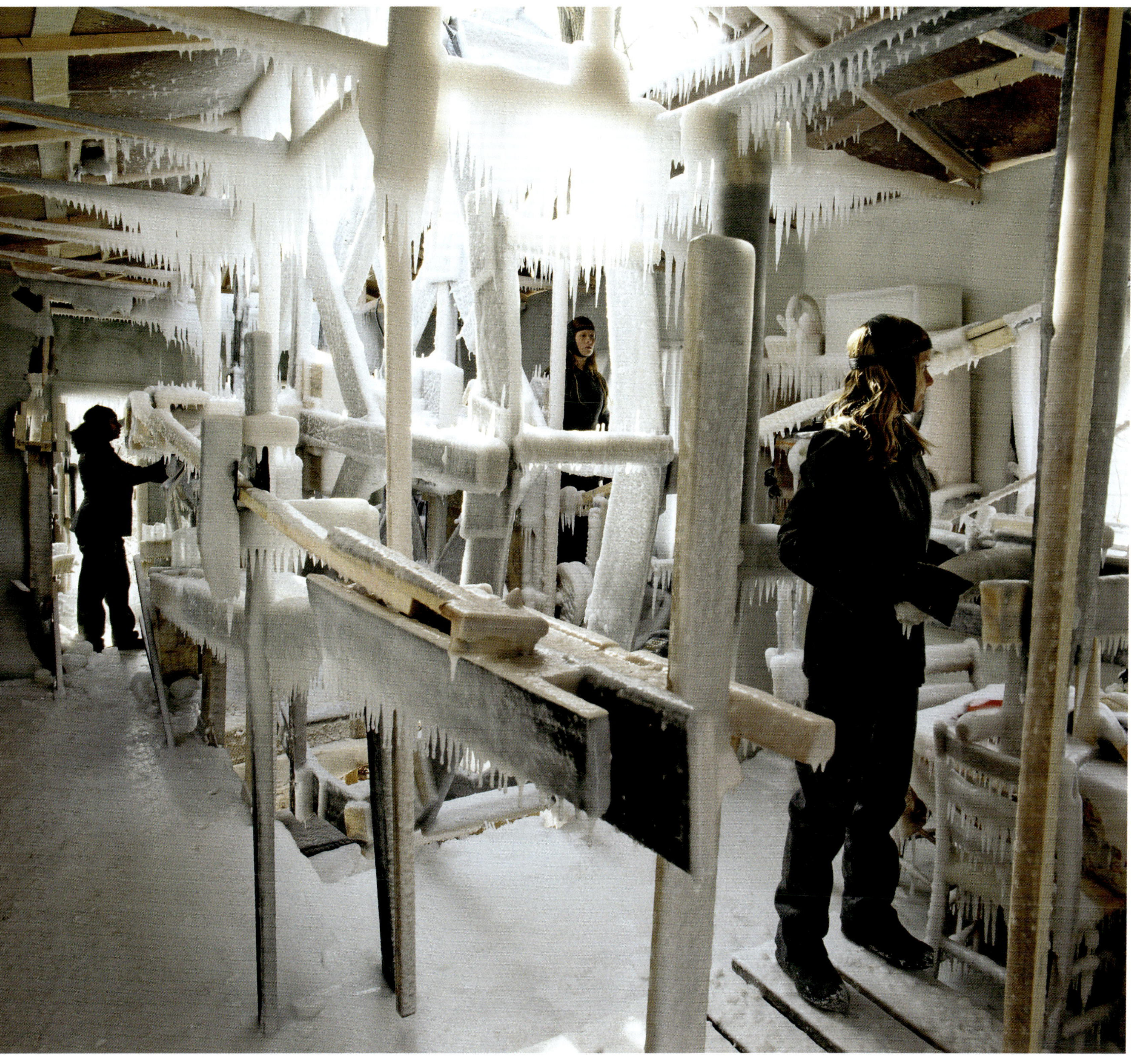

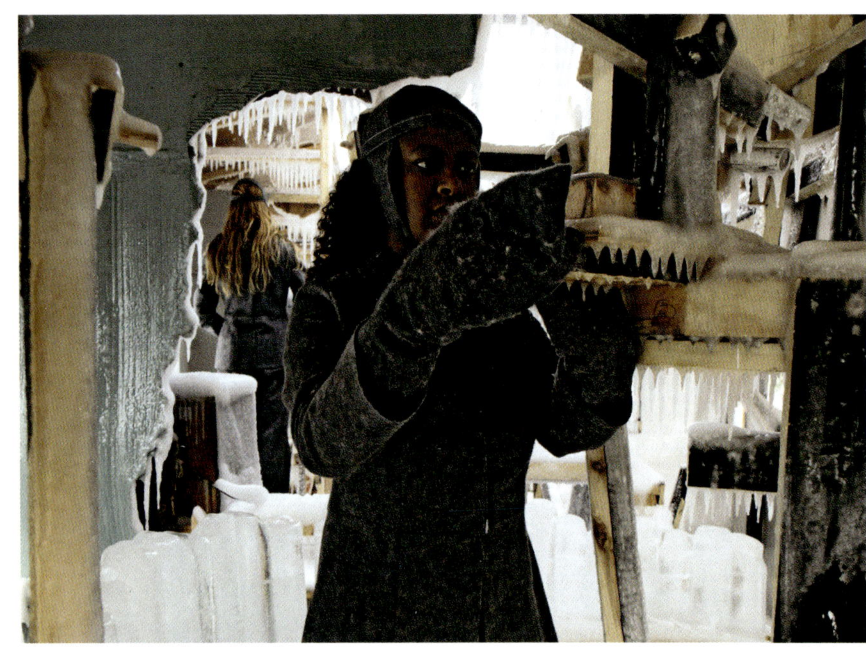
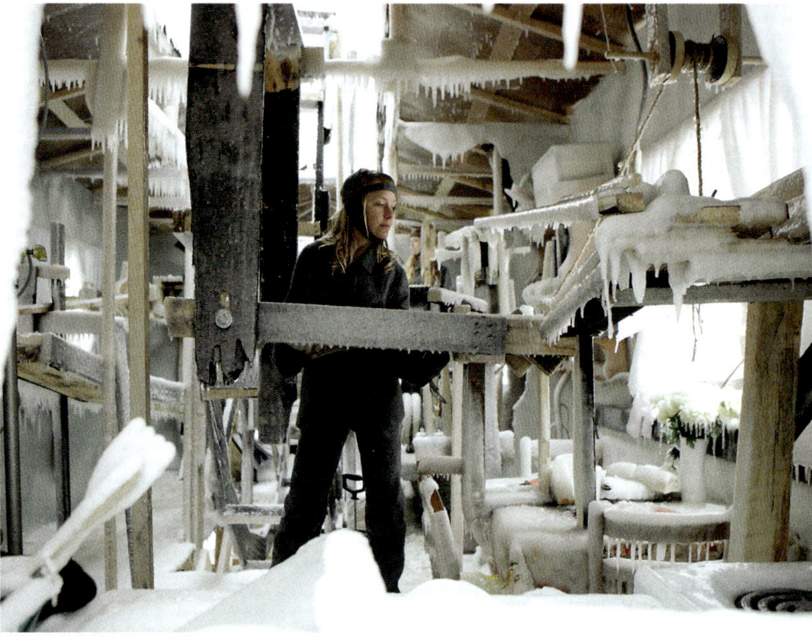
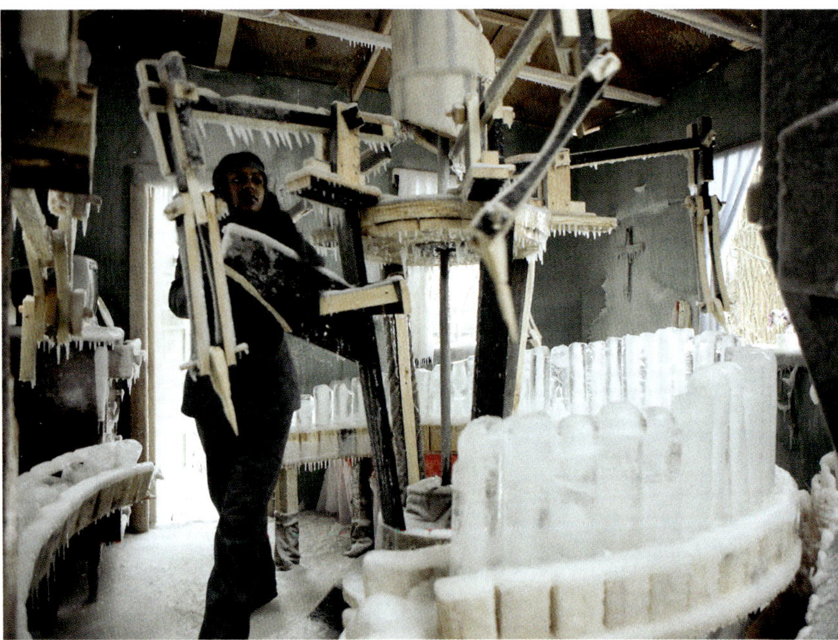
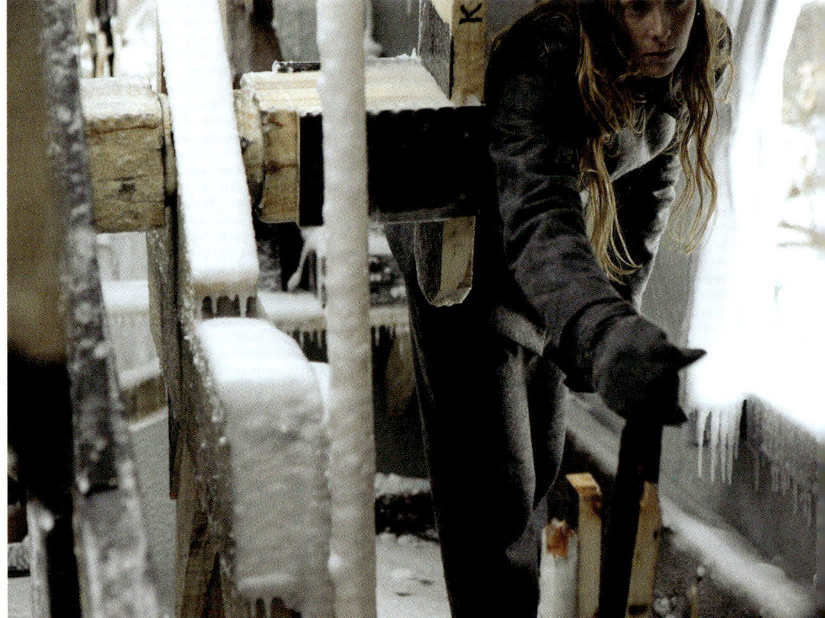

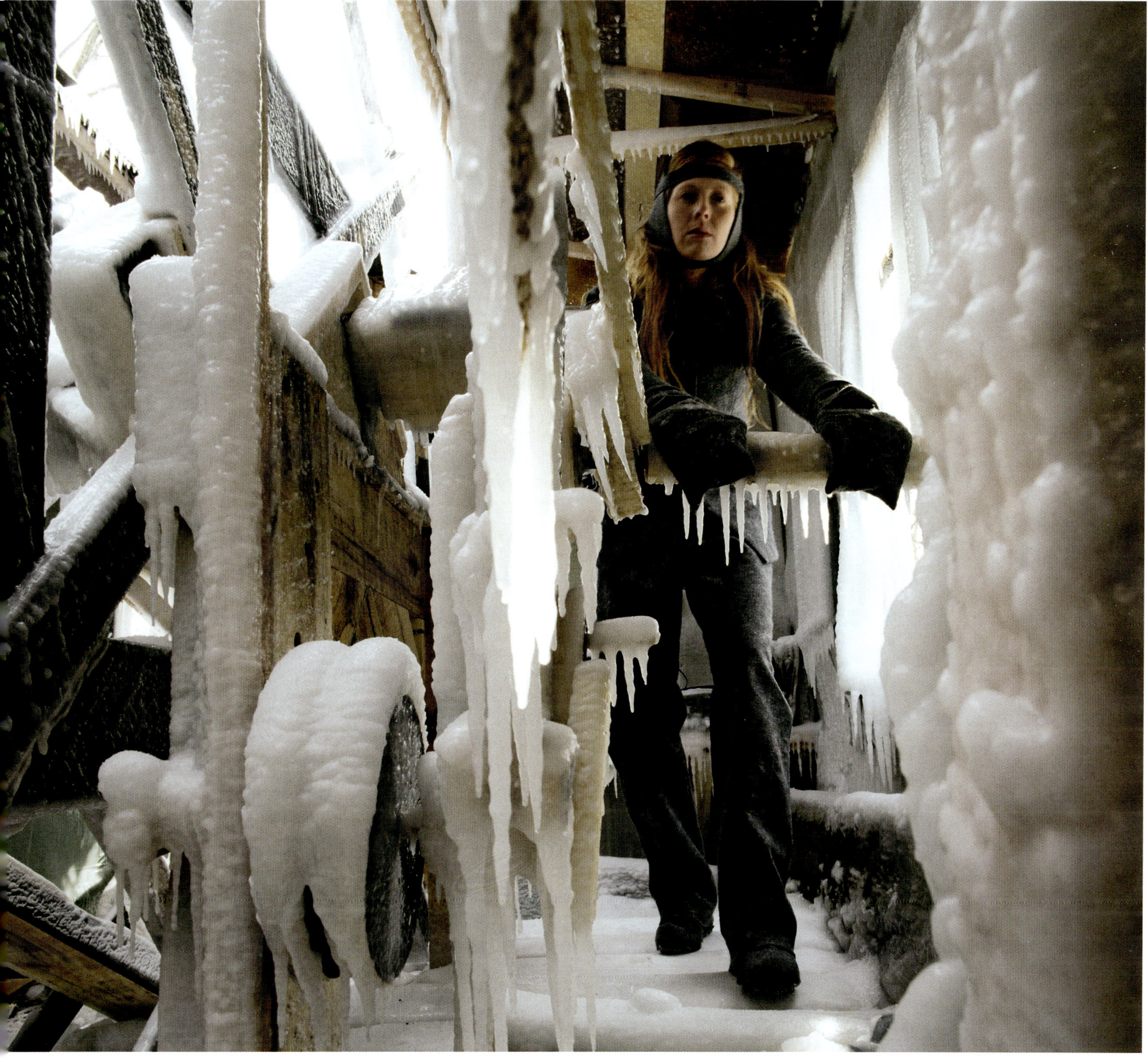

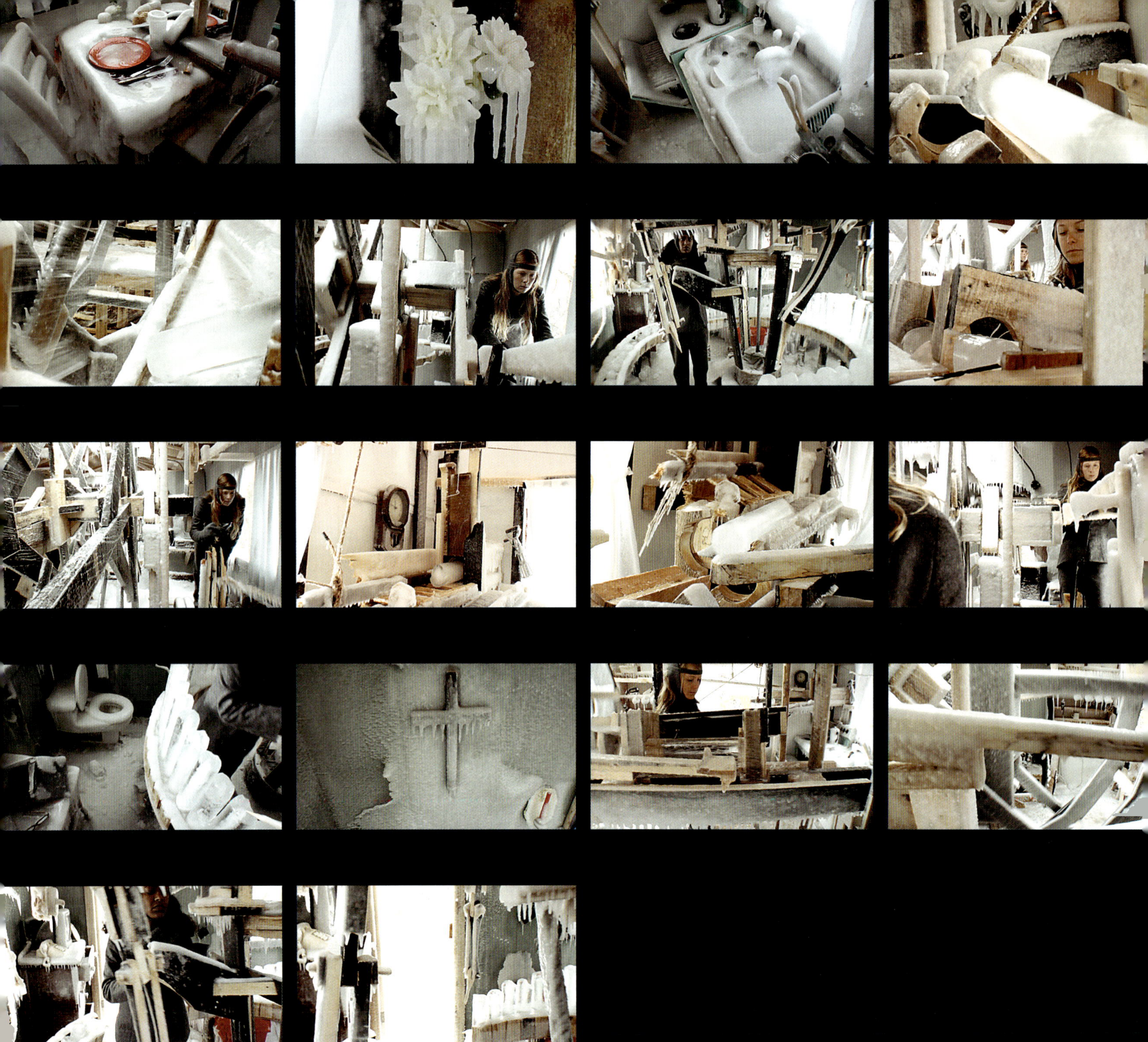

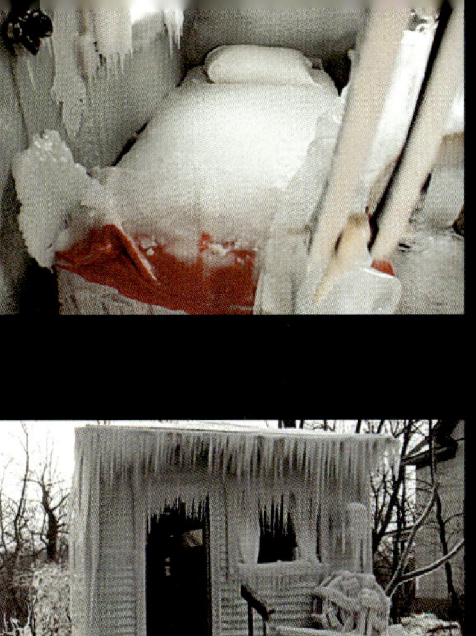
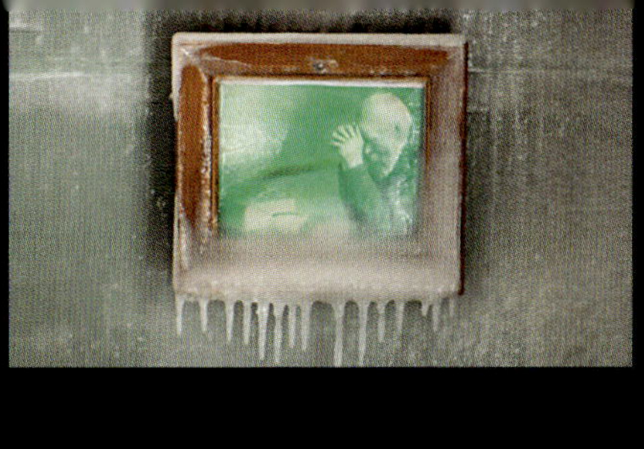
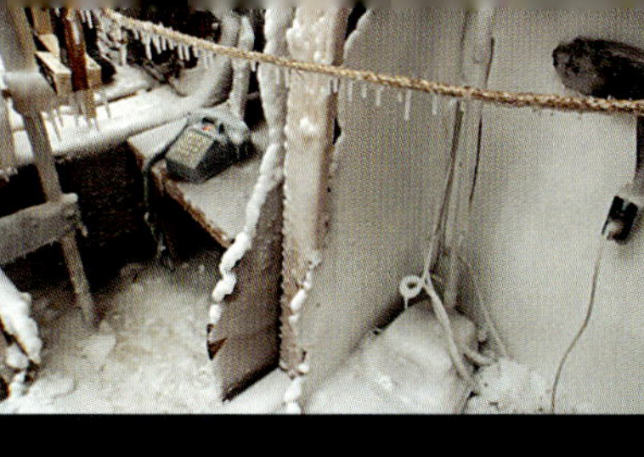
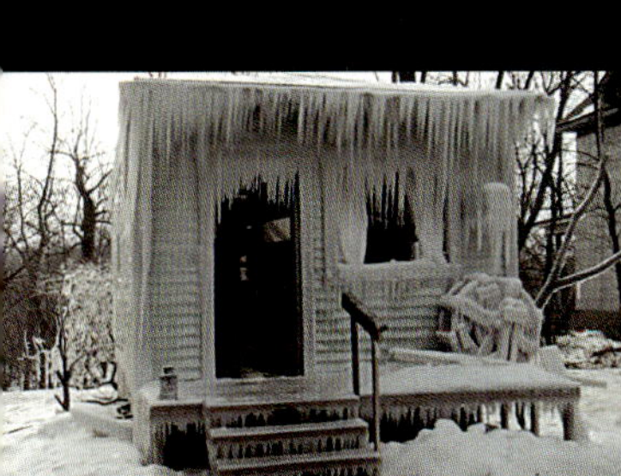
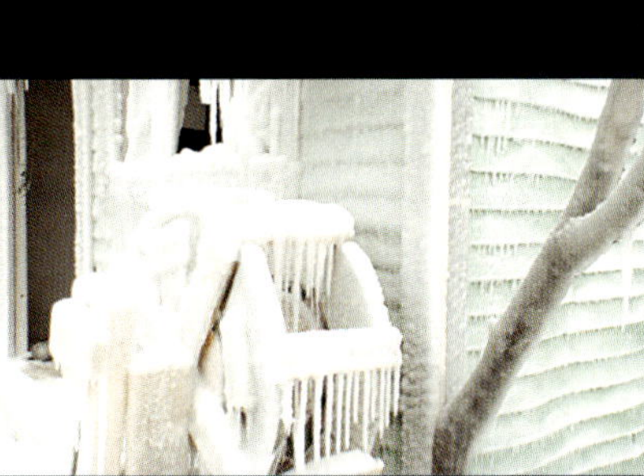
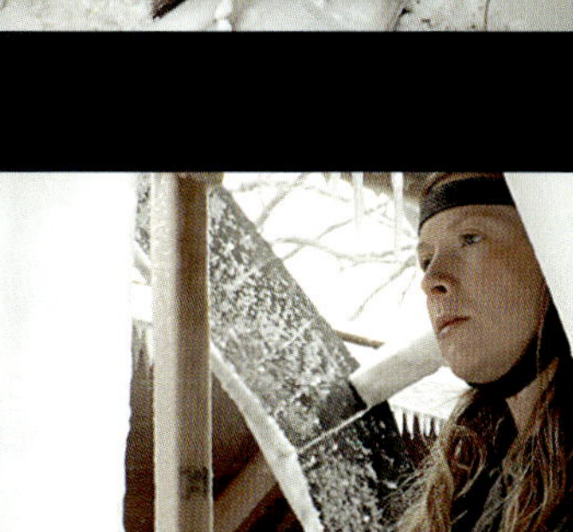
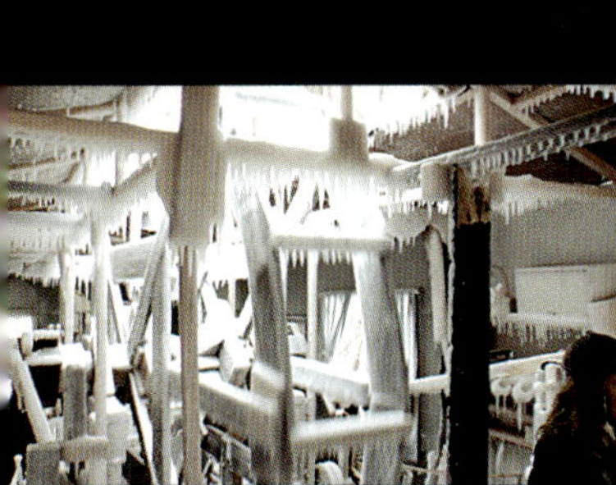
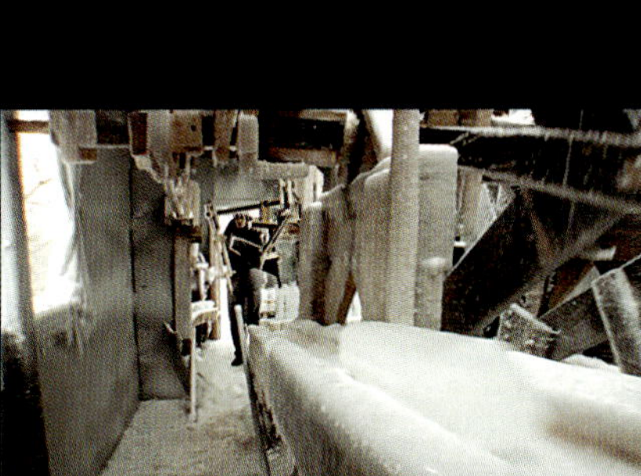
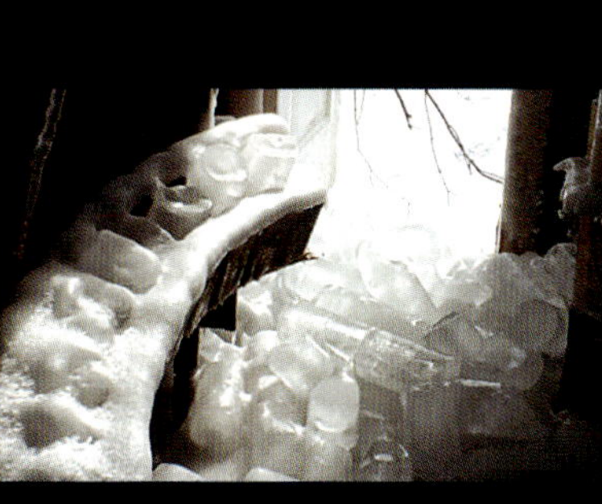
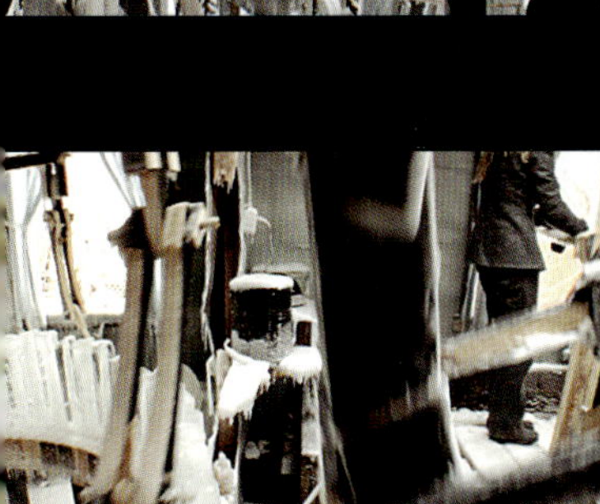
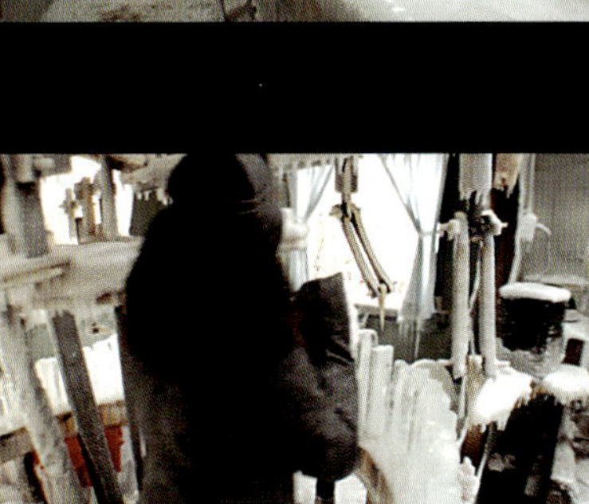
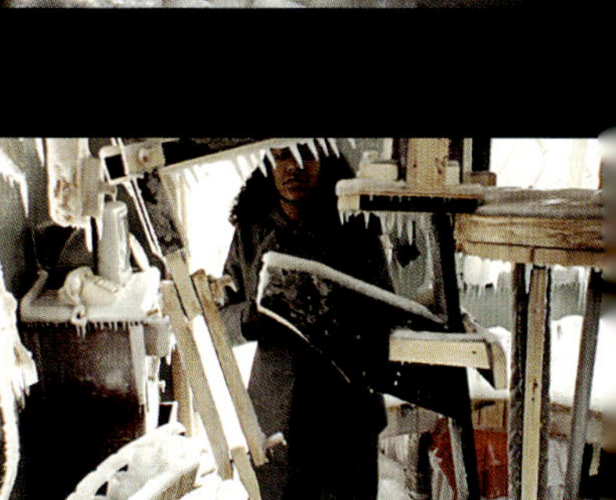

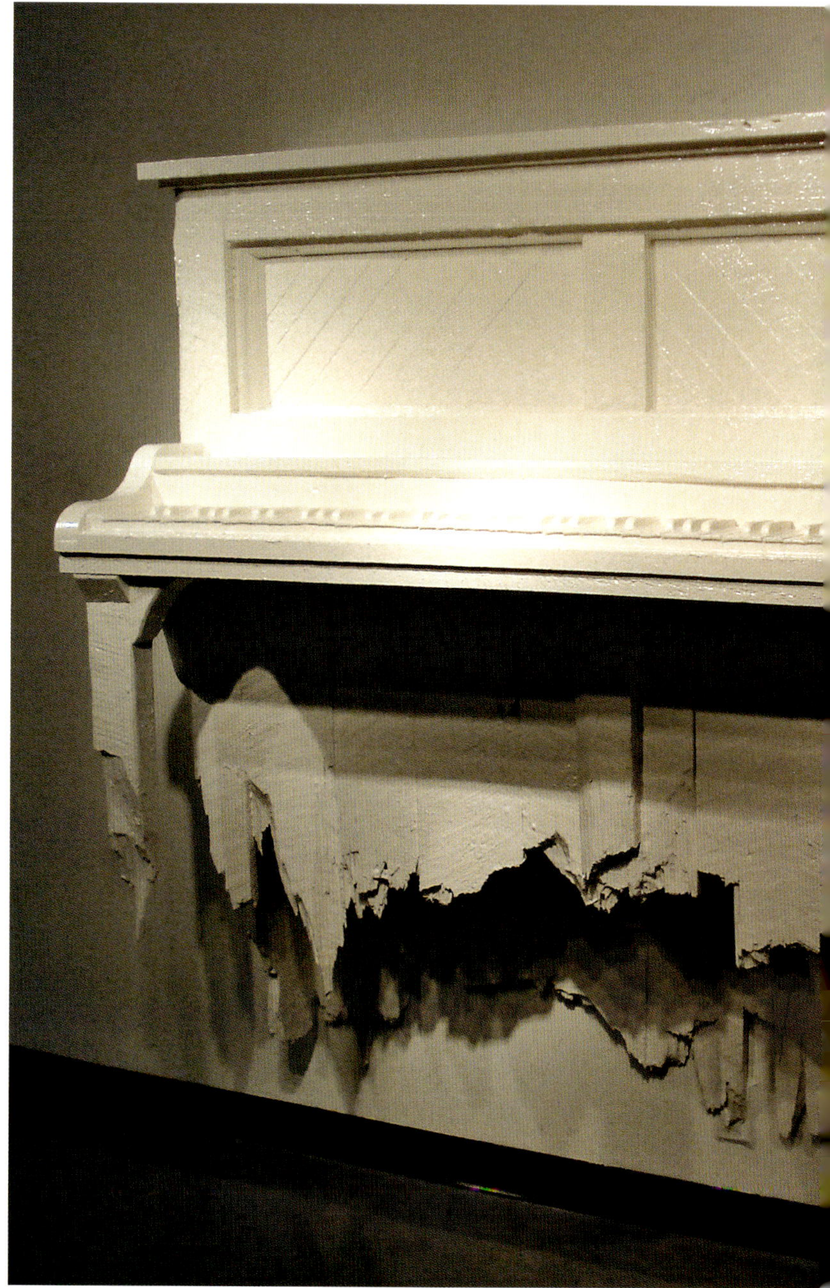

The Price of Freedom (Weldon Irvine)

Painting * 2007 * Black paint on plywood,
single shot with a .22 caliber rifle * 60 x 60 x 5 cm

Piano * 2007
Wood, high-gloss white paint * 150 x 180 x 90 cm

Installation views at Katherine Nash Gallery, Minneapolis, MN

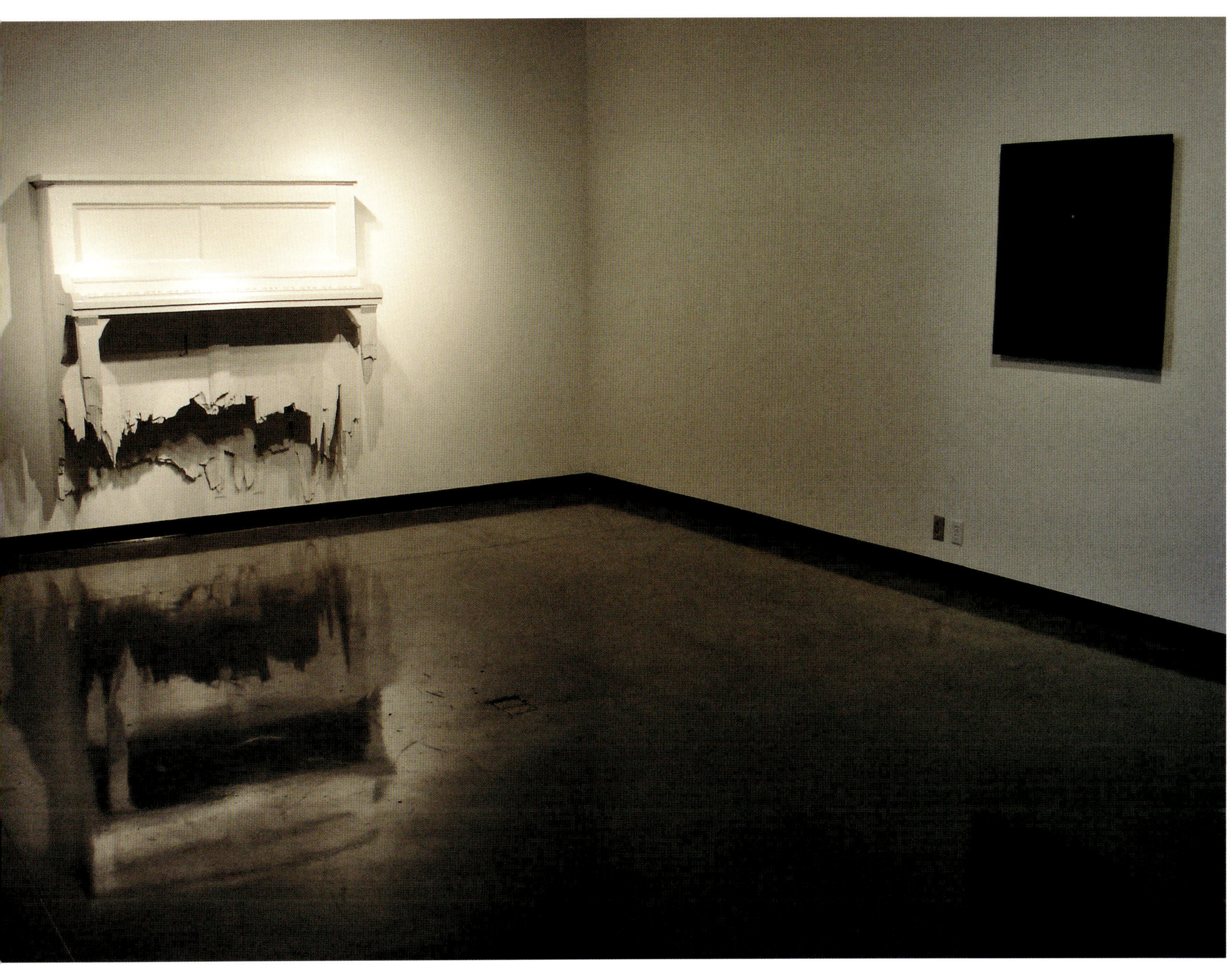

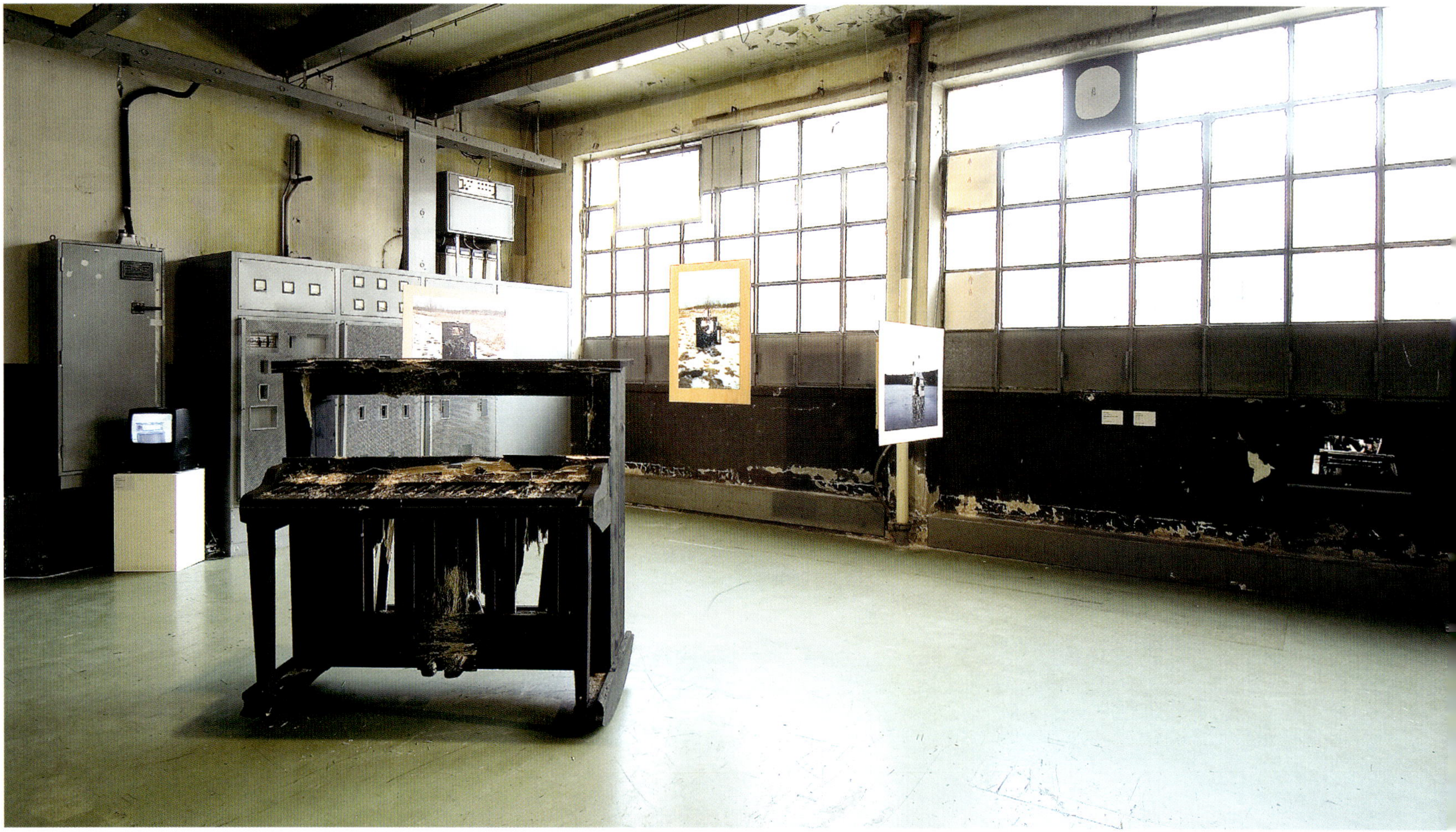

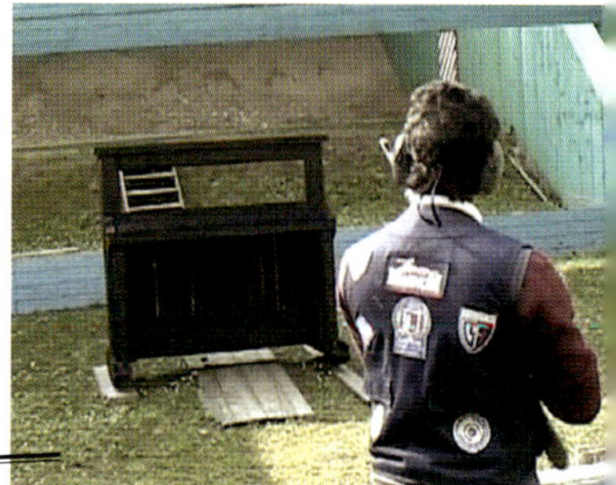

Shotgun Piano

Black Piano • 2007 • Wood, black paint, shot by shotgun
172 x 148 x 112 cm • Installation view
Space Control, Assab One, Milan

Shotgun Piano (Milan) • 2007 • Video
Running time: 2:10 min. • Video still

Page 101
Shotgun Piano #2 (Milan) • 2007
C-print mounted on board, shot by shotgun • 81 x 110 cm

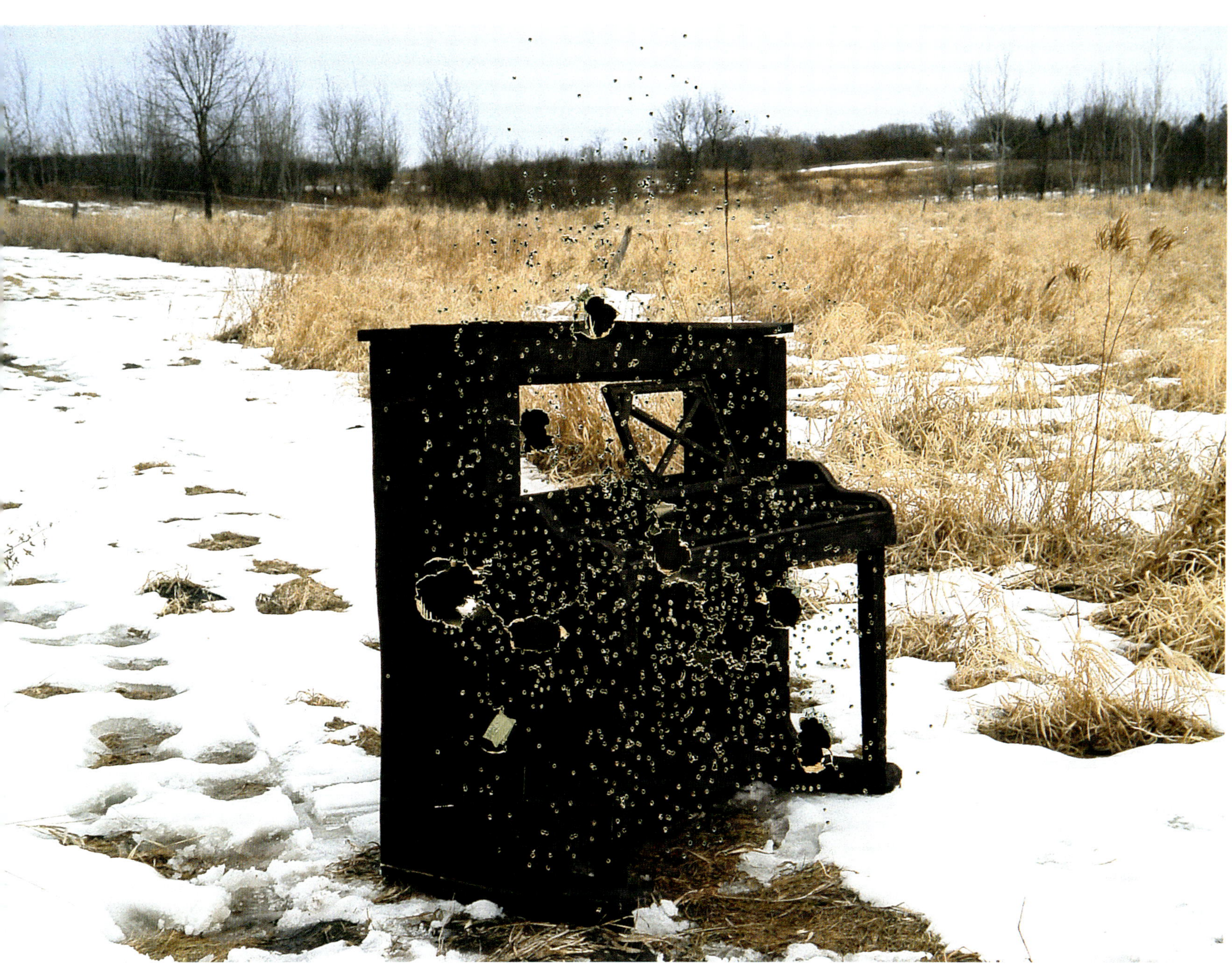

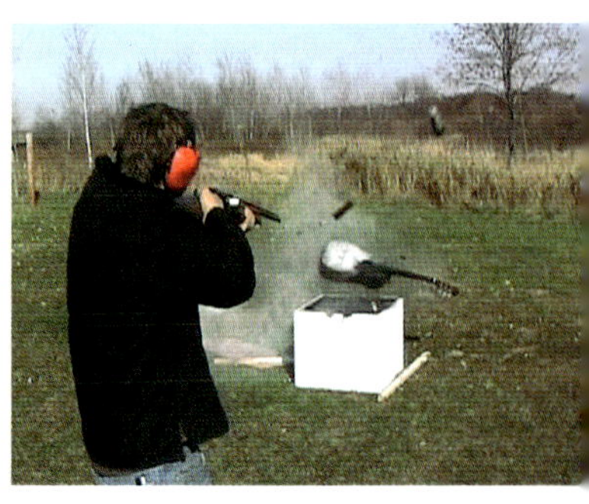

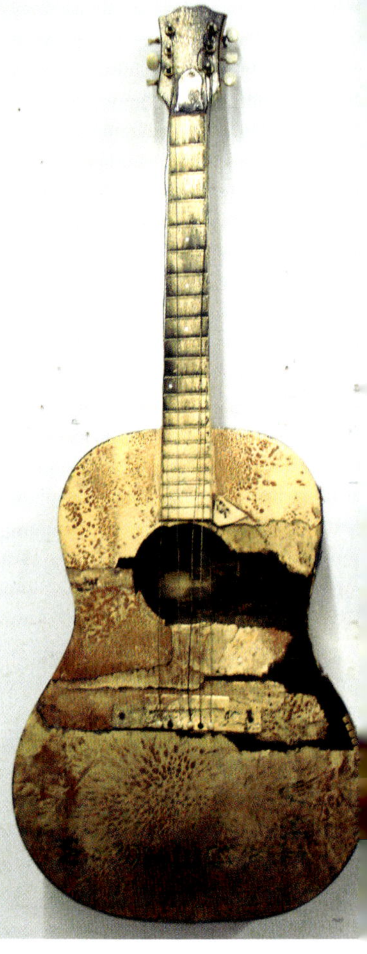

Shotgun Guitar

Shotgun Guitar • 2006
Performance and video • Running time: 2:02 min.
Video still with Chris Larson

Shotgun Guitar Gold • 2007
Guitar, gold spray, shot by shotgun • 100 x 35 x 10 cm

Page 103
Shotgun Guitar • 2006
Guitar, spray paint, shot by shotgun • 100 x 70 x 13 cm

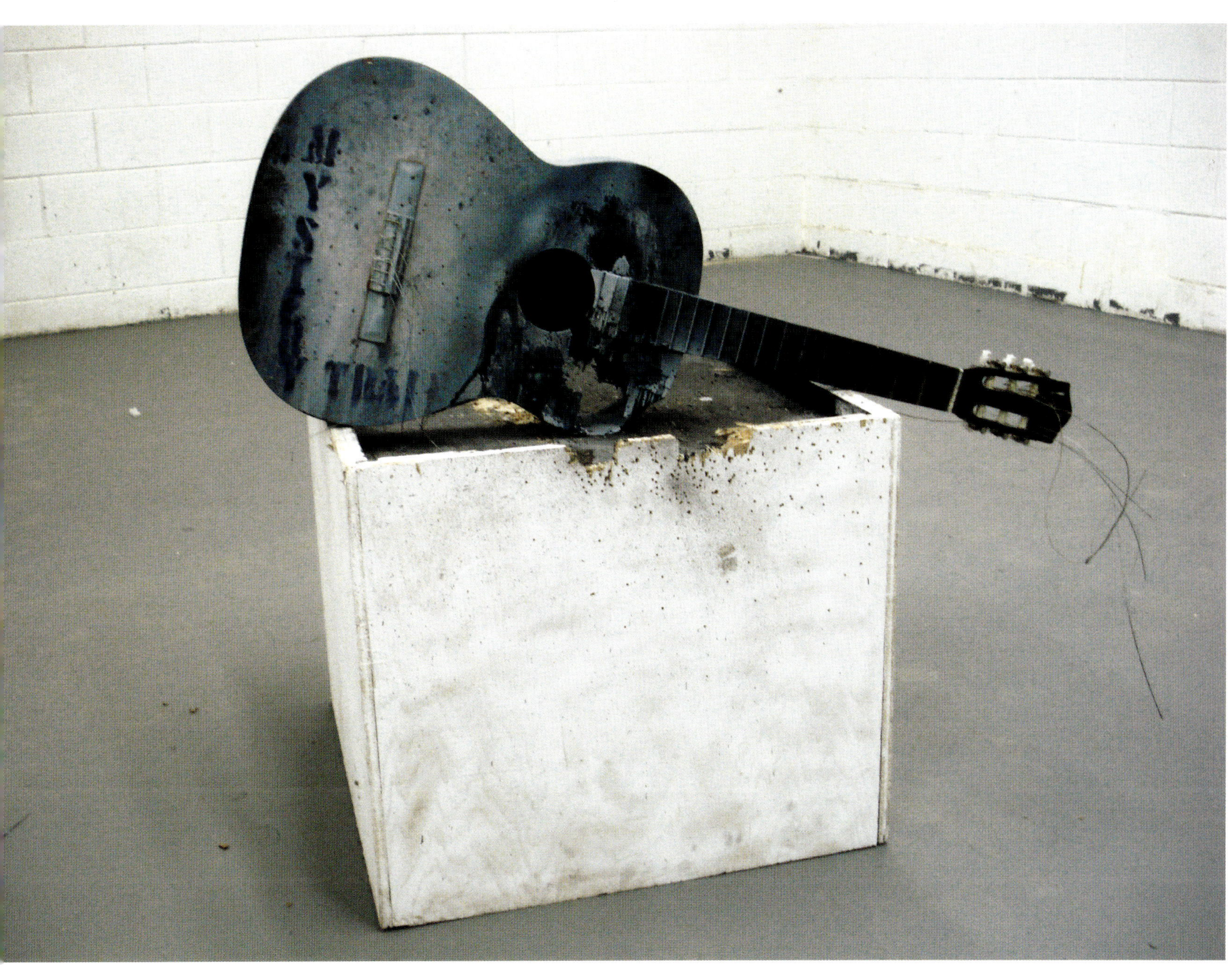

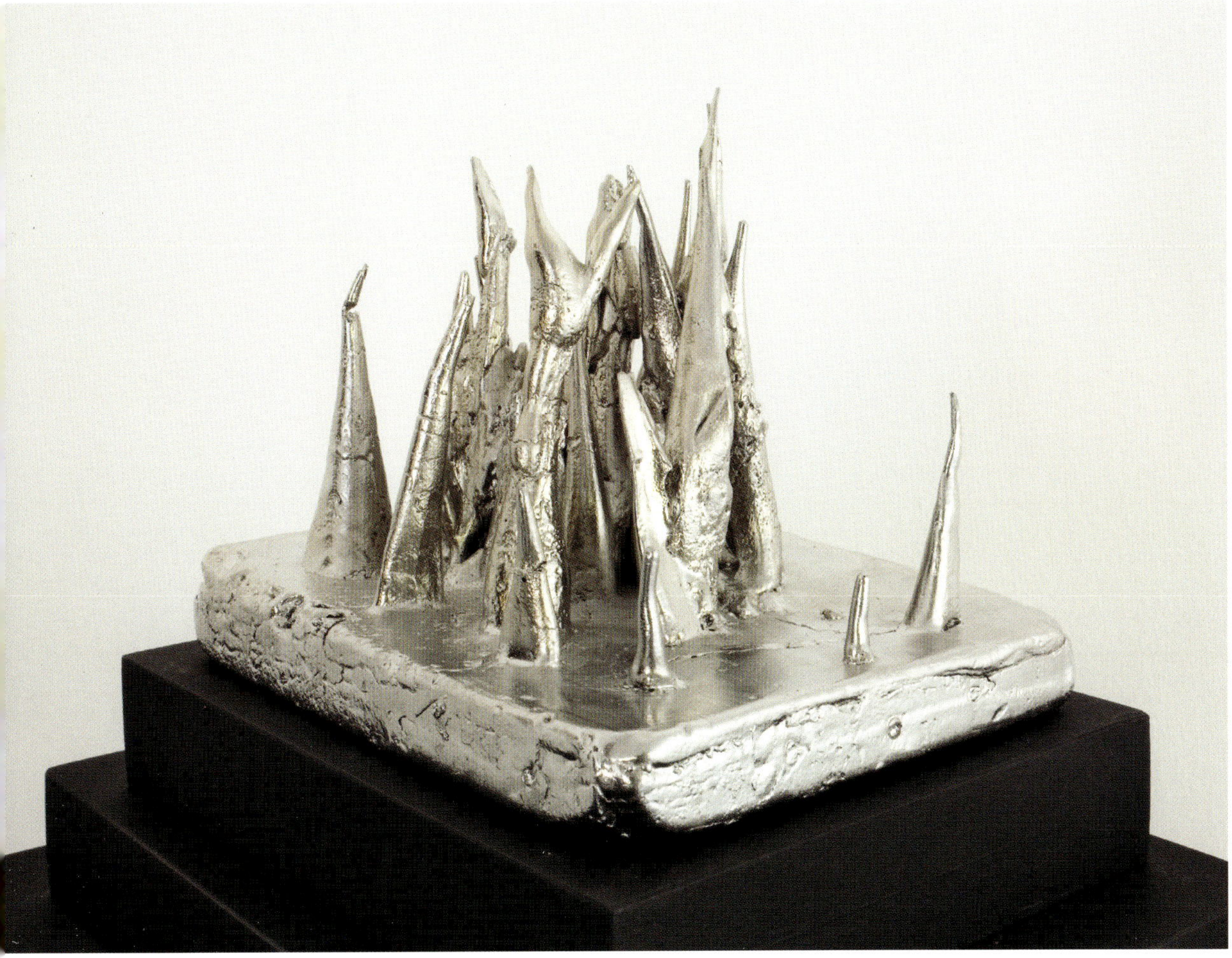

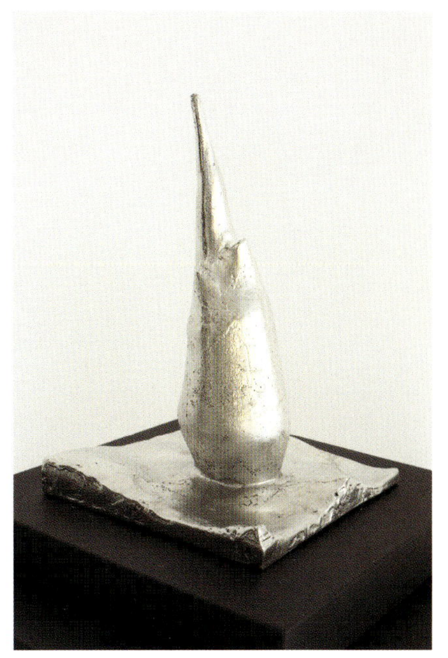

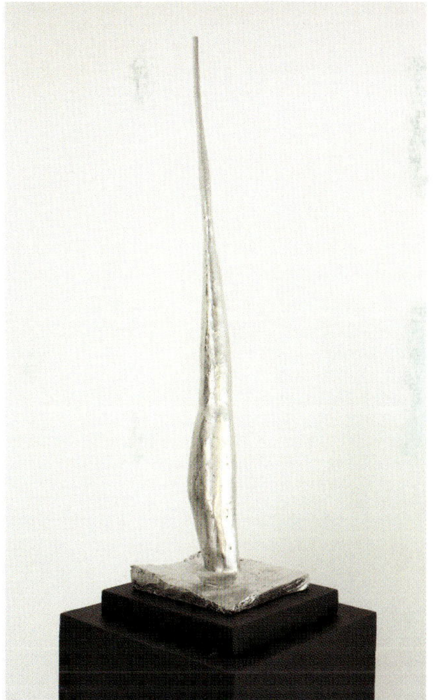

Blast

Blast/Nevermind # 2 ∗ 2007
Cast made from a gunshot into a block of wet clay, shot with a 12-gauge shotgun ∗ Stainless steel ∗ 13 x 15 x 25 cm

Blast/Cosmic Vortex # 1 ∗ 2008
Cast made from a gunshot into a block of wet clay, shot with a .22 caliber rifle ∗ Stainless steel ∗ 25.4 x 20.3 x 20.3 cm

Blast/Selbstporträt als ein Soldat (Blast/Self-portrait as a Soldier) ∗ 2008
Cast made from a gunshot into a 4-foot block of wet clay, shot with a Ruger .40 caliber handgun ∗ Stainless steel
86.4 x 20.3 x 20.3 cm

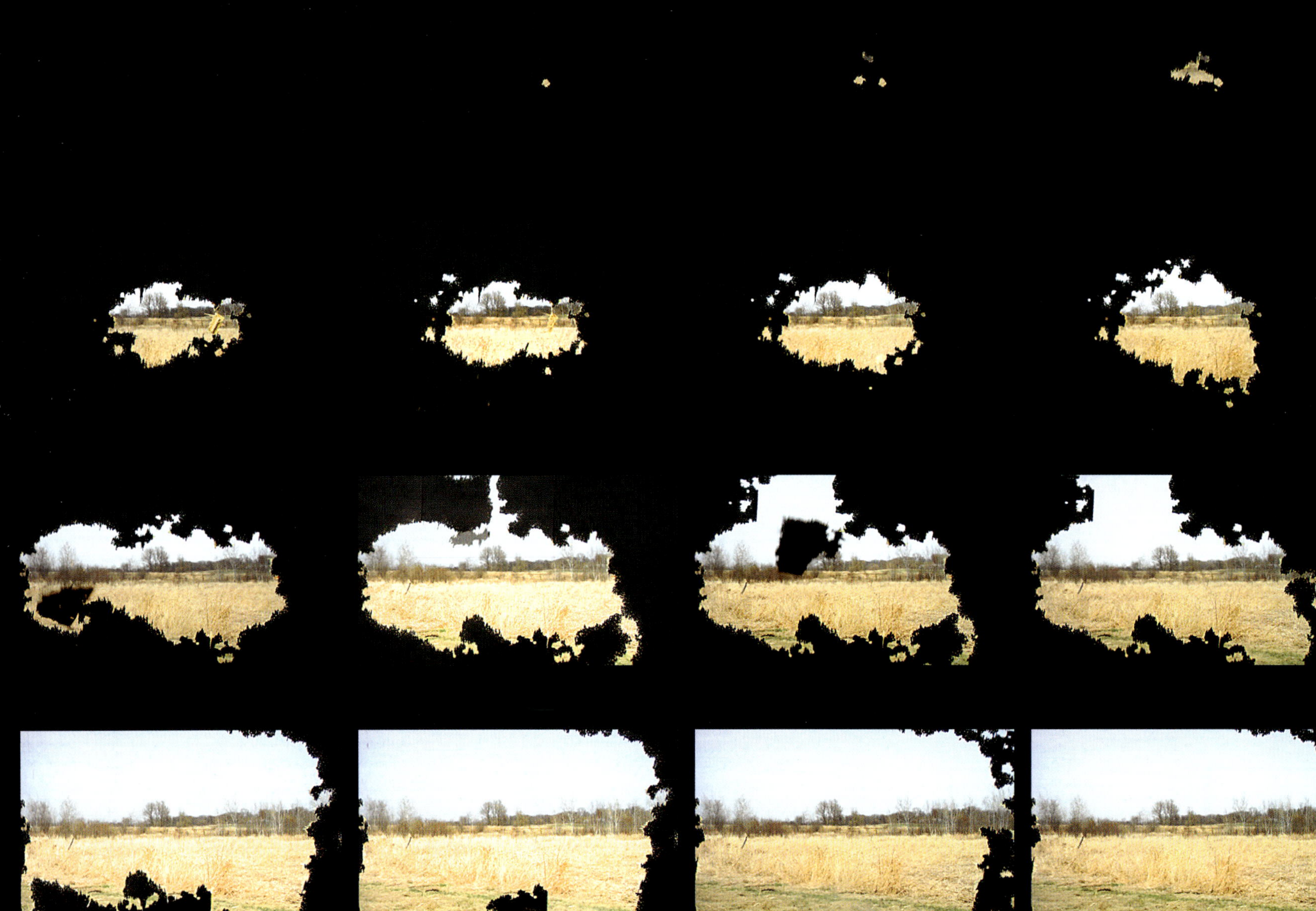

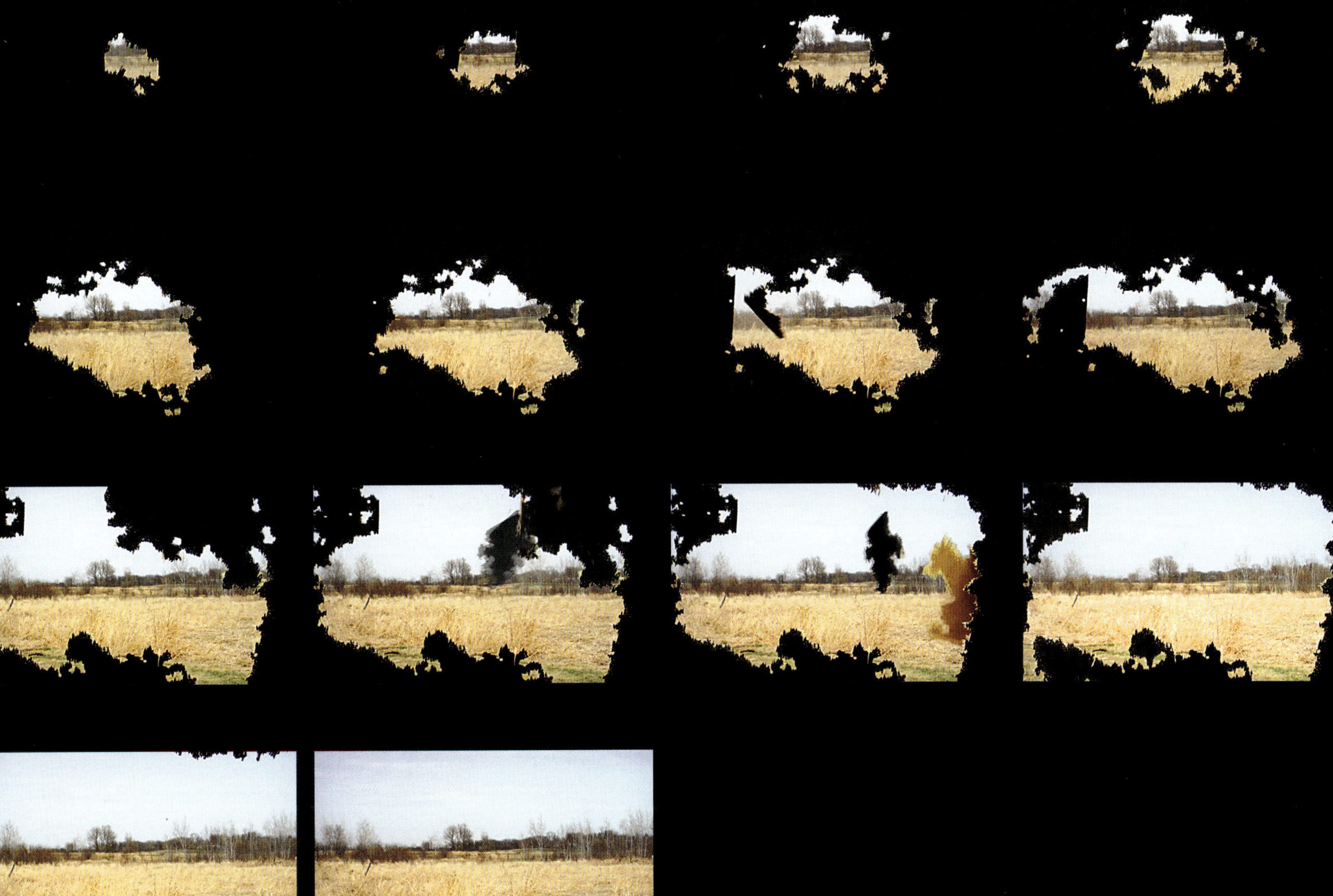

Shotgun Landscape

2007 * 240 x 480 cm sheet of painted black plywood shot
759 times with a 12-gauge shotgun
HD DVD * Running time: 15:49 min.
Video stills

Chris Larson

Born in 1966 in St. Paul, MN
Lives and works in St. Paul, MN

Education

1992 Masters of Fine Arts, Yale University School of Art, New Haven, CT

1990 Bachelor of Fine Arts, Bethel College, St. Paul, MN

Solo Exhibitions and Performances

2009 Burnet Art Gallery at Chambers, The Luxury Art Hotel, Minneapolis, MN

2008 magnus müller, Berlin, Germany
Rochester Art Center, Rochester, MN
Art Basel, Video Section, Basel, Switzerland
Screen Spirit_Continued #8, Städtische Galerie im Buntentor, Bremen, Germany

2006 *Crush Collision*, magnus müller (with Harald Hermann), Berlin, Germany
Crush Collision, Minneapolis Institute of Arts, Minneapolis, MN
Shotgun Shack, Creative Electric Studios, Minneapolis, MN

2004 *Pause*, Rare Gallery, New York, NY
Film Sculpture Drawings, Franklin Art Works, Minneapolis, MN

2002 *Bogus Brook Township*, Rare Gallery, New York, NY

2001 *The Gostrol Colony*, Rare Gallery, New York, NY

2000 *Saturday Night, Sunday Morning*, Art in General, New York, NY
Washington Pavilion of Arts and Science, Visual Arts Center, Sioux Falls, SD

1997 Grand Arts, Kansas City, MO
Spotlight Gallery, Katherine E. Nash Gallery, University of Minnesota, Minneapolis, MN

1996 *Chris Larson Sculpture*, College of Visual Arts, St. Paul, MN
Chris Larson: Recent Work, Minnesota Museum of American Art, St. Paul, MN

Selected Group Exhibitions, Film Festivals

2008 *Surreale Welten*, Sammlung Scharf-Gerstenberg, Staatliche Museen zu Berlin – Stiftung Preussischer Kulturbesitz, Berlin, Germany
YoHoY, curated by José Springer, Indianilla Art Centre, Mexico City, Mexico

2007 *BÄNG! Forum für junge Kunst*, curated by Sönke Magnus Müller, Ideal Forum, Berlin, Germany
Not your Parents' MTV: Music Videos from Hell, Postmasters Gallery, New York, NY
SAD, Weisman Art Museum, Minneapolis, MN
Space Control, curated by Sönke Magnus Müller, Assab One, Milan, Italy
Enchanted, Revealing the Fantastic and Metaphysical, Katherine E. Nash Gallery, University of Minnesota, Minneapolis, MN
9. Februar 2007, magnus müller, Berlin, Germany
New Orleans Revisited, Walker Art Center, Minneapolis, MN

Idiot Joy Showland: An Evening of Film and Video by Artists, IFC Center, New York, NY; Video Festival, Dallas, TX; The Center for Contemporary Art, Tel Aviv, Israel

2006 *Contemporary II*, curated by Maria Rosa Sossai, Magazzino d'Arte Moderna, Rome, Italy
Scarecrow, curated by David Hunt, Postmasters Gallery, New York, NY

2005 *Jerome: Hill and Foundation*, The Museum of Modern Art, New York, NY
Jerome Hill Centennial: A Filmmaker and His Legacy, Walker Art Center, Minnesota, MN
Crash. Pause. Rewind, Western Bridge, Seattle, WA
Minets à Polis, Cohan and Leslie, New York, NY
A Celebration of Minnesota Artists: 90th Anniversary Collection, The Minneapolis Foundation, Minneapolis, MN
From<To, Minneapolis College of Art and Design, Minneapolis, MN

2004 *The Ludovico Treatment*, curated by David Hunt, MüllerDechiara, Berlin, Germany
4 x 4, Plug In, Institute of Contemporary Art, Winnipeg, Canada
Slice and Dice, Visual Arts Gallery, New York, NY

2003 *Druid: Wood as a Superconductor*, Space 101, Brooklyn, NY
New York Video Festival, Lincoln Plaza, New York, NY
City Mouse, Country Mouse, curated by David Hunt, Space 101, Brooklyn, NY
McKnight Artists, Minneapolis College of Art and Design, Minneapolis, MN

2002 *Art New York*, Kunstraum auf Zeit, Linz, Austria

2001 The Minnesota Artists Exhibition Program, Minneapolis Institute of Arts, Minneapolis, MN
Midway Contemporary Art, St. Paul, MN

2000 *Fast*, Grand Arts, Kansas City, MO

1999 *Cause and Effect*, Forecast Public Artworks, St. Paul, MN

1998 *Sculpture on Site*, Walker Art Center, Minneapolis, MN
Material Matters, Janet Wallace Fine Arts Center, St. Paul, MN
Faculty Exhibition, Winona State University, Winona, MN

1997 Minnesota State Arts Board, St. Paul, MN

1996–97 Franconia Sculpture Park, Franconia, MN

1995 Yale University Art Gallery, New Haven, CT
Art in Space, Intermedia Arts, Minneapolis, MN

1993 *The Jerome Five*, Minneapolis College of Art and Design, Minneapolis, MN

Honors and Awards

2006 Bush Artist Fellowship, Bush Foundation, St. Paul, MN

2004 Jerome Media Fellowship, St. Paul, MN
Artist Assistant Fellowship Grant, Minnesota State Arts Board, St. Paul, MN

2002 McKnight Artist Fellowship, Minneapolis College of Art and Design, Minneapolis, MN
Jerome Media Fellowship, Jerome Foundation, St. Paul, MN

1999 Louis Comfort Tiffany Foundation Fellowship, New York, NY
Forecast Public Arts Commission, St. Paul, MN

1998 Bush Artist Fellowship, Bush Foundation, St. Paul, MN

1997 Artist Assistant Fellowship Grant, Minnesota State Arts Board, St. Paul, MN

1995 Jerome Installation Arts Commission, Intermedia Arts, Minneapolis, MN

1994 Artist Assistant Fellowship Grant, Minnesota State Arts Board, St. Paul, MN

1993 Jerome Foundation Fellowship Grant, Minneapolis College of Art and Design, Minneapolis, MN

1992 Alice Kimball Traveling Fellowship, Yale University, New Haven, CT

Selected Articles

2008 Schuster, Peter-Klaus, "Kunstjuwel für Berlin. Sammlung Scharf-Gerstenberg," *Tagesspiegel* (July 10)
Brillson, Leila, et al., "Demolition Man," *Surface* (June)
Begemann, Dieter, "Wilde Maschinen, stille Landschaften," *Weser Kurier* (June 6)
Heinz Hock, Marikke, "Chris Larson — Crush

"Collision" at Städtische Galerie im Buntentor," *Punkt. Kunst im Nordwesten* (Summer)
Bruggaier, Johannes, "Ein Organist über dem Höllenschlund," *Kreiszeitung online* (June)

2007 Kupka, Mahret, "Bäng! Art Forum auf der ideal 4," *http://www.modabot.de* (July 30)
Lambert, Olympia, "Pulse New York—Part 2," *http://lamgelinaoly.blogspot.com* (March 6)

2006 Vacura, April, "Massive Crush. Artist Chris Larson Exhibits with a Bang," *The Wake Student Magazine* (November 29)
Nero, Stephanie, "Artist Gives Form to Every-day Collisions of Culture," *St. Paul Pioneer Press* (November 26)
Abbe, Mary, "Smash-Ups," *Minneapolis Star and Tribune* (November 24)
Askari, Sarah, "I'd Stay Away from That There Shotgun Shack," *City Pages* (November 15)
Robinson, Walter, "Art Fair New York," *http://www.artnet.com* (September 28)
Wheeler, Claudia, "Geschmacksache/ Galerierundgang," Kulturradio am Vormittag (July 26)

2004 Douglas, Kris, "Reviews Nationwide," *ArtUS 4* (September–October)
Briggs, Patricia, "Reviews, Minneapolis, Min-nesota," *Art Papers* (September–October)
Roberts, Chris, "State of the Arts," *MPR* (May 20)
Abbe, Mary, "Free Time Full Page," *Minneapolis Star Tribune* (May)
Smith, Rod, "A-List," *City Pages* (May)
Klefstad, Ann, "Art Review: Arms and the Boy: Chris Larson at Franklin Art Works," *MNArtists* (April 30)
Fallon, Michael, "Reviews," *The Rake* (April)

2003 Wilson, Michael, "Reviews, Chris Larson, Rare, New York," *Frieze* (March)

2001 Curcio, Robert, "Reviews, Chris Larson, Rare," *Sculpture*, Vol. 20, No. 8 (October)
Abbe, Mary, "Reviews, A Lot Going On," *Minneapolis Star Tribune* (August)
Knighton, Andrew, "Review, Rosemary Fiore, Chris Larson," *New Art Examiner* (July–August)
Valdez, Sarah, "Review of Exhibitions, Chris Larson at Rare," *Art in America* (July)
Johnson, Ken, "Art in Review, Chris Larson, The Gastral Colony," *The New York Times* (March 9)

1998 Briggs, Patricia, "Sculpture on Site," *Artforum* (November)

Permanent Collections

Kemper Museum of Contemporary Art, Kansas City, MO
Minneapolis Institute of Arts, Minneapolis, MN
Sammlung Scharf-Gerstenberg, Staatliche Museen zu Berlin – Stiftung Preussischer Kulturbesitz, Berlin, Germany
Walker Art Center, Minneapolis, MN

Contributors

Kris Douglas is chief curator of the Rochester Art Center. Also a writer, he has published essays in journals such as *Contemporary*, *ArtUS*, and *Tema Celeste*.

Marc Glöde is a film scholar and curator, who is active in a wide range of projects including numerous film series such as Art Basel, Wild Walls Film Festival and Experimenta Mumbai/Bangalore, as well as exhibitions in contemporary art (Los Angeles, Berlin, New York). He is widely published within the field.

Sönke Magnus Müller is an art historian and owner of the gallery magnus müller in Berlin, Germany, which represents Chris Larson.

Tamatha Sopinski Perlman is a writer and program associate for the Minnesota Artists Exhibition Program, an artist-run curatorial department at the Minneapolis Institute of Arts.

Wayne L. Roosa is professor of art history and department chair at Bethel University, St. Paul, MN, and chair of the New York Center for Art and Media Studies in New York City.

Sarah Stauder is executive director of the Rochester Art Center.

Credits

All works by Chris Larson:
Courtesy of gallery magnus müller, Berlin, and the artist

With gratitude to the following collectors for allowing images of works from their collections to appear in this publication:
Allen Adler and Frances F. L. Beatty, New York, NY
Ralph and Peggy Burnet, Minneapolis, MN
Brooke Garber Neidich, New York, NY
Horst Köhn, Vienna, Austria
Ken and Barb Larson, White Bear Lake, MN
Private collection, Berlin, Germany
Private collection, Los Angeles, CA
Private collection, Paris, France
Peter and Annie Remes, Minneapolis, MN
Cole Rogers and Carla McGrath, Minneapolis, MN
Beth Rudin DeWoody, New York, NY
Sammlung Scharf-Gerstenberg, Nationalgalerie, Staatliche Museen zu Berlin – Stiftung Preussischer Kulturbesitz, Berlin, Germany
Jason Spafford, Turtle Lake, WI
Jay and Ellen Swanson, Minneapolis, MN
Bill and Ruth True, Seattle, WA
Walker Art Center, Minneapolis, MN

Photo Credits:
All photos: magnus müller gallery, except:
Akg-images: p. 11 (top)
Askari, Sarah: pp. 62–63
Dennehy, Dan: pp. 39, 44–45, 83
Green, Warwick: pp. 42–43
Kelly, Donna: pp. 80–81, 82 (black piano)
Paffrath, Ludger: Cover, front endpaper, pp. 7, 65–75, 79, 101, 105 (left), back endpaper
Sferra, Rik: pp. 17, 22–23

Colophon

This catalogue is published in conjunction with the exhibition
Deep North

Rochester Art Center, Rochester, MN
September 27, 2008–January 17, 2009

gallery magnus müller, Berlin
October 25–December 6, 2008

Burnet Art Gallery at Chambers, The Luxury Art Hotel, Minneapolis, MN
Spring, 2009

Edited by Sönke Magnus Müller
Concept: Cristina Steingräber, Julika Zimmermann
Editing: Kris Douglas, Constanze Korb
Copyediting: Anne O'Connor
Translations: Allison Plath-Moseley
Graphic design: Anja Lutz Book Design
Typefaces: Humanist 777, Vineta, Giddyup
Reproductions: LVD Gesellschaft für Datenverarbeitung mbH
Production: Stefanie Langner
Paper: Galaxi Supermat, 170 g/m²
Printing and binding: sellier druck GmbH, Freising

Chris Larson is represented by magnus müller gallery in Berlin www.magnusmuller.com

Published by
Hatje Cantz Verlag
Zeppelinstrasse 32
73760 Ostfildern
Germany
Tel. +49 711 4405-200
Fax +49 711 4405-220
www.hatjecantz.com

Hatje Cantz books are available internationally at selected bookstores. For more information about our distribution partners, please visit our homepage at www.hatjecantz.com.

ISBN 978-3-7757-2232-2

Printed in Germany

Cover illustration:
Shotgun House (Milan), 2007
C-print mounted on board, shot by shotgun, 90 x 66 cm

Front endpaper:
Black Hole Shotgun, 2007
Luan plywood painted black and silver, shot by shotgun, 56 x 43 x 2 cm

Back endpaper:
Shotgun Blackhole, 2007
Luan plywood painted black and shot at close range with a 12-gauge shotgun, 61 x 61 x 5 cm

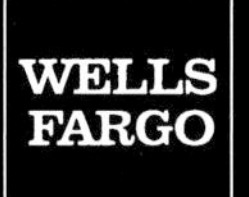

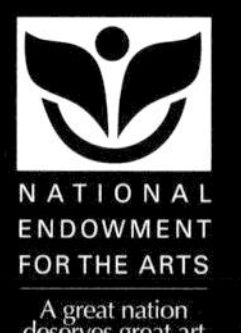

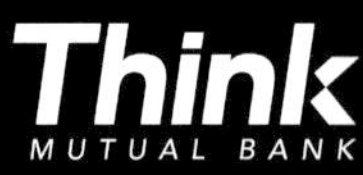